BLACK GATHERING

BLACK GATHERING   *Art*

BLACK OUTDOORS: Innovations in the Poetics of Study
A series edited by J. Kameron Carter and Sarah Jane Cervenak

Ecology, Ungiven Life SARAH JANE CERVENAK

Duke University Press
Durham and London 2021

© 2021 DUKE UNIVERSITY PRESS All rights reserved
Designed by Courtney Leigh Richardson
Typeset in Warnock Pro by Copperline Book Services

Library of Congress Cataloging-in-Publication Data
Names: Cervenak, Sarah Jane, [date] author.
Title: Black gathering : art, ecology, ungiven life /
Sarah Jane Cervenak.
Other titles: Black outdoors.
Description: Durham : Duke University Press, 2021. | Series:
Black outdoors | Includes bibliographical references and index.
Identifiers: LCCN 2020054726 (print)
LCCN 2020054727 (ebook)
ISBN 9781478013556 (hardcover)
ISBN 9781478014478 (paperback)
ISBN 9781478021773 (ebook)
Subjects: LCSH: American literature—20th century—History
and criticism. | American literature—African American
authors—History and criticism. | African American art—20th
century. | African American aesthetics. | African American
women authors. | African American women artists. | African
American artists. | Womanism. | Ecocriticism. Classification:
LCC PS153.N5 C39 2021 (print) |
LCC PS153.N5 (ebook) | DDC 810.9/89607300904—dc23
LC record available at https://lccn.loc.gov/2020054726
LC ebook record available at https://lccn.loc.gov/2020054727

COVER ART: *Denver*, 2008. © Xaviera Simmons.
Courtesy the artist and David Castillo, Miami.

For Gayl Jones

ACKNOWLEDGMENTS

Thank you for being here. I want to say that first.

Black Gathering is sister to *Wandering*, my first book. I was thinking about gathering in Leonardo Drew's art soon before my first book was published. They go together. My wonderful editor Courtney Berger at Duke University Press has supported me and these books from the beginning, and I'm tremendously grateful to her. As well, I thank the anonymous readers for their time, encouragement, insight, and enormously helpful feedback. Thanks to Sandra Korn and Lisl Hampton for their support throughout the book's production process. Thank you, Leslie Watkins, for copyediting the book. I thank Sarah Osment for preparing the index.

Indeed, the lives of these two books are threaded, and so the folks I thanked in the acknowledgments to *Wandering* are also the ones I thank now along with others who have since shown me kindness and support.

Thanks to my colleagues at UNC Greensboro: Tara Green, Leila Villaverde, Daniel Coleman, Danielle Bouchard, Lisa Levenstein, Kathy Jamieson (now at CSU-Sacramento), Cerise Glenn, and Mark Rifkin. As with *Wandering*, Danielle Bouchard showed me as well as this book much kindness and generosity, graciously reading drafts and letting me work at her home when I needed some space and time to finish. After I got tenure, I was lucky to get a one-semester research leave from UNC-Greensboro's College of Arts and Sciences, which gave me additional time to work on chapter 1.

I'm thankful for my son's day care teachers who cared for him while I taught and wrote.

Thanks to the people who came and listened to the presentations I gave connected to the book: Duke University's Gender, Sexuality and Feminist

Studies Department and Northwestern University's Colloquium on Ethnicity and Migration. Small portions of this book's chapters were also presented at the American Studies Association, Modern Language Association, National Women's Studies Association, and Arts of the Present annual conferences. I thank those in attendance for their warm reception.

Thank you to friends and colleagues from beyond UNCG: Amber Jamilla Musser, Chelsea Frazier, LaCharles Ward, Keguro Macharia, Meg Driscoll, Juana María Rodríguez, Tao Leigh Goffe, Patricia Nguyen, Amirio Freeman, Fahima Ife, Rachel Zolf, Ashon Crawley, Tiffany Lethabo King, Leon Hilton, Adler Guerrier, R. A. Judy, Brent Edwards, Joshua Bennett, Maya Stovall, Calvin Warren, Christina Sharpe, Carter Mathes, Chandan Reddy, Petero Kalulé, and S*an Henry Smith. I want to acknowledge and also thank Jared Sexton here for his great essay "All Black Everything," where I first encountered Claudia Rankine's beautiful poem "After David Hammons."

I sincerely thank the wonderful poets Samiya Bashir, Nikki Wallschlaeger, and Gabrielle Ralambo-Rajerison for their kindness, their words, and for their generosity in permitting me to reprint entire poems and passages. Thank you to Nikki Wallschlaeger and to Samiya Bashir and Nightboat Books for giving permission to reprint their beautiful book covers.

Thank you to the visual artists. Thank you Xaviera Simmons, Leonardo Drew, and the estate of Clementine Hunter for permission to feature your art. Here I thank Claudia Mattos with David Castillo Gallery, Melissa Diaz, who supplied Leonardo Drew's images, and Kassie Edwards (NMAAHC) who helped facilitate the connection with Thomas Whitehead (Cane River Art Corporation) and Stan Broome, Esq. (whom I also thank), who provided the images of Clementine Hunter's art.

Prior to going into COVID-19 quarantine, I visited the Gayl Jones archive at Boston University, where I had the privilege of reading through some of her published and unpublished poetry and prose. I'm so thankful for my experience there and want to thank archivist Jane Parr for her help in arranging my visit.

Kevin Quashie and Jennifer Nash were supporters of this book for a long time; Kevin moderated a panel on Gayl Jones that I was on and has been so kind and supportive of my writing and thinking. Jennifer Nash, who has become a wonderful friend over the years, read this book in multiple forms, multiple times, and I'm so, so thankful to her. Thanks to my friend Samantha Pinto for reading portions of the manuscript and for being a great supporter. I met the great writer Renee Gladman in person at a conference in Manchester, UK; we've since been in contact, and she was kind enough to read my Gayl

Jones chapter, which was wonderful. I thank my friend La Marr Jurelle Bruce who also read an early bird version of the Jones chapter.

I'm so thankful to have met, to have learned from, and to have become friends with Ren Ellis Neyra and Dixa Ramírez. Our text conversations undulating between the astrological and the feline have been filled with laughter and provided great sustenance.

Thanks to J. Kameron Carter, my friend and collaborator since 2014. Seems like our friendship came from or moved by way of study groups, filled with cake and laughter. The Black Outdoors working group series and eventual book series were beautiful events and have been a beautiful process of learning from and with others in the imagination of something new. Thanks to our fellow band members, Candice Benbow and Matt Elia, for always being supportive and always ready to have an impromptu cake/pie party.

Thanks to my teacher and friend Fred Moten and to my dear friend Kathryn Mathers.

Finally, I thank my family. My mom and sisters and my best friend Mercy. My dad died two months after *Wandering* came out. The plastic-wrapped hardcover book collected dust as it sat unwrapped on his coffee table. I picked it up the day we were emptying his house before the bank took it. He might have been the only person on the planet to buy the hardcover. But the fact that it stayed wrapped in that plastic and was around, along with the lonely furniture, after he died is something for which I still have no words.

My husband, Marc, and my son, Edison, are my whole heart. I'm at peace and smile so big when I'm with them.

Thank you for reading.

Another Beginning

In 2010, African American visual artist Xaviera Simmons completed and installed her work of art called *Harvest*. Standing approximately eight by nineteen feet tall, the installation comprises 231 wood panels on which are painted a variety of words and phrases (see figure I.1). Such words as *gold, flowing silk, blue,* and *arabic* adorn some panels, while phrases like "an evening of cards," "open sky," and "of the possibilities for joy" appear on others. As a composite, it is a beautiful ensemble of earthly life and experiences, a kind of patchwork that suggests a loose coming together, some kind of deregulated togetherness. A gathering.

Interestingly and ironically, considering the artwork's title, if there is a harvest in this ensemble, it's unclear where it is. Unlike a harvest, which is often coextensive with a homogenous yield, Simmons's artwork offers instead a world of different, seemingly unrelated, variously flourishing forms of life. Nothing and no one appears in a locatable space-time, just life blooming in the marked planks that come together as an uncategorized ecology of their own. A gathering of some kind where the word's (*gathering*) own shape-shifting capacity to be either (or simultaneously) noun or verb, a collectivity or state,

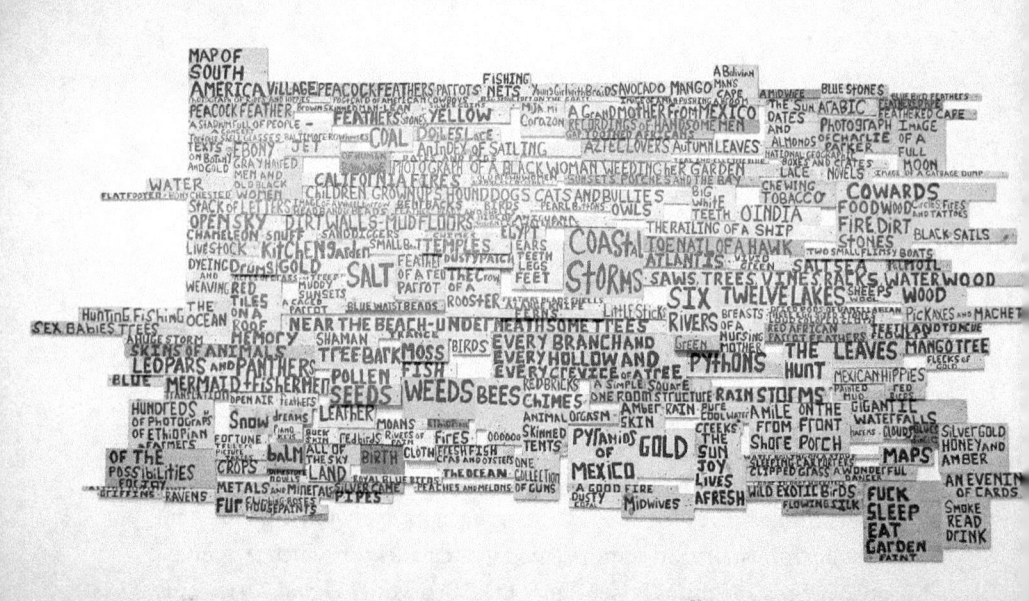

FIGURE I.1. Xaviera Simmons, *Harvest*, 2010. Courtesy of the artist and David Castillo.

a relation or act of coming together animates the ungovernable, uncategorizable energy infusing this art.

Most directly, while phrases like "greyhaired men and old black women" and "Mexican Hippies" affix planks without an accompanying predicate, events such as "fuck sleep eat garden paint" or "of the possibilities for joy" are not wedded to an easily locatable subject. The separation here arguably engenders a certain fugitive movement where togetherness is unmoored from the enclosures of category and purpose. Moreover, like an aerial view of earth swirling as undifferentiated swashes of green and blue, *Harvest* is a flourish of building materials remaining unbuilt, unconsolidated, and uncategorized. Social life in *Harvest* orbits into and out of view as verbs disappear and reappear from and without their proper subjects and half-indicated socialities bloom as an earth without enclosure.

I begin with Simmons's installation because in some ways it seems like a beginning, another imagination of earthly relation that pushes against capture. Unfinished sentences, unlocalized movement and activity, people living within and outside the limits of name and category, a vision of earth that isn't. In *Harvest*, earthly living moves by way of a seemingly uncoordinated ensemble of gatherings, and the aesthetic ruse of Simmons's installation is that, despite the title's extractive/consumptive implications, the art and the living within remain ungivable and, in turn, neither knowable nor takable.

In *Black Gathering*, I engage with Black artists and writers who've aestheticized and poeticized a relation between togetherness and ungivable living. Toni Morrison, for example, concludes *Beloved* (1987), a novel about un/surveilled Black gatherings, as "not a story to pass on" (Morrison 2004, 323). Fellow writer Gayl Jones joins Morrison by not *giving* words to her characters; instead, she listens to how they arrange their lives. Both writers join up with sculptor Leonardo Drew in moving out of the way of the various togethernesses flourishing on the page and the canvas. As Drew shares about his abstract installations of weathered everyday objects, "The work will pull you by the nose. You know that you don't have all the answers, and the unknown is the best place where you would want to be as an artist, not knowing. That actually leads you to ask questions, and it continuously feeds itself" (quoted in Weiss 2016).

It is precisely this nonteleological openness, unenclosed words and stories, insistently unfinished canvases and sentences where Black life and Blackened living seemingly come together through a kind of release.[1] I assert that the writers and artists surveyed in this book, in some ways all together, speak to as well as formally experimentalize another relation to fleshly and earthly togetherness, what Gayl Jones might describe as saying the beginning "better than [it was said] in the beginning" (Jones 1975, 54). Within the context of Jones's *Corregidora* (1975), where the quote appears, a Black woman blues singer named Ursa lives with slavery's long h/arm, finding that its violence, its perverse logic of Black women's sexuality as given over haunts her songs. She grapples with, and often discovers in her dreams, how *their* ownership of her family changes her music and how singing itself changes what release might mean; "Let me give witness the only way I can. I'll make a fetus out of grounds of coffee to rub inside my eyes. . . . I'll stain their hands. Everything said in the beginning must be said better than in the beginning" (54).

Ursa's witnessing moves by way of a different comportment toward flesh and earth, an understanding of both (here, womb and coffee bean) as extractively imbricated, and how their imaginative gathering in her eyes, their gathering which becomes a haunted song she releases, makes for a vision they can't take. All of this prefaces the main character's instruction that *everything said in the beginning must be said better than in the beginning*. In *Corregidora*, Black art makes for another imagining of relation, one that indicts anti-Black and anti-earth extraction and alchemically transforms their presumptively shared give-overness into untakable music. What the main character attunes us to is how Black art has long provided another dream of beginnings, deregulated, unownable arrangements different from those imposed by the world slavery made.

Ursa's song, like Xaviera Simmons's *Harvest*, aestheticizes other beginnings where Black life moves as if flesh and earth were neither givable nor ownable. Such aesthetics of ungiven life are, as Gayl Jones instructs, how new beginnings are formed. Beginnings that might respond to the enduring violences of a fictionalized, white Enlightenment narrative of the earth's beginning. For example, according to seventeenth-century patron saint of liberal humanism, John Locke (2015, 120), "in the beginning, all the world" was America, and such beginnings were ordained by god's *giving* of the earth to men: "God, who hath given the world to men in common, hath also given them reason to make use of it to the best advantage of life and convenience. The earth and all that is therein is given to men for the support and comfort of their being" (110).

Moreover, for Locke, such use of the earth was inextricable from gathering, which was inextricable from ownership. Indeed, according to the philosopher, "all the world" began with the "first gathering"; in the chapter "On Property" from his *Two Treatises of Government* (1689), this "first gathering" describes man's presocial relation to the earth (2015, 119). Locke ponders: "He that is nourished by the acorns he picked up under an oak, or the apples he gathered from the trees in the wood. . . . I ask then, when did they begin to be his? When he digested? Or when he eat? Or when he boiled? Or when he brought them home? Or when he picked them up? And it is plain, if the first gathering made them not his, nothing else could" (111). Significantly, Locke's rationalization of self and earthly ownership is bound up with the question of labor: "He [who] hath mixed his labour with, and joined to it, something that is his own" (111). Such a claim, on its face, both brutally hopes to justify settlement and expropriation while also suggesting that the enslaved Black and Indigenous workers of the land had divine right to it and, by implication, their own flesh. But, as is common in Enlightenment rhetorics about freedom's universality, anti-Blackness makes explicit the Age of Reason's brute and terrible particularity. That is, the father of liberalism himself was also a chief architect of the Carolina colony within which both Black and Native "slaves made up a significant portion of the population from the beginning," such that "by 1672 'between one fourth and one third of the colony's newcomers were Negroes.'" By 1710, "promotional literature for the colony . . . included '2 Negro slaves as a requirement . . . in order to live comfortably' in Carolina" (Hinshelwood 2013, 577, 579). By making the ownership of Black people a requirement for settler comfort and by naturalizing the colony's existence precisely through recourse to a fear of war, of being surrounded, Locke sanctioned the unhoming of Blackness and indigeneity as settler home's prerequisite.[2]

Moreover, after Locke declared "all the world was America," a move that at once rationalized Black people and earth as ownable and givable and brutalized the expression of gathering as extraction, the logic of the gift buttressed life and freedom's expression. That is, Locke's theory of beginnings, as Black and Native studies scholars Cheryl Harris, Joanne Barker, and others have argued, provided a political theory for the purported founders of the United States, who "embraced Lockean labor theory as the basis for a right of acquisition because it affirmed the right of the New World settlers to settle on and acquire the frontier. It confirmed and ratified their experience" (Harris 1993, 280).[3] Moreover, as feminist scholar Mimi Nguyen demonstrates, the notion of the gift forges a "genealogy of liberalism" extending from Locke to the present: "Under modern humanism, th[e] individual is understood to be 'free' on the condition that he or she act autonomously[;] . . . the consciousness of the modern subject thus proceeds through self-referential enclosure as a precondition for rational action and contract with like others, including wage labor, marriage and family deemed the most natural of such forms, through which *possessive ownership* is perceived as a historical necessity for human freedom" (Nguyen 2012, 11–12).

Saidiya Hartman joins Nguyen here in arguing that this history of (white) self-possession, or holding property in one's self, "presumes particular forms of embodiment and excludes or marginalizes others" (Hartman 1997, 122). Put differently, even after emancipation and the alleged gift of Black freedom, the history of American self-possession centrally moves as the capacity of whiteness to keep Blackness held, that is, in holding. Such figuration of Black freedom as propertied self-possession, moreover, depended on a continued anti-Black and anti-earth figuration of gathering. As Hartman demonstrates, compelled Black self-regulation manifested through the equating of quasi-bound (often, agricultural) labor with civic responsibility: the coercive gathering of earth moved in relation to the coercive gathering of self. In her seminal *Scenes of Subjection: Terror, Slavery, and Self-Making in Nineteenth-Century America*, Hartman continues by arguing: "Indebtedness was central to the creation of a memory of the past in which white benefactors, courageous soldiers, and virtuous mothers sacrificed themselves for the enslaved. This memory was to be seared into the minds of the freed. Debt was at the center of a moral economy of submission and servitude and was instrumental in the production of peonage. Above all, it operated to bind the subject by compounding the service owed, augmenting the deficit through interest accrued, and advancing credit that extended interminably the obligation of service" (Hartman 1997, 131). It is through her engagement with the rhetoric and writing of "missionaries, teachers, and Freedmen's Bureau officials, and Northern entrepreneurs," particularly their advice on what so-called responsible freed Black living should *look* like, where Hartman finds indebtedness a common theme (127). To be free was not only to have received a gift, something givable, but the expression of such freedom was legitimate only if one could paradoxically demonstrate a measure of coercive self-regulation in its exercise. Keeping oneself together, via the "moral economy of submission," moreover, was bound up with the quasi-forced capitalist extraction of the earth (130).

What is more, as Hartman argues, Black gathering's movement outside of anti-Black and anti-earth spatio-temporalities of capitalist regulation figured as a civic threat. Reflecting on narrative accounts by recently freed Black people, she (Hartman) argues that: "Freedom did not abolish the lash . . . the habitual exercise of violence, in particular, Klan attacks on black homes—against freedpeople forced them to 'mostly hide out in the woods.' If blacks assembled, they were accused of sedition" (140). Instructively, this figuration of deregulated Black gathering as Black sedition, from slavery to the present, has long been integral to the generalization of a white ecology. A *white ecol-*

ogy is a fictionalized imposition of anti-earth and anti-Black narratives of the earth and Black people as given over to propertied regulation and inscription, theoretically sanctioned, according to Bernd Herzogenrath, in the text of "Western (white) Metaphysics," notably that of John Locke (Herzogenrath 2013, 4). Through anti-Black forms of gathering (as extraction) and regulation, such a generalization of white ecologies has attempted to privatize and regulate a free relation with the self and the earth.

Notably, before Herzogenrath's recent theorization of white ecology's enduring pretense to metaphysical generality (from Locke to the present), Nathan Hare's landmark 1970 essay, "Black Ecology," centered racism's enduring impact on Black people's access to healthy places for gathering ensured by clean air, water, and housing. Hare indicts mainstream environmentalism's unmarked investment in what he calls "white ecologies." Citing a 1965 federal water pollution report, Hare (1970, 2) argues, "In the realm of white ecology pollution closes your beaches and prevents your youngsters from wading, swimming, boating, water-skiing, fishing, and other recreation close to home."

Tellingly, according to Hare, in a report on the impact of contaminated oceans on (white) leisure and extraction, a 1960s governmental call for environmental awareness and remedy ignored pollution's impact on the Black working class. Given that public beaches were not desegregated until 1968, the report doesn't say how an investment in the generality of white ecology always already violently policed Black gathering. According to environmental sociologist Dorceta Taylor (2002, 27): "Blacks were barred from using other city parks and living in other neighborhoods. [Chicago's] Marquette Park, which had a public beach, was guarded to ensure that Whites had exclusive use of the facilities. When Whites used fear, intimidation, and vigilante tactics to deny Blacks use of recreational facilities, the police did not protect the rights of Blacks."

Taylor's and Hare's attention to the distinction between white and Black ecologies, then, powerfully attunes us to the tenacious whiteness at the heart of mainstream environmentalism and how discourses of pollution, for example, sustained an enduring ethos against Black gathering even as the purportedly race-neutral discourse of contaminants was being advanced. Moreover, Hare's "Black Ecology" is regarded as a key text that identifies and extends the need for environmental justice activism. As Taylor (2002, 28) writes, "During the 1960s and 1970s, Blacks throughout the country also organized campaigns to reduce pollution, improve sanitation, clean up neighborhoods, and reduce the incidence of lead poisoning in African American communities." While

Black Gathering is not a history of Black art focused on environmental justice, it engages with Black literary and visual arts of the environmental justice era (1970s–present). Arguably extending the terms of environmental justice, the art surveyed in this book powerfully elaborates some possible but, per Morrison, not-to-be-passed on shapes of gathering as Black ecological desire.[4]

Equally important, Black writers and artists have illuminated how a certain figuration of the aesthetic, a certain relationship with the aesthetic, integrally buttresses such presumption of the earth and Black flesh's given-overness to inscription. On the notion of a "white ecology" in the text of Western metaphysics, Herzogenrath writes:

> In the Beginning was the Word, and the Word was with God, and the Word was God. But where did the word fall, where did it leave its trace? Where did it echo, resonate? So, before the word, there must have been some background, some canvas, some blank page? As Deleuze and Guattari have it, "Significance is never without a *white wall* upon which it inscribes its signs and redundancies." So, in the beginning was the White. Uniform, indistinctive whiteness. And God wrote. The omniscient author had no writer's block. Facing the absolute whiteness, always following the Golden Ratio, he separated light from darkness, the waters from the land, night from day, and so on. (2013, 3)

Recall that Locke, too, mobilized a Genesis narrative, asserting that God gave over the earth (and people) to men "in common" (2015, 113). Then, not only did the earth and the universe become figured as given-overable, but as Herzogenrath argues, this given-over-ness is inextricable from a violent figuration of the aesthetic. In Locke, the word's meta-inscriptional force moved coterminously with an extractivist, fundamentally anti-Black and anti-indigenous ethos. And the earth figured as canvas and pen for gathering's reductivist definition.

Even still, against such violent aesthetic instrumentalization of Black people and nonhuman life toward liberal personhood's vile anti-Black origins, Ursa's elusive song bespeaks other arrangements. In *Black Gathering*, I engage writers and artists who theorize and aestheticize gathering's essentially deregulated kinesis at the meeting ground of ungiven people and ungiven earth. Here, I join scholars Camille Dungy and Kimberly Ruffin. Dungy's anthology, *Black Nature: Four Centuries of African American Nature Poetry* (2009), and Ruffin's monograph, *Black on Earth: African American Ecoliterary Traditions* (2010), center Black writers and poets who were "investigating the alignment between man and nature long before the popularity of contemporary ecopoetics" (Dungy 2009, xxii) and who reflect "a deep knowledge about the human and nonhuman consequences of social systems" (Ruffin 2010, 20). At the same time, though, the writers surveyed in this book push the question of Black ecology past what might figure as physical nature all the way into the domain of astrophysical and quantum vitalities. I consider how deregulated togethernesses undulate in sentences, images, and artistic arrangements that pulsate against enclosure, extending the ecological beyond even its own regulative pretense. That is, a Black ecology, where *ecology* derives from the Greek word *oikos*, "a fundamental unit, a household, a collectivizing space, a gathering of people and things," moves by way of an aesthetic that's visible and invisible, earthly and cosmic, phantasmatic and imaginative (Cohen 2013, xvii). There's a kinetics of returning—spatially, temporally, astrophysically—to other possible horizons of togetherness, a vision conjured by artistically *saying the beginning better than it was said in the beginning.*

For scholar Christina Sharpe, these other horizons might accrue at the interface between atmospheric and poetic distillation, ecoaesthetic openings for gathering with self and earth in the unshareable space-time of "hold and release" (Sharpe 2020). In a recent column in the online magazine *Jewish Currents*, Sharpe is one of "three poetry readers [who] reflect on a poem they've been holding close during this difficult time" (Sharpe 2020). Sharpe characterizes her engagement with Canisia Lubrin's recent poetry collection, *The Dyzgraph*ˣ*st* (2020), as a "sitting with" (Sharpe 2020), a form of aesthetic dwelling and cohabitation taking place in the midst of the COVID-19 pandemic quarantine and global protests against anti-Black state violence. As Sharpe relates:

> A word might hold you close when the world does not, gerund; it might measure the distance between what is and what might be. Open to this old/new word/world that was always there and that was "big enough for all of us."
>
> In the midst of all of the sacrifices (and the sacrificed)—and all that is being made and unmade by masses of young, queer, trans, disabled Black people organizing and gathering in order to insist a habitable wor(l)d into being—I come back to "Dream #5." And by the time I land in its final line, "How rude of me to force you on the thing that springs blood," some suspension breaks, some clarity returns. I have been gathered.
>
> My breath has been taken away and then given back. (Sharpe 2020)

For Sharpe, Black gathering moves across what is taking place in the streets—"masses of young, queer, trans, disabled Black people organizing and gathering"—and amid the wordly arrangements within Lubrin's poetry (Sharpe 2020). Concerning the latter, "a sitting with," a being with Lubrin's poetry, describes other aesthetic possibilities for Black gathering during a pandemic that disproportionately impacts (and is instrumentalized to perversely criminalize) Black people's already regulated rights to be together and to survive such togetherness. Sharpe's "sitting with," then, weighed down by the enclosure of spectacularized Black suffering and the hyperpolicing of its refusal, elaborates gathering's possibility to make other ways of being with the world. Precisely, for Sharpe, a being with Lubrin's long poem, which "works with and at what survives TransAtlantic slavery" (Sharpe 2020), joins her time with clouds (which, as she acknowledges, remind her daily "to breathe, and to look up and out") to bespeak another iteration of Black gathering as integral to survival as that which unfolds in the streets. Sharpe's brilliant elaboration of Black gathering's aesthetic travel evokes the healing potential of some deregulated togetherness ethereally linking sky, street, and page.

In that way, Sharpe's writing and its earthly canvas move as part of a larger Black aesthetic tradition traveling alongside what figures as Black gathering's political expression. As Black people gather in the streets to protest state violence and as Black people have always gathered in spite of the state's incessant prohibitions against such gathering, white supremacist violence moves (and has moved) with deadly force to interrupt Black togetherness. Even still, Black gatherings happen; some livingness, with neither sanction nor extraction, manages to get through. The artists and writers in this book aesthetically honor and acknowledge this, and their artworks might be seen as offerings of respite and for (cosmically expansive levels of deregulated) reassembly, which Sharpe also acknowledges, even as white supremacy's murderously interruptive force sees fleshly/earthly separation as its raison d'être.

Put another way, through non-pass-on-able scenes of cloud and poem dwelling, quilting, and sharing, the immeasurable quantum communique between earth and cosmos and the unfinished arrangements of words and objects, Black artists and writers experiment with togetherness without ownership. Moreover, as indexed by Sharpe's communion with poetry, activism, and atmosphere, aesthetic engagements with Black social life's multiplicity put pressure on form itself such that pages and canvases become occasions for a different kind of relational praxis. In this regard, other kinds of engagement with such art are required.

As a student of Black studies, performance studies, and Black feminist theory, and as someone committed to the abolition of whiteness (as racialized, gendered, and sexualized property and as propertizing apparatus), which imbricates and animates the "extractive view," I argue that Black gathering's aesthetic enactments provides instruction on a nonpropertizing, nonauthoritative relation to the craft of writing about art itself (Gómez-Barris 2017).[5] As Jared Sexton (2014, 593) writes, "Abolition is the interminable radicalization of every radical movement, but a radicalization through the perverse affirmation of deracination, an uprooting of the natal, the nation, and the notion, preventing any order of determination from taking root, a politics without claim, without demand even, or a politics whose demand is 'too radical to be formulated in advance of its deeds.'" Arguably gathering bears a similar kinesis to what Sexton calls "the perverse affirmation" of indeterminacy itself. This undecidabilty, at once indicating a noun or verb, a being or making, potentiates fugitive capacity; in that way, such undecidability when it manifests in and as Black literary and aesthetic practice must, as Édouard Glissant might say, be respected.[6] That is to say, part of what it means for me as someone who benefits from whiteness is to not just engage Black social and aesthetic thought in its delimitation of abolition's political and ethical shape but to think about how the commitment to abolition through a sustained engagement with Black studies refuses reading strategies enacting the very propertizing and extraction otherwise critiqued.

In other words, as each chapter queries how the arts of writing, sculpture, and painting engender the possibility of form as a place for relationality's reimagination and safeguarding, I'm committed to not attempting some false analytic resolution of Black gatherings' indeterminate meanings and ambulation. Most directly, the artists and writers surveyed in the book advance another ecological and architectural imagination into some undisclosed coordinates where the release of earth from its fraudulent ownership is coterminous with the release of flesh. Such forms of release, the inherent fugitivity of *gathering* as a term, flourish in the recesses of property's afterlife, theorized by innovative assemblages of language, found objects, paint; Black gathering potentiates exits out of the extractive view and into realms that are nobody's business. In that way, I hope that this book contributes to ongoing conversations about contemporary Black feminist and abolitionist ecopoiesis and the role of aesthetics (and aesthetic analysis) in sustaining and concealing a nonextractive view. Moreover, I'm interested in how an engagement with Black gathering's deregulated kinesis as a way to imagine fleshly/earthly togetherness at abolition and anti-extraction's meeting ground calls on my belief in another geological ethos, what Audre Lorde and Kathryn Yusoff might respectively describe as "language [as correlated to rock] crazure" and the "epoch making" capacity of "black poetics" beyond the space-time of this writing (Lorde 1980, 8; Yusoff 2019, 19).[7]

Returning to Simmons, to suggest that *Harvest* might flourish as gathering is to believe in (but not look for) its unseen/unfracked depths of undisclosed place and activity, unindicated space-times of interspecies relation—"wild exotic birds," "pythons," and "rainstorms." When the human is indicated in the mosaic of wood planks, they are often Black and Brown, the people historically extracted from, perversely harvested, so that the earth could be. That is, capitalist agriculture's very world-historical conditions are settler colonialism and chattel slavery, flesh and earth gathered up so that the world could be turned over and broken up for a profit. As Black feminist scholar Tiffany Lethabo King (2016, 7–8) argues: "Under slavery and conquest, the Black body becomes the ultimate symbol of accumulation, malleability, and flux existing outside of human coordinates of space and time. Rather, Blackness is the raw dimensionality (symbol, matter, kinetic energy) used to make space."

But in *Harvest*, Black and Brown people show up as human insofar as that humanity ambles in the unelaborated recesses of the artwork's own unlocalizable socialities. In the middle of *Harvest*, for example, there's a panel that tells of "a photograph of a black woman weeding her garden" while, elsewhere, an "old black women" and a "grandmother from Mexico" are named as quickly as they are dispersed. Once more, the omission of certain elaborations bespeaks a fugitive gathering at the heart of *Harvest*. Just as communions run out of and away from category, togethernesses otherwise vitiated by agents of extraction manage to flourish as a half-told story. In *Harvest*, fugitive life moves as beginnings that ripple past the enclosures indicated by the artwork's very name, gathering in and with the ungiven earth otherwise.[8]

These gatherings with earth otherwise and more particularly the aesthetic depictions of Black women in a variety of outdoor locales are arguably a central theme of Simmons's photographic oeuvre. For Simmons, while the Black woman subject of her photographs is often herself, *she* becomes a different character depending on where a photo is taken, be it cane fields, forests, a canyon's valley. She shares, "I see the landscape at this point as both the most fertile and the most basic ground to overlay the characters that come to me when I engage with these environments" (quoted in Despain 2012). Simmons's reflection here suggests that art, and with it the land, enacts the possibility of another imagining, one where known artist and (perhaps) location might be re-created differently together. An artful interaction with the environment potentiates a dream of another relation. In Simmons's artwork, otherwise pursued and surveilled flesh and earth are somehow cast outside the harvester's reach, as the photos intimate the possibility of unendangered togetherness.

In the photo titled *Denver* (2008), for example, a Black woman stands alone in a creek, her skirts underwater. She holds a fishing pole, cast outward with the end of the line invisible. Behind her is an uncultivated field, some towering pines, and a mountain. The river flows around her ankles (see figure I.2). There is no evidence of impending arrest or extraction, no diggers of a pipeline visible or policers accusing her of trespass. No one to interrupt her activity or presume, divinely, juridically, otherwise, that she and the earth belong to them. In the space/time/ecology of this photo, relationalities flourish without definition or interception.

I argue that the space/time/ecology of this photo suggests a possibility of gathering with and on earth without the threat of someone else's overdetermination, an intrusive presumption of harvestability. As with Simmons's installation *Harvest*, in *Denver* there's relationality without explanation and assertions of earthly life that come through without category. In *Denver*, something and someone flourishes within the frame's safekeeping—a Black gathering made possible by a kind of ecological protection engendered by art.[9]

Here I believe in the ecology of the photograph, installation, and watercolor painting the same way Sonya Posmentier believes in poems. In *Cultivation and Catastrophe*, Posmentier (2017, 4) advances, "Poems sometimes mimic or approximate organic forms and processes often associated with enclosure, preservation, self-sustainability, and internal relation, forms that can exceed their own boundaries, and that may in turn yield new models for social and ecological relation." I also believe in poems and particularly how they can, like photographs, sculpture, and paintings, "yield new models for social and ecological relation" (4).

Indeed, scholars in Black studies and Native studies, along with twentieth- and twenty-first-century Black women writers and poets, have long engaged the intersection of anti-Black and anti-earth violence toward "new models for social and ecological relation." To backtrack, when I first started thinking about gathering in relation to anti-Black histories of property and propertied personhood, I was in a series of study sessions with my friend J. Kameron Carter, sessions which eventually formalized into a speaker series at Duke University called Black Outdoors: Humanities Futures after Property and Possession (2016–17). During this time I began to more fully con-

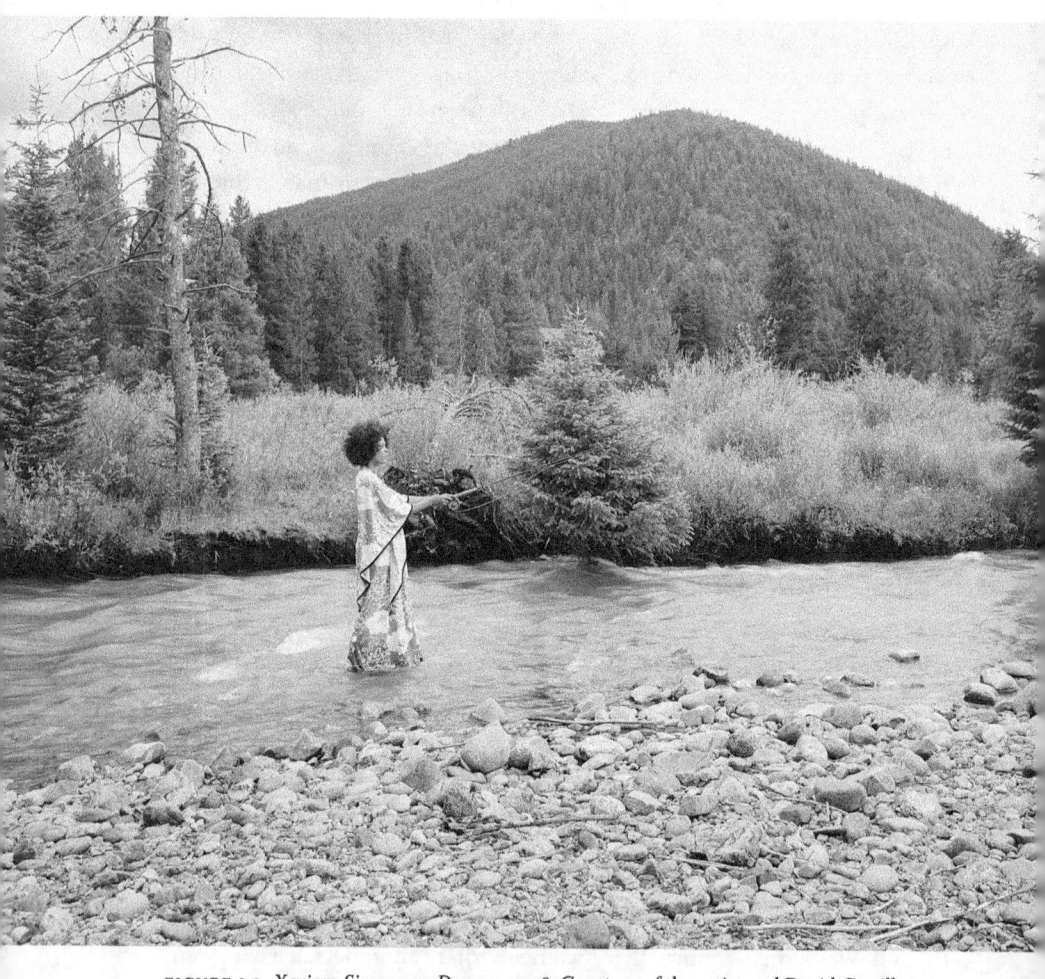

FIGURE 1.2. Xaviera Simmons, *Denver*, 2008. Courtesy of the artist and David Castillo.

template Black studies in relation to critical ecology literatures. The writings of Anna Tsing, Saidiya Hartman, Fred Moten, Denise Ferreira da Silva, and others figured centrally as we grappled with the ways that these scholars' engagements with the world's end, the violence of the Anthropocene, attune us to the practices of intra-racial and inter-species forms of togetherness long flourishing otherwise. Key concepts advanced by these scholars include the anti-cultivationist view of more-than-human togetherness from a mushroom on the forest's floor (Tsing 2015), propertied personhood's integral anti-Blackness (Hartman 1997), Black studies' earth-saving mandate (Moten 2017c),[10] and Black feminist artists and writers' unorganization or deorganization of the world toward "difference without separability" (Ferreira da Silva 2016). Moreover, as I was working on this book while reading and thinking alongside these scholars, I was also reading and writing in relation to Black women artists like Xaviera Simmons, Dionne Brand, and Wangechi Mutu, who gesture toward while creating ecologies in their photography, poetry, and collages alike, where Black women characters interact with the natural world without regulation, highlighting while also subverting a relation between the mutual precarity shared by uncaptured Blackness and earthliness. The book emerges out of this sustained thinking and study, done together and alone, even though alone is never what it seems to be.

Black Gathering is divided into two parts: part I, Gathering's Art, and part II, the Art of Gathering. This distinction, while in keeping with *gathering*'s meanings as a noun or a verb, is kind of impossible. That is, *gathering* as noun (a collective, a party, and so on) and *gathering* as verb (bringing together) shape-shift into each other. For example, the brief sentence "People are gathering" could suggest either an event or an activity; *gathering* indicates some kind of elusive arrangement, an artful ecology of ungiven life.

In chapter 1, I engage Toni Morrison's *Beloved* (1987) and Nikki Wallschlaeger's *Houses* (2015) to argue for Black women's centrality to conversations on ecoaesthetics. Although they are often underacknowledged if not unacknowledged, Black women writers have long illuminated how the world slavery made, in its juridico-philosophical sanctioning of "whiteness as property," brutalized experiences of ecology, of home (Harris 1993). Even so, writers like Wallschlaeger and Morrison crucially imagine the possibilities of home beyond property. In their art, Black gatherings ecoaesthetically intercede in and against property's terrors and depravations. So, thinking with *ecology* as derived from *oikos*, I interpret *Beloved* and *Houses* as enacting all the term's definitions while elucidating how *oikos* doesn't require the conditions of extractive gathering and the propertizing of self (Cohen 2013, xvii). Across these texts, there is an imagining of gathering's artfulness, of its artistic capacity to change an environment, to etherealize home as rearrangements of color, light, texture, and image that, in turn, illuminate and suspend property's disruptive violences. Arguably, both books imagine another kind of living, another kind of house and oikos, unmoored from an assertion of ownership or presumptive givenness. Both authors poeticize oikos and home less from the vantage of property than from an ecoaesthetic vantage, the complex interface between what gathers in a room and what might artfully release as some ungivable time together.

In chapter 2, I explore how writers Samiya Bashir and Gabrielle Ralambo-Rajerison engage classic physics and astrophysics, respectively. They join Morrison and Wallschlaeger in precisely these ecoaesthetic and ecopoetic contemplations of Black social life in the wake of anti-Blackness's enduring assault on fleshly, interspecies, extraplanetary, and more-than-human relationality.[11] Drawing on branches of science that, as Ashon Crawley (2017, 48) writes of quantum physics, offer "mode[s] of study that verif[y] the fact [that] there are things that happen in the world, in the universe, that are not easily perceptible to human flesh," Bashir and Ralambo-Rajerison offer meditations on Black gathering that posit the deep connections between earth and cosmos. In many ways, I argue that, the authors surveyed in this chapter poetically dwell with the universe's beginnings and, following Jones, try to say them better. That is, both Bashir and Ralambo-Rajerison poeticize around the fluctuations of dark matter, which even astrophysicists conclude is what proceeded the fictionalized beginning forged by god as creator; Blackness, in their writings, moves as both earthly, "enfleshed" (and degraded in that enfleshment) experience and as a kind of energetic and cosmological surround for otherwise regulated relationality (Weheliye 2014, 14). Moreover, in keeping with the question of how gathering makes an environment, I advance that the authors' artful engagements with Black gathering enact a cosmoaesthetics and a cosmopoetics. That is, through unconventional arrangements of words, particularly the spacing between them (Bashir) and between passages (Ralambo-Rajerison), I believe that the writers cosmoaestheticize poems as parallel galaxies. As poet Amy Catanzano (2011) argues, "Quantum poetics investigates how physical reality is assumed, imagined and tested through language at discernible and indiscernible scales of spacetime." While neither Bashir nor Ralambo-Rajerison identifies their art as "quantum poetics," per se, their conceptual deployment of terms common in quantum and astrophysics, along with the errant spacing between and around words and passages, arguably alludes to what Catanzano calls the "something else" quality of the poem. In other words, if, following Catanzano, the poem, is not just writing but a play of "indiscernible scales," showing how language always points to an extraempirical elsewhere, then might the spacing around words also allude to a something beyond the page? An immeasurable space-time that shows up as an emptiness, a pulling of words apart? This chapter considers how the poetry of Bashir and Ralambo-Rajerison makes of emptiness, the emptiness between words, another occasion for cosmoaesthetic and cosmopoetic cohabitation.

Again, the first part of this book considers how gatherings make or art something, be it a poetic experience of galactic relation or a sense of home against property's artificial enclosures. The second part considers Black gathering's relation to ungiven life through artistic practices of bringing together. I begin by discussing how writer Gayl Jones engages language and then how sculptor Leonardo Drew arrays artificially weathered objects in order to elucidate how unforeseen arrangements might unsettle life's assumed givenness to word and category. I see both Jones and Drew as gathering, although not necessarily toward something recognizable; in fact, their gatherings put pressure on the impulse to name and know. What their gatherings potentially do is activate the possibilities of a togetherness that exceeds understanding and, in some ways, the logic of social and economic value. In their art they raise the question of forms of togetherness ungivable to axioms of reason and category and of forms of togetherness that thrive precisely because they evade regulation.

Moreover, the artists surveyed in the first part elucidate how togetherness creates an environment, more livable surroundings—gathering as a group or family—and the artists in the second part express the definition of gathering as a bringing together. The first definition indicates a place of arrival; the second suggests an activity without clear or predictable end or form. Put differently, *gathering* in part I emerges as a noun, as an effect of an arrangement of an author's writing and wordly (along with spatial) arrangements. What Morrison does in *Beloved*, for example, in her deeply beautiful engagement with flora and fauna, is conceivably transform the book into an earthly environment for the (formerly) enslaved characters of her novel. The novel, I hope more than think, is a gathering, a literary materialization of an earth where characters can live rather than merely survive. Moreover, the novel bears spaces for characterological and imagistic togetherness in its prose and across its pages, and harbors experiences of gathering to remain, as per its author's instruction, elusive to transfer at book's end.

In part II, I attend to the act of *gathering*, where its status as verb is highlighted by the abstractional practices of both Jones and Drew. In their work, there's arguably an interest in the materiality of words and objects—wood and cotton, for example, in the case of Drew—as locus of relationality rather than in the possible worlds those arrangements yield. In particular, in chapter 3, I consider Jones's early writing as forms of aesthetic experimentations that attempt to listen, without interfering, to where social life might build and move in Black erotic and "cripped" turns of speech (McRuer 2004, 59). That is, her (Jones's) unanticipatable arrangements of language, alphabetic letters, and tense arguably suspend a giving over of social life to presumptively normative linguistic arrangements. In that way, her characters thrive beyond others' understanding even as they contend with the violence of others' sentencing.

In chapter 4 I contemplate how Drew's gathering of artificially weathered, everyday objects questions the relation between gathering and economic systems of valuation. Particularly in Drew's installations, everyday objects—kids' toys, a high-heeled shoe, the feathers of a dead bird, for example—are artificially weathered, often painted in monochromes of black and white, and arranged into nonfigurative installations. Such arrangements move by way of gathering's kinetic openness. That is, there is an unfixedness to Drew's installations, as materials thickly bob on the surface of the canvas while the illusion of decay indicates an impending collapse, where everything might fall together.

Finally, *Black Gathering* concludes with a brief meditation on the mid- to late twentieth-century artistic career of former sharecropper Clementine Hunter. In 1955, Hunter completed murals commissioned for a structure on Melrose, a working twentieth-century plantation in Natchitoches Parish, Louisiana. On the walls of what was alternately remembered as a storehouse and a prison for enslaved people, Hunter painted scenes of Black people gathering: different tableaux feature Black women sharecroppers gathering cotton and pecans, people assembling for church services and baptisms, some nighttime dancing. On the walls of a building arbitrarily named African House, the walls of a plantation are repainted by someone managed, someone whose own ancestors were violently gathered so that those walls could hold life apart. Mothers from children, lovers from lovers, the feel of grass on unfettered flesh.

In ornamentalizing the building with an ungivable painterly vision, of Black gathering, these powerful murals not only work in the interest of togetherness's deregulation, but somehow they also change the atmosphere in which they appear.[12] This is complicated. The murals are on the interior of a plantation. To view them requires the purchase of a ticket for a plantation tour, the monies of which ostensibly support the very anti-Black, anti-earth structure's maintenance and touristic vitality. Still, what would it mean to think of that muraled wall as an ecology that harbors Black memories, feelings, desires, and dreams? The feel of a painter's brush, the unscaled images and memories that ambled in her mind, the molecular breakdown of wood that somehow makes its way into the night sky. Indeed, along with the work of other writers and artists surveyed in this book, Hunter's murals suggest that Black gatherings, through artistic innovation, might transform the very terroristic ecologies within which they move or, at the very least, might engender private harbors where besieged flesh and earth could live together differently. Indeed, in reflecting on why I arrived at *all* these writers and why all of them *together*, I kept coming back to the common denominator of home. Each writer and artist gestures to home: its elusiveness in Simmons; its dual comforting and terroristic character in Morrison, Wallschlaeger, and Jones; along with its quantum and molecular immeasurability in Bashir, Ralambo-Rajerison, and Drew; and in Hunter, its infinite re-canvassing.

While the first chapter engages home in relation to property's terroristic anti-Black shapes, there are ways that home appears again and again through the art and literature surveyed here. As if through opening something on the page and canvas and into flight, home joins other words, like a bird in murmuration, indexing not just the possibility of Black gathering as deregulated social life but also a deregulated social life that's somehow protected. In that way, perhaps what art does, in safeguarding the presences and histories it names and evokes, is honor their ungivability, even if ownership and enclosure come knocking and try to have their say.

PART I. GATHERING'S ART

1

"FOR A WHILE AT LEAST"

Toni Morrison, Nikki Wallschlaeger,
and the Ecoaesthetic Shapes of Home

A tall door rises up into this nothing; its hardware is heavy, secure. No bell invites your hand. So you stand there, perhaps, or move away, and later, sticking your hand in your pocket, you find a key that you know (or hope) fits the lock. Even before the tumblers fall back you know you will find what you hoped to find: a word or two that turns the "not enough" into more; the line or sentence that inserts itself into the nothing. With the right phrase, this sense becomes murky, becomes lit, differently lit. . . . More important, however, is that the writer who steps through that door with the language of his or her own intellect and imagination enters uncolonized territory, which she can claim as rightfully her own—for a while at least.
—TONI MORRISON, "On *Beloved*"

Beloved (1987) is a novel loosely based on the story of Margaret Garner, a young enslaved woman who, in 1856, killed her child in order to save her from being returned to a plantation. Describing the content of the tiny news article in which she first encountered Garner's name, Morrison (2019, 283) writes, "What is already there is simply not enough." Soon after this realization of a looming nothing, *a not enough*, Morrison describes the making, the poetic and aesthetic act of crafting *Beloved*, as at once alchemical and ecological. "A *tall door rises up into this nothing*" (283). Some space around that sentence seems necessary. Something and someone congregates there.

Returning to Morrison's account, *Beloved* begins as a door. On one side is the author with a question, a question about Black women and motherhoods long denied, of gatherings long interrupted.[1] On the other side, according to Morrison, is the "uncolonized territory, which she can claim as rightfully her own—for a while at least" (283). When I first read this assertion, I puzzled over the notion of the book as a gesture of aesthetic colonialism, particularly because the novel conceptually agitates against colonialism in its reimagining of Black and earthly togetherness after/despite slavery's encroachments. But once you get to the novel's end, the last two pages, in fact, Morrison (2004, 324) instructs her readers: "It was not a story to pass on. . . . By and by all trace is gone, and what is forgotten is not only the footprints but the water too and what is down there. The rest is weather. Not the breath of the disremembered and unaccounted for, but wind in the eaves, or spring ice thawing too quickly. Just weather." If *Beloved* blooms as a door and what is on its other side is by definition uncolonized, then might its non-pass-on-ability and the very disappearance of the novel's namesake at book's end—the mourned child at its center—suggest that what's uncolonized remains untrammeled flourish. Indeed, what I think Morrison elucidates is how the book form can both enact and dissipate colonizing doors and walls: a door aesthetically conjured and later not to be passed on. Arguably, what Morrison asserts by way of *Beloved* is an aesthetic that advances a momentarily doored environment as nondominion, as uncolonizing, and, in so doing, she prevents a presumptive (aesthetic) logic of the earth as given over to authorial colonization, to a leaving of doors where they weren't before.

Moreover, this notion of home, environment, oikos, as a mode of relation that doesn't drop a door on an ant colony without warning assuredly honors the earth as ungiven. *Beloved* sustains ungivenness, paradoxically, through an offering to Garner. That is, through communing with the "not there" and "never enough," Morrison merges the ecological and the aesthetic to advance an unextractive ecoaesthesis. Considering Malcolm Miles's recent theorization, for example, of the concept of the "eco-aesthetic" to think art practices forged at the crossroads of ecology and aesthetics, I contend that Black women writers have long engaged ecoaesthetically in the face of violence and theft and have done so by arting different practices of gathering.

To be sure, for Miles, the European Enlightenment and post-Enlightenment philosophical conversations on aesthetics and ecology have been shaped by mutual interests; that is, the "relation of the subject to other subjects/

objects . . . key to an ecological approach [is also] the central problem in rational aesthetics" (Miles 2014, 3). The question of nature's objectification via the disinterested spectator idealized by Immanuel Kant, for example, haunts Enlightenment discourses on aesthetics, thus bespeaking a larger investment in the earth's rational, perceptual subjection (56). Moreover, Kant's musing about the aesthetic, particularly the sublime, is inextricable from one's deeply racialized, gendered capacity for its appreciation in/as nature.

Still and instructively still, the anti-Blackness integral to the Enlightenment era's enslaving colonialist, violent devouring of the earth and Kant's estimation of one's capacity to rationally evaluate such aesthetic shifts go unremarked in Miles's analysis. Indeed, even though historically unacknowledged in this text on ecoaesthetics, slavery was often survived through an ecoaesthetic imagination. Black women writers like Morrison have long engaged and provided that philosophical analysis, deploying the aesthetic toward an antiextractive, decolonial ecological imagination; in *Beloved*, Morrison attends to how loving the earth and loving Blackness are integral to an antislavery, ecoaesthetic imagination. As Morrison indicates in the passage cited at the beginning of this chapter, this otherwise ecoaesthetic imagination moves by way of a door that momentarily becomes a home, the gift of lavender and a fugitive people brought together. So, too, the home at its center, 124 Bluestone Road, is a work of art, the work of a novelist who powerfully honors homemaking as a Black woman's ecoaesthetic practice undertaken by characters and writer alike: an art practice, homemaking, that sustains the characters "for a while" and that doesn't extract from the people and earth it imaginatively and momentarily builds with. Indeed, by book's end, what Miles (2014, 14), after Nicolas Bourriaud, calls "relational aesthetics" undulates as a house that fades, with everything "look[ing] sold" into an untraceable human presence, just "wind in the eaves" (Morrison 2004, 319, 324).[2]

Similarly, though appearing almost thirty years later, Nikki Wallschlaeger's poetry collection *Houses* (2015) can be seen as joining Morrison in honoring-by-doing nonextractivist ecoaesthetic work, particularly regarding the notion of home as a nonpropertizable work of art. The collection consists of forty-six one-page poems named after differently colored houses: "Pink House," "Red House," "Mint Green House," and so on. Each poem, as its own unit or gathering space, through accretion, associatively muses about the color of the house. Often, for example, color pops up in different phrases that speak to, among other referents, tones of skin, aluminum siding, and earth, contributing poignantly to what we might call a synesthetic or an ecosynesthetic life of the particularly colored house poem. In the first poem, "Pink House," for example, the first three sentences are short and deceptively simple: "Pink houses are nice. A nice house. A red worm shitting berries" (15). A sweetness about the house soon turns into a kind of bitterness, where the illusion of simplicity is precisely that. At poem's end, the presumptive resident is "Certainly a homebody. Certainly an estranged somebody, tearing pink in/the spring. I cannot post how flowers yell, but how was my baby's day at / school? Brown/pink cheeks of children weather" (15). The first three lines of the poem's final passage speak to that pink house's resident, who is estranged, "certainly." The narrator's own estrangement, perhaps in talking about the house itself, is powerfully expressed: "I cannot post how flowers yell." The pain in this poem, ostensibly shared by estranged people and torn flowers alike, forms the background noise of this "nice house for / you, a pink house . . . a chokecherry tree in back / for the kids to climb" (15). Interestingly, the singsong music of a real estate sale, the transfer of property, is weighted down by the poet's evocation of a "chokecherry tree"; here Wallschlaeger names the same tree Morrison imaginatively conjures as the shape of slavery's violent imprint on the scarred back of her main character, Sethe. Whether or not this is deliberate, Wallschlaeger and Morrison both link a notion of house as property with the violences of flesh and earth's brutal ownership.

Yet, as with *Beloved*, *Houses* formally, conceptually, and aesthetically elaborates communal living and intimacies, attending to the possibilities of a nonbrutalizing, nonextractivist, and interspecies sociality in home's sometimes improper name: "I cannot post how flowers yell but how was my baby's day at / school? Brown / pink cheeks of children weather" (15). Here, a concern about a child's day connects to the unconsumable, unknowable rage of flowers. Love for new blooms and young life phantasmatically connects the precarity of brown-cheeked children with the cultivated flowers around a "nice home." The narrator's care for both complicates the language of surface and property, what niceness says and doesn't say about how vulnerable children and flowers experience a home.

Again, both *Houses* and *Beloved* imagine the possibilities of home beyond property. Across these works of art, Black gatherings seem to ecoaesthetically intervene in and against property's violences and devastations. *Beloved* was published in 1987, 130 years after Margaret Garner killed her daughter rather than return her to slavery. The novel mythically time travels, imagining Garner's fictionally alternative life, directing the "lonesome fugitive" (Moten 2008, 202) to all the momentary places, addresses, kitchens, and frozen lakes where she can be at home (finally) with her stolen daughter, even if just *for a while*.

Moreover, *Beloved* elucidates how oikos doesn't require an extractive gathering and propertizing of self and earth as its conditions. As with Wallschlaeger's *Houses*, in *Beloved* Morrison offers another imagination of house and oikos, one unmoored from an assertion of ownership or presumptive givenness. In these authors' works, oikos emerges less from the vantage of property than from an ecoaesthetic vantage, the "relational aesthetics" of home (Miles 2014, 14), where home might momentarily harbor the possibilities of ungiven living.

And even though not acknowledged in Miles's elaboration of the concept of the ecoaesthetic, Black women writers have long contemplated the intersection of ecology and aesthetics. Such ecoaesthetic imagination arguably manifests in how oikos travels across and as a range of gatherings within unowned, shared spaces: rented rooms (Gayl Jones), community centers (Toni Cade Bambara), haunted houses and overgrown forests (Toni Morrison).[3] These writers dwell with the eco, unmooring it from the propertized logic of *dominion*, to elucidate how oikos might coalesce in a stare at the swollen red ceiling of a kitchen occupied only *for a while*. Black women writers like Morrison and Wallschlaeger seemingly ask: How might the ecoaesthetic engender other possibilities of "relational aesthetics" beyond logics of property and dominion/domination, which, in turn, might also change how we study or know (logos) the shape of gathering and oikos itself?[4]

Indeed, such unmooring of gathering from ownership moves in the words spoken by Margaret Garner herself. Again, Morrison's encounter with the news article ostensibly featuring Garner's thoughts about the murder prompts the reflection with which this chapter began; the newspaper clipping where "what is already there is simply not enough." In the clipped article written by a priest who met with Garner when she was incarcerated, he (the priest) writes:

> I inquired if she [Garner] was excited almost to madness when she committed the act.
>
> No, she replied, I was as cool as I now am; and would much rather kill them at once and thus end their sufferings than have them taken back to slavery and be murdered by piece meal. (Bassett 1856)

To be sure, to ask the question of madness here is to ask a question of property's normativity, one of fences dividing mothers from children.[5] But yet, after his query, the priest moved beyond the prison house of mad/not mad to recognize Garner's refusal of such fencing, of her children's slow murder by the plantation's housework, as the gathering wish embedded in the "passionate tenderness of a mother's love" (Bassett 1856).

Perhaps it is this enduring unfathomability of Garner's infanticide as gathering desire that inspired the ecoaesthetic work of art that Morrison made and, in some ways, left to be unmade. Not to be passed on. Not to be owned or transferred, evicted, or understood. Ecology innovated from within by those imagined to be oikos's impossibility, its underside and enabling conditions. If slavery made a home and, with it, installed a logic of property that presumed the given-over-ness of Black people, of unperceived nature, Black women writers have long been de-architecting that home toward other practices of deregulated togetherness. Through gathering's art, writers like Morrison and Wallschlaeger deploy ecoaesthetics to at once elucidate home as a place of innovation, a practice, and another way to imagine nonextractive doors and walls protecting the life within and "outside" "for a while."[6]

Beloved

"124 was spiteful" (Morrison 2004, 3). The prized street address that opens *Beloved* is audibly sick of itself. Harboring the thick terror and sadness of slavery, its unceasing grip on those who thought escape might hold life at its end, 124 Bluestone Road can't stop running. Dishes break, floorboards shake, the floor shoves. In the front room, a pool of light descends like a siren, announcing the ghostly presence of a baby killed in the collision between slavery's flesh- and earth-killing machine and the "motherlove" that endangers it and of which it is afraid (155).

The house was once a harbor for fugitives escaping Kentucky whom found the free state of Ohio on its front stoop. It was loaned to a recently freed woman, Baby Suggs, by an abolitionist couple who allowed her to reside there in exchange for work. And though we find out later that Suggs hoped the house would be a place for her entire family to gather, all the reader knows from the beginning is that Suggs's borrowed house is coming apart at the seams. Buckling under slavery's life-destroying pull, its sick logic of Black flesh-as-interminably given over, of children destined to be given to those who will never cease giving them over, "124 was spiteful." As Morrison reveals in the novel's introduction, Beloved, Garner's mythic child, "walked out of the water, climbed the rocks," and was moving furniture from the beginning. Changing the look and feel of the house. "And everybody (the characters) knew it" (xviii).

Early on, for example, Paul D, a former slave from the Sweet Home plantation that Sethe, 124's principal tenant, also came running from, notices how 124's ecosystem functions according to the whims of whose name is not on the title. From his initial entrance into the house, Paul D felt the presence of the evicted trying to come home, "a pool of red and undulating light that locked him where he stood" (10).

> "You got company?" he whispered, frowning.
> "Off and on," said Sethe.
> "Good God." He backed out the door onto the porch. "What kind of
> evil you got in here?"
> "It's not evil, just sad. Come on. Just step through." (10)

The outside, what's shut out by the false conceit of a door—the racially particular "[non]divisioning of inside and outside"—weighs down the kitchen (Cuevas 2012, 608). "Every sense he had told him the air above the stairwell was charmed and very thin" (Morrison 2004, 13). Not only does the house bear the weight of what and who evades its enclosures, but it (the house) also finds difficulty keeping the owned and ungiven earth apart. As spectral yet soaking wet girls make kitchens glow, their living sisters carry the scents of forests on their skin.

What is more, after 124 started to shut her heart down, Baby Suggs (the girls' grandmother) spent her last days in the keeping room, in a sickbed, warming herself with the threaded earths of her own making. In her room, the quilt lay "over an iron cot, made up of scraps of blue serge . . . the full range of the dark and the muted . . . in that sober field, two patches of orange looked wild—like life in the raw" (46). In the novel, as the outdoor feel and smell of earth lingers on grandchildren's skin, other ecologies bloom in the blanket that warms the home's dying, heartbroken, senior resident. A small shard of beauty provides a refuge and place of gathering for the former fugitive such that while the house pitched and protested, Suggs gathered color. Against the home, she homed.

> Baby Suggs didn't even raise her head. From her sickbed she heard
> them go but that wasn't the reason she lay still. It was a wonder to her
> that her grandsons had taken so long to realize that every house wasn't
> like the one on Bluestone Road. Suspended between the nastiness of life
> and the meanness of the dead, she couldn't get interested in leaving life
> or living it, let alone the fright of creeping-off boys. Her past had been

like her present—intolerable—and since she knew death was anything but forgetfulness, she used the little energy left her for pondering color.

"Bring a little lavender in, if you got any. Pink, if you don't."

And Sethe would oblige her with anything from fabric to her own tongue. (4)

Even though there wasn't much that Baby Suggs could do about the home clamoring not to be one, she enjoined her family into creating other arrangements: "Bring a little lavender in." The making of the quilt, which appears here and there in the novel and brings special comfort to the baby who wanted them all gone, remains one of the last remnants of a gathering at the story's conclusion. Indeed, the quilt moves throughout the novel not just to blanket the characters but to offer beauty, a different aesthetic of gathering for those exhausted from property's grip. After Suggs's death, the creation stayed behind with the besieged living; for example, after the ghost—now a young woman—walked out of the water to be with her mother, the quilt comforted her exhausted body: "she seemed so totally taken with those scraps of orange" (65). And later, Morrison writes that Beloved's desire to have the quilt near her stemmed from "its smelling like grass and feeling like hands" (92). Arguably, this making, gathering's art, how gathering arts, speaks to Baby Suggs's larger ecoaesthetic praxis; as a character, Suggs facilitates gathering amid fabric and flesh, a kind of housework against the violence of the home slavery built. This art smells like untrammeled earth and feels like hands; in *Beloved*'s case, these are hands that comfort and hold without harming her.[7]

Moreover, the image of hands and earth coming together to artfully innovate the environment, the feel of a room, the feel of the outside world, connects with Suggs's cultivation of other deregulated gatherings within and along the outskirts of the house. Suggs, before she died, was an "unchurched" preacher who, from time to time, "took her great heart to the Clearing—a wide-open place cut deep in the woods nobody knew for what" to make something holy with the men and women who hid amid and with the trees (102). In the novel, the Clearing flourishes as a place of prayer and gathering for a loose group of formerly given over Black men and women; there they came together to let it all go. Powerfully, the literary account of the Clearing evokes a history of enslaved people's mobilization of the "African practice of meeting in secret wooded places" while suggesting the role of the wild, of the wilderness, of the un—given over in some kind of loving reassembly (Glave 2010, 56). As Dianne Glave writes in *Rooted in the Earth*, "The wilderness was a place to roam and hide for a moment's peace from slaveholders, or it could be a means of permanent escape. It was also a source of both sustenance and healing as slaves hunted animals and gathered medicinal plants" (2010, 8).

In that way, inasmuch as *Beloved* begins by and grapples with slavery's unhoming of Black life, at the same time it highlights the antislavery tradition of crafting shelter and relation, momentary households, in an ungiven world. And in Morrison's novel, Baby Suggs's gathering in the woods is deeply aesthetic; in some ways, as with the quilt, it is a gesture of aesthetic reinstruction for those whose appreciation of beauty was highly regulated and defiled. Morrison seemingly knows and writes and makes accordingly; in the Clearing, Suggs preaches to the gatherers, instructing them to love their "flesh. . . . Feet . . . need to rest and to dance" (Morrison 2004, 103–4). Her sermon moves into a dance directed by the music made by her fellow gatherers. That gathering in the woods arted; togetherness itself made something that her daughter-in-law Sethe hoped still lingered in the space remaining after the gatherers were long gone (104).

This scene and others illuminate how Sethe and Baby Suggs hoped for, and at times believed in, the ecoaesthetic, the aesthetic of otherwise ecological desire that Black gatherings made. Baby Suggs, for instance, came to look for the homes stitched (not claimed) across fabric and sky after sadly realizing that 124 Bluestone Road could not protect her. "Bring a little lavender in" follows what we know happened to the house, how the ghosts of slavery changed it. Twenty-eight days after Suggs's daughter-in-law showed up, the weight of slavery's violence (at the interface between the trespassing footsteps of the slave-owning protectors of "whiteness as property" and the fugitive mother who otherwise believed in home) shut the house down: "There is no bad luck in the world but whitefolks. 124 shut down and put up with the venom of its ghost. No more lamp all night long, or neighbors dropping by. No low conversations after supper" (105).

Moreover, after Suggs's death and in the midst of the house that pitched and evicted, Sethe still looked for the "spaces that that long-ago singing had left behind" (104). What the quilt on the wrought-iron bed promised, how it kept Beloved awake and comforted. It is these ecoaesthetic movements, bright patches of color and memories of sound in a "wide-open place cut deep in the woods," that quite literally transform the environment, with what's unowned becoming a momentary safe harbor (102). And the characters know it; they go looking for it, stay awake for it. They go outside looking for it, Sethe in the Clearing and her daughter Denver in those "emerald rooms" yielded by the thicketed trees beyond the house. For Denver, for example, in those "woods, between the field and the stream . . . five boxwood bushes, planted in a ring" stretched together to make a room outdoors (34). "Veiled and protected by the live green walls, she felt ripe and clear, and salvation was as easy as a wish" (35).

Again, as the slowly evicted try to make home elsewhere, in the recesses of long-gone sounds and the trail of green light, sometimes they, like Baby Suggs, try to craft it in the very hostile oikos from which they run. Returning to the character of Sethe, her ongoing ecoaesthetic interventions against the homes slavery made begin at the plantation proper, known with brutal irony in the novel, as Sweet Home. In *Beloved*, housework appears as both subjection and ecoaesthetic wish, and it is entangled in Sethe's memory; for example, the beauty of the earth, its radical blooming against/despite/within the plantation's bloodied enclosures manifests in the beautiful trees that emerge in her traumatic memory of sexual assault, along with the comfort of the yellow flowers and myrtle brought by her into the slave master's living room.

> Although there was not a leaf on that farm that did not make her want to scream, it rolled itself out before her in shameless beauty. It never looked as terrible as it was and it made her wonder if hell was a pretty place too. Fire and brimstone all right, but hidden in lacy groves. Boys hanging from the most beautiful sycamores in the world. It shamed her—remembering the wonderful soughing trees rather than the boys. Try as she might to make it otherwise, the sycamores beat out the children every time and she could not forgive her memory for that. (7)

According to Kimberly Ruffin (2010, 29), Morrison's featuring of the rolling green here, as with her description of the Clearing, indicates how "enslavement did not obliterate the potential for multiple, often positive associations with the natural world." Indeed, in Sethe's memory, the yet-to-be logged trees, that lush unfettered green, reminds her of the presence of beauty, of ecoaesthetic possibilities, in the midst of terror—life, newness, promise, something unknowable to the brutalized, formerly harvested young woman.[8] Here is at once Morrison's honoring of histories of African American environmental imagination and ecoaesthetic practice while artfully offering a vision of shared, not given-over, life: how gathered myrtle might feel in the hand of the owned one, how a different gathering might ecoaesthetically transform a horrible living room, "for a while at least." Perhaps the novel is Morrison's gathering wish for the woman claimed and without claim, a gesture of unharvestable possibilities, of the possibility of the unharvestable, of unextractable homemaking on the run, in the heart. Moreover, Morrison's artful insistence on flora and fauna's unenclosable movement, their "rolling out," suggests an ongoingness of earth as a space of beauty, intimacy, momentary safe-harboring, and creativity that endures, even as property insists on being the final word.

With respect to these intimacies, what *Beloved* advances are the ways that the story of slavery, the story of property's violent gathering of flesh and earth, might have been and still might be somehow survived by what Anna Tsing (2013, 36) calls "more than human socialities." These socialities, where "many histories, human and otherwise, come together," evoke the other possibilities and potentials for gathering seemingly foreclosed by the instrumentalization of gathering as ownership. Flesh and forest collected for another's profit. Indeed, as Morrison and Tsing argue, such gatherings, long present before ownership's brutal history, endure despite property's trampling. So, too, these otherwise gatherings, following Tsing and Alexander Weheliye (2014, 32), not only potentialize a Black feminist "disarticula[tion] of the human from Man," but they move humanity's relational capacity into an ecoaesthetic dance with other vast relationalities. Such relationality, in deprioritizing neuronormative human capacities of communication and representation, not only recenters the freedom and world-making stories of plants and animals but also unmoors that social life from the entrapments of understanding. This is powerful in the context of a (neo)slave narrative in that, following Tsing, the tyranny of understanding is a Kantian legacy, which propertized and racially humanized the shape of understanding's legitimate expression. In other words, being able to *understand* the world and perversely recognize its beauty not only figured as white, propertied man's cognitive endowment but underwrote the claims he made of and about it; being rational and sensible, in Kant as well as in Locke, is the racially and gendered particular feature of the self-determined homeowner. But in *Beloved*, such propertied *understanding* of flesh and earth destroys socialities, human and more than human. While Morrison novelistically attends to the violence, she also poetically and aesthetically gestures to other, unpropertizing relationalities in which fugitive life often lives together without sanction or explanation. For instance, just as her main character Sethe somehow knew that the red kitchen was sad, she somehow also knew that sharing "a little lavender" with her mother-in-law would make the older woman's remaining time more livable (Morrison 2004, 4).

Once more, I think that *Beloved* formally and conceptually grapples with how the often word-collapsing experience of environment moves as the aesthetic, the feel and sound of unowned gatherings. Another example of such an unowned gathering arrives in the elusive account of the birth of Sethe's second daughter, Denver. Notably, as Denver shares in the novel, to get to the "part of the story she liked best, she had to start way back: hear the birds in the thick woods, the crunch of leaves underfoot; see her mother making her way up into the hills where no houses were likely to be" (36). It is in and amid the uncultivated, the uncleared leaves and thick, thick woods, wild onions, and with the "raggediest-looking trash you ever saw," white girl Amy Denver, that Sethe birthed her second daughter (38).

A fugitive mother, on the run, with a now-fugitive child emerges as an impossible relationality, at once fettered by the dogs on their tail while protected by a novelist keeping the plantation's love-killing forces at bay. Indeed, this ecoaesthetic account of a fugitive slave giving birth in the thick, thick woods is not the story of the historical Margaret Garner that Morrison shares having learned. Unlike the novel, the historical accounts do not attend to how the thick woods might have felt, or smelled, to the fugitive woman.

Perhaps that momentary unfettered relationality, the feel, look, and promise of it, remains on the unenumerable ("not to pass on") list of reasons why murder was (preferable to) the plantation. Said differently, I think that Morrison's description of Sethe's birthing experience is an ecoaesthetic and eco-ethical gesture toward Garner, as otherwise gatherings are protected and advanced through an extended aesthetic engagement with the wooded place of a hunted child's arrival.[9] Describing the place, Morrison writes of the surrounding, "spores of bluefern growing in the hollows along the riverbank [that] float toward the water in silver-blue lines [and are] hard to see unless you are in or near them, lying right at the river's edge when the sunshots are low and drained. Often they are mistook for insects—but they are seeds in which the whole generation sleeps confident of a future. And for a moment it is easy to believe each one has one—will become all of what is contained in the spore: will live out its days as planned" (99). This writing disappears as Morrison's gift to Garner, her Black feminist wish, to poetically enact a space-time where ungiven flesh and ungiven earth can "live out" their days "as planned" and to do so of their own design. What is more, I believe that one of *Beloved's* aesthetic lessons is in how gathering enacts, among other things, art's formal and conceptual protection of the laboring mother "for a while at least." That is, the time Morrison takes to dwell with the spores, with their color, their low-lyingness, their profoundly beautiful, future orientation, is time away from the laboring mother, who outside of claims made by the most protective of authors, might achieve some unwritten sleep nearby, "confident of a future." No "patroller came and no preacher," no one to round up the gathering and what they elusively made together (100).

So terribly, then, when Sethe's captors, most notably schoolteacher, arrive at her house to take back that life, to give it over, to presume that it was given over, it is instructive that before Sethe heard "No," "she heard wings: Little hummingbirds stuck their needle beaks right through her headcloth into her hair and beat their wings" (192). Here, on the edges of world's end, outside the presumptive protections of a home, unfettered relationality between ungiven flesh and ungiven earth rebel against the plantation's perverse homemaking conceit. And amid the birds' tiny flapping, in order to have a chance at a new life, a child was murdered and subsequently spirited away to a lake's private harbor.

But still, even still, the book begins with the child coming back, walking out of the water, to be with her mother. And even as that touch from Beloved was said to feel like those evictional, wall-shattering tears from the other side, Sethe embraced them for the way they smelled like the milk recently drunk by a newborn (115). That embrace helped Sethe imagine that she could make a household, a Black feminine gathering, just like the one promised to her when she arrived at 124. Poignantly, after Sethe recalls those twenty-eight days she lived with her mother-in-law and all of her children together, twenty-eight days before schoolteacher came and her baby left again, she and her kids go ice skating (109). With Denver and Beloved, the baby who came back, they went out to the woods and danced and spun on the ice. When they were finished:

> Both of them had an arm around her waist. Making their way over hard snow, they stumbled, and had to hold on tight, but nobody saw them fall.
>
> Inside the house they found out they were cold. They took off their shoes, wet stockings, and put on dry woolen ones. Denver fed the fire. Sethe warmed a pan of milk and stirred cane syrup and vanilla into it. Wrapped in quilts and blankets before the cooking stove, they drank, wiped their noses, and drank again. (206)

Here, this house, this angry house, is artfully reimagined by Morrison as a refuge, a safe harbor, a place to get warm. Close to the fire, they sit "wrapped in quilts," huddled together amid woven textures, enjoying the house made together. This quilt, this pulling together, comforts and warms, arguably expressing an ecoaesethetic desire, powerful enough to "settl[e] [the] pieces into places designed and made especially for them" (207).

Maybe, even "for a while," these furtive gatherings amid harmed and "stolen life," once given over flesh and yet to be logged trees, is the household, the housework of which Black feminist poet June Jordan once spoke, the kinds of intimacies and creativities engendered by people and earth being together differently (Moten 2018). During an interview with Jordan, Black feminist critic Alexis De Veaux (1981, 82) mused:

> For June, poems are housework. They're done at home, like women's more traditional work: raising children, making quilts, tending collard green gardens, doing hair in the kitchen on weekends, cooking, sewing, giving music lessons. June sees no distinction between doing these things and working as a writer. "What has been called women's work traditionally includes the nurturing of young people, maintaining a house, providing the wherewithal so that people can keep going. . . . I would be very proud if people found in my poetry things that were as useful to them as a decent breakfast before they go to work."[10]

Following De Veaux's assessment of Jordan, poems, and perhaps creative writing more broadly, are forms of house-making that alchemically forge the unpropertizable or uncommodifiable "wherewithal so that people can keep going." Wherewithal, as what nurtures relation and passage, powerfully asserts a conjunction of location and togetherness, a gathering in time, a gathering across times. It is an offering made within the alchemical and ecological *while* engendered by the poem, what arrives on the other side of the pen that is a door, a home where you can come and go, a borrowed home on the page, the quilt, and in the mind. Wherewithal is perhaps the unencumbered yield of Black women's creative work, what inflects the social significance of *Beloved* and *Houses* as literature that reaestheticizes home to illuminate its ongoing shaky foundations and crafts living rooms where the evicted might get a "decent breakfast."

That's seemingly why, for Baby Suggs, the beginning of the end was when *"they came into [her] yard"* (211). As "Baby Suggs leaned back into the peppers and the squash vines with her hoe . . . she smelled another thing. Dark and coming" (Morrison 2004, 163). She smelled the tramplers of earth coming to gather up the flesh imagined to be divinely given to them. Tramplers of Suggs's yard, trampling the gathering she made and was making. Maybe what she smelled coming was an end to the furtive gatherings amid fugitive women and children, formerly enslaved women, and the peppers and squash with which they crafted some momentary relation. Amirio Freeman (2018), in his beautiful words about the significance of gardening for Black queer world-making, intones here: "Lesson one: from my grandfather's garden, I have learned that moving beyond just survival requires leaning into faith. Faith in your continued existence. Faith in the fact that the life you have cultivated will continue to be, uninterrupted. Faith in the capacity of spaces of death to be transformed into expanses of life."[11]

The little garden that Suggs nurtured, just like the Clearing and the quilt, was another place where togetherness was an act of faith. And even as the book and the home at its center are haunted by the "coming thing," Suggs leaning into the peppers bespeaks that faith as well as the ecoaesthetic "expanse of life" (Freeman 2018) with which it is entwined and with which the novel ends. That is, Morrison's conclusion of the story, the conclusion of the story of a different attempt at gathering, a different exercise of homes and housework, was not of a trampled home and its evicted tenants. Rather, it ends at another gathering place, a delicate harboring of an ungiven space-time when flesh moves with water moves with trees moves with weather. It ends with the more-than-human socialities, somewhere outside gathering as ownership, where a sad ghost finds rest. It ends with another cradle crafted by a quiet earthly ensemble—"not the breath of the disremembered and unaccounted for, but wind in the eaves or spring ice thawing too quickly" (Morrison 2004, 324). An unfenced arrangement, dreamed by an author with an imaginary key. An arrangement that welcomes the wet, evicted child's return while another household is conjured without "a trace of human inhabitation" (Duke Franklin Humanities Institute 2016).

And true, before the conclusion, it gets sad. Really sad. Before Beloved has to go, the household they all made together starts to wear them down. The "hurt of the hurt world" (Morrison 2004, 35) makes it so that they try to pull from each other, like two people straightening a quilt. After a while, the struggled-over fabric starts to lose its own gravity. But before that and before Beloved is returned to the spirit world, she is offered novelistic time to gather. That is, in two short chapters of writing without punctuation, Morrison experiments with the periodless sentence to let Beloved ecoaesthetically dream: to dream a relation with her mother, the water, the air, with other people without harm or interference. The following quote is from one of these chapters:

I AM BELOVED and she is mine. I see her take flowers away from leaves she puts them in a round basket the leaves are not for her she fills the basket she opens the grass I would help her but the clouds are in the way how can I say things that are pictures I am not separate from her there is no place where I stop her face is my own and I want to be there in the place where her face is and to be looking at it too a hot thing. (248)

Later, toward the end of Beloved's vision, she shares how she continued to wait for *her*.

I am in the water and she is coming there is no round basket no iron circle around her neck she goes up where the diamonds are I follow her we are in the diamonds which are her earrings now my face is coming I have to have it I am looking for the join I am loving my face so much my dark face is close to me I want to join she whispers to me she whispers I reach for her chewing and swallowing she touches me she knows I want to join. (251)

In this four-and-a-half-page experimental chapter, where the writing is distinct from the rest of the novel in its punctuationless sentences and stream of consciousness musing, Beloved dreams her life differently. Here we see her perspective in ways that the view eludes us. Her time spent in the water, where her dripping, fleshly self emerged, is detailed in a dream sequence. Here Morrison describes Beloved's view underwater, not centering on what she missed, but instead offering a vision of her mother's whole life, from when she "wore the iron circle" to the time when she did not (251). In this passage, the child sees her enslaved mother, remembers the Middle Passage that she herself did not endure and perhaps even felt the earth's own ungiven beginning as a fiery ball, a "hot thing" (248). Unmoored from property, spectral life moves here across time and space, the beginning and the end of the world, driven by the desire "to join." In some ways, this is Beloved's ecoaesthetic imagining, a vision of Black gathering formed through the removal of all punctuation and separation. Periodlessness in this passage seemingly makes for flesh moving bumpily together, the earth moving close to the flowers, the brutal displacement of child from mother upended by their entering the "diamonds" as one.

Arguably, Beloved's repeated "I want to join"—powerfully given its own time, a chapter of its own, and even the visible extra spacing in the text itself—highlights how this novel experimentalizes Black gathering. Through collective dwellings in diamonds and with the orange of a quilt, to private moments in the green light of overgrown trees, to wordless family time, the novel aesthetically enlarges the ecological beyond property. As Morrison reveals, on the other side of that door are other shelters, clearings, cities made from fabric, uncultivated "emerald closets," and beds thatched from kindling (62). There are places and experiences that not only provide respite and recovery for flesh burdened by its presumptive wildness but that also usher other forms of togetherness past the raucous places where enclosures have their say. Home's riotous exclusionarity bespeaks the social life it can never really contain, protect, or govern. These are the social lives and shapes of gathering that ecoaesthetically craft other forms of Black environmental relation beyond ownership's terrors. Moreover, across the novel, Black gathering creates another environment and feeling of home, "for a while at least." Something the characters seek out, even after "all trace" of its makers are gone.

In the following section I engage another writer who also uses language to create a feeling of a home, an unenclosable aesthetics of gathering that lingers like "wind in the eaves" or in the inaudible song of blooms pulled too soon. Poet Nikki Wallschlaeger joins Morrison in crafting homes in another fictional neighborhood, somewhere near the one momentarily doored on Bluestone Road. Her poem gatherings, like 124, bear the weight of oikos's world-historical violence while imagistically, structurally, and linguistically creating hidden corners and gardens where some other togetherness becomes possible.

Houses

Nikki Wallschlaeger is a contemporary poet whose 2015 collection *Houses* prompted me to consider how it might poetically grapple with the concept and the materiality of home. I find that *Houses* beautifully joins Morrison's *Beloved* in defamiliarizing and unfolding the complex racial, sexual, ecological, and economic "relational aesthetics" that build a poem home (Miles 2014). That is, across the collection, differently colored house poems unfold as a series of sentiments, textures, intimate and impersonal lyricisms on the improper beauty of togetherness. Using short phrases and sentences that move like a stream of consciousness about each residence, Wallschlaeger precisely poeticizes how particular classed, raced, gendered, and sexualized figurations of (American) belonging haunt and lyrically regulate the life that finds itself attached to each home. So, too, what seems to sneak in, as if from the house poem's backdoor, is an unextractable sentimentalism surrounding each residence.

Moreover, among other formal innovations, Wallschlaeger uses color to foreground the difference that difference makes in the dialectics of property and trespass animating the promiscuous reach of property management in a postbellum world. That is, in *Houses*, color refers both to a chromatic range of paint donning and differentiating each house's exterior and to the name of its corresponding poem. Poem titles include, for example, "Red House," "Black House," "Cerulean House," "Pink House," "Grey House," and "Glitter House." Following critic Eric Sneathen (2015), this precise variegation works alongside the enclosures suggested by the poems' own formal composition. Sneathen argues further that the composition, what he calls the house as poem, repeats a hegemonic operation of housing itself, as "its list-likeness . . . nouns without verbs" and disavowed "fragmentation" seemingly close in on the life that hopes to gather there.

This notion of the house poem as enclosure, though, contrasts with the rainbowed, all-inclusive poem neighborhood advanced by the collection as a whole. Wallschlaeger offers each house poem as a brightly colored fragment, a different reflection and refraction of (home) ownership's chromatically singular experience. That is, the oscillation between *every* color presented in the book's table of contents and the collection's *particular* lyrical chromatic riff at once illuminates homeownership's mythic figuration as equal opportunity while elucidating the central value of color in concretizing such opportunity's racial, sexual, economic, and ontological specificity. Precisely, in the three poems I engage here, questions and experiences of Blackness persist as structuring tensions uprooting each person's relationship with where they reside. For instance, around houses named "Green" and "Black," anti-Blackness moves in such evictional-sounding phrases as "death rows roll," "invisible house," a "dampness," and an "American doing the foreign thing in an African country" (Wallschlaeger 2015, 20, 21). Yet the final poem, "My House," represents a tonal shift in the overall collection.[12]

Unlike the rest of the collection, "My House" lacks reference to a home's third-person residents and associates along with a potentially localizable property marker/address given in the series as specific color. Rather, the poem consists of a range of holdings: "holding bees," "holding you in the air" (74, 75). With this final poem, I consider the stakes of a Black woman poet's artful holding on to the immaterial as Black gathering's expressive reach into unavailable feeling. Put differently, I offer that, in "My House," Wallschlaeger lyrically crafts oikos as a kind of affective field and, in turn, defamiliarizes and reimagines the possibilities of "relational aesthetics" beyond a visible address. At the end of *Houses*, gathering coalesces in and as ethereal, textural, and sentimental forms of unowned, earthly relation—flowering as pop-up living rooms on the page and in the air—even as signs of foreclosure threaten from just around the corner.

Indeed, the idea of the home and, in particular, the ecoaesthetic feel of a home happen in *Houses* through gathering. As with *Beloved*, gathering in *Houses* arts, it poetically makes an invisible architecture, unsteadied with good, bad, and indescribable feelings. Yes, sometimes the homes themselves, again referencing Sneathen, appear as particular kinds of enclosures. And, sometimes, the terseness of a phrase devastates by what it doesn't say or attend to such that the house poem feels like most enclosures, stifling. Yet still, through certain other turns of phrase and in the midst of what seems like an aesthetic vision of homes as violently oikic, something else seems to move. A swish of uncertainty, an assertion of fuckoffedness, that I/we're going to get together regardless. Through an unanticipated, unplaceable image or a foundation-unsettling word like *maybe*, I imagine some other tenderness getting through, disrupting enclosure so that togetherness might be practiced otherwise.

Before proceeding to the first poem, I'd like to dwell a bit on the cover of *Houses* because it powerfully gets at this comingling of enclosure and gathering as it arts togetherness otherwise (see figure 1.1). To begin, the cover features, front and center, a red tray table holding a redbrick lunch tray against a red wall. Both sit on a large red-white-and-blue doily. Next to the tray is a thin, white plastic vase in which stands a plastic red-stemmed and leaved rose. The rose towers high, reaching the latitudinal line of the book title. The pretty sky-blue title *Houses* seemingly blooms like a cornflower against the red wall.

When I initially sat with the cover, I sensed a coziness, a gesture of warmth and fanciness crafted from seemingly inexpensive, what some might call cheap or gaudy, items. Like how a doily transforms a microwaved plate and plastic cup into a special event. The tray table too suggests a kind of care, perhaps, for someone who is unable to or doesn't feel like sitting at the dining room table. Maybe. That is, the cover image calls up from the collected poems an ecoaesthetics of housework, some unseen labor of care that might momentarily change the feel of home.

When I asked Wallschlaeger about the cover image, she shared that the cover is "a commentary on American life—TV trays, the patriotic doily, etc. as an institution of sterility."[13] Later returning to the image, not only did I see

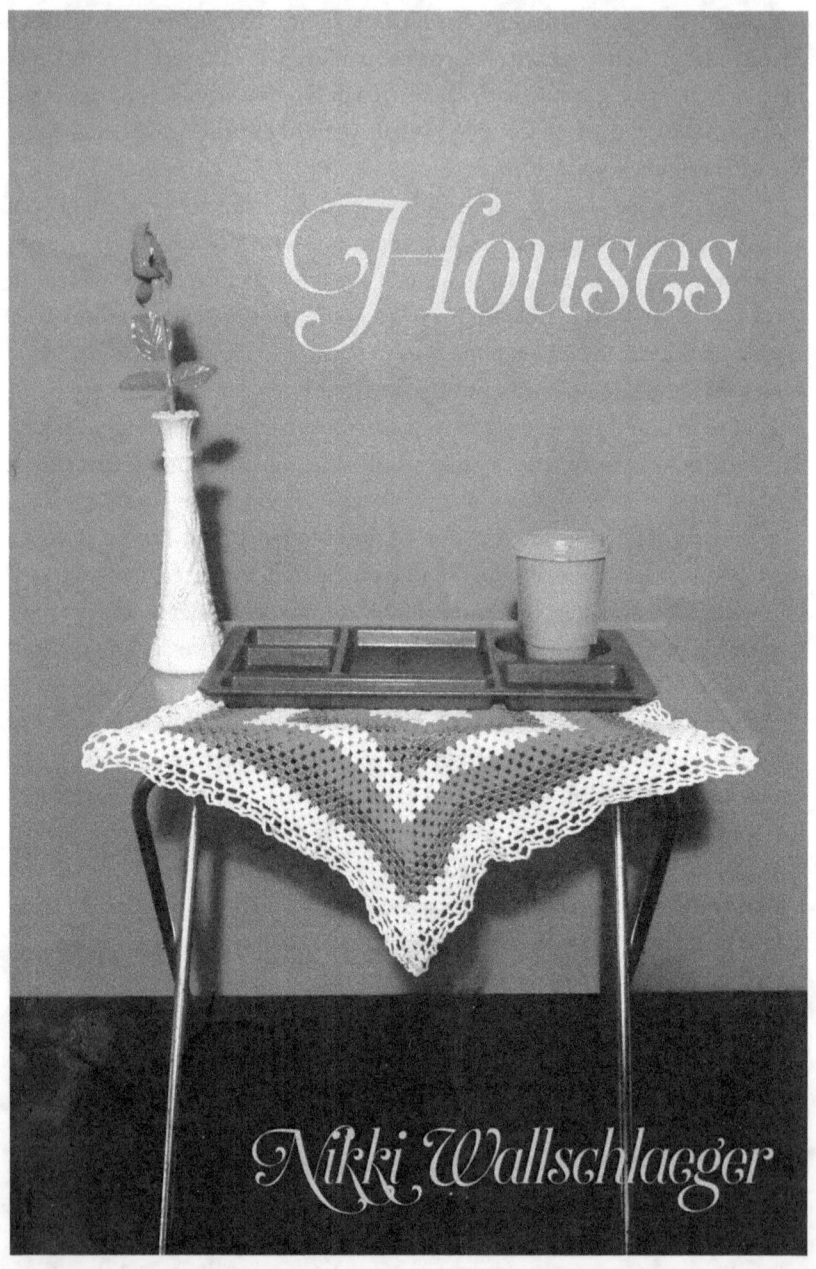

FIGURE 1.1. Cover photo of *Houses* by Nikki Wallschlaeger; cover photographic design by Nikki Wallschlaeger, 2015; photograph by Brian Wallschlaeger, 2015. Courtesy of the author.

how Americanness comes through, as the author described, as sterility and deprivation (the absence of food on the tray) but also how that staged patriotic energy eerily resembles the unspeakable red silence of Sethe's kitchen. Americanized sterility perhaps is oikos as property's violent, ecological imposition and reddened effect.

Yet, even still, there's that doily and the pretty plastic rose to spruce up what looks like a plate of absence. *Houses*, as a collection, feels to me like that portable tray and rose along with the absence and emptiness to which it might be trying to respond. Put more directly, I argue that the poems' formal prose structure, its gathering of sentiments, images, and scenes, ecoaesthetically arts a sense of a home where sterility's life-neutralizing movements are met by an unextractable abundance. Powerfully, what Wallschlaeger's poems elucidate, along with Morrison's *Beloved*, is how gathering might feel like enclosure, might sound like enclosure but can just as easily shape-shift into some other feeling of togetherness. For instance, an unanticipated tonal shift, the placement of a phrase in just the right place, like Baby Suggs's placement of orange squares in that "sober field," can change a room, making space for another way of being together (Morrison 2004, 46).

Turning to the collection and beginning in the order in which they appear, the poem "Green House" tonally begins with enclosure, riffing on the dialectic of saving and killing the earth suggested by the double significance of the title itself. That is, a greenhouse describes an architecture of ecological efficiency and enhanced vitality, a building made of glass used for plants needing warmth and protection. But *greenhouse* also announces conditions of unvitality, the man-made emissions and gases contributing to the suffocating operations of earth's atmosphere. According to scientists Eugene Takle and Don Hofstrand (2015), the naturally existing greenhouse gases responsible for planetary warmth, like water vapor and carbon dioxide, are short-lasting. That is, they don't stay in the atmosphere long and eventually move into deep space, thereby allowing the earth to restore a climatic balance. However, with the rise of fossil fuels, the destruction of forests, and increasing carbon dioxide emissions from cars, the earth's carbon dioxide expenditure exceeds what its plant life can reabsorb, creating a residual atmospheric surplus that results in global warming. In line with the arguments thus advanced in this chapter and following Sylvia Wynter's argument on the "coloniality of being/ truth/power/freedom," it is the "man" made itself, shorthand for the "ethnoclass Man versus human struggle" (Wynter 2003, 260–61), that kills the earth. That is, following Wynter:

The struggle of our new millennium will be one between the ongoing imperative of securing the well-being of our present ethnoclass (i.e., Western bourgeois) conception of the human, Man, which overrepresents itself as if it were the human itself, and that of securing the well-being, and therefore the full cognitive and behavioral autonomy of the human species itself/ourselves. . . .

The correlated hypothesis here is that all our present struggles with respect to race, class, gender, sexual orientation, ethnicity, struggles over the environment, global warming, severe climate change, the sharply unequal distribution of the earth resources (20 percent of the world's peoples own 80 percent of its resources, consume two-thirds of its food and are responsible for 75 percent of its ongoing pollution with this leading to two billion of earth's peoples living relatively affluent lives while four billion still live on the edge of hunger and immiseration), . . . these are all differing facets of the central ethnoclass Man vs. Human struggle. (260–61)

In "Green House," what Wallschlaeger does, formally, conceptually, and beginning with the enclosure-referring word itself, *greenhouse*, is separate the "green" from the "house." This underscores the poet's ecoaesthetic attention to the movements of disavowal, the protection and eviction of life secured when a call for earthly and self-preservation are twinned operations, and where such preservation smuggles in the violences of regulation and extraction. Assuredly, I see these larger thematic questions swirling around the house poem, which I'll quote in full below. After which I'll engage in a close reading to see how much the poem, like the more conventional term *greenhouse* itself, traps in (or restrains) the vitality of those who live there while also using language to secure energy's release. "Green House," in some ways, poetically dwells in the ether between its titular words, asking after the violences that happen when they're pushed together and the possibilities that move when green is left alone and with a little distance from a potential architecture of enclosure. Perhaps the space between "Green" and "House" is filled by breath, a space where Wallschlaeger seemingly asks how dwelling there might enact a less violent togetherness than one that presumes such room(s) is not possible at all.

Let us now turn to the poem itself, "Green House," presented in full as follows:

Steam house. Spring before grass cutters, the best time. Thick before drought and angry man management, he must gut the grass on the weekends, imagine the scandal if not. What will the neighbors think, I think nothing. Don't bother. Don't bother the sod, push mower. Go green with upcycled link purses, I am that auctioneer w/other epidurals made possible to me in part by gas.

So he gets out his lawn mower anyway, paints his house in acceptable olive, not green, green like new grass, that would be too confrontational, too many risks of dandelion patty cake. City citation says no food gardens allowed on front lawns, city citation says I can't puff naked across my lawn. What will the neighbors think about my hairs. Maybe you shouldn't be bothered by looking.

Nonsense, says man in powdered bone who believes in modified tomatoes, but green tomatoes are good. Without his placards. Behind the scenes people make recipes out of green things, make livings out of weeds wild and uncultivated just so, hidden somewhere. No dogs allowed in the secret countries, you have to know someone. Would angry man tell on the guerillas of green feet? Maybe so, maybe not

Maybe he tried it in college and now offhandedly works networking parties playing I don't know what a bong is. We laugh. Oh, how we laugh and the quotas brighten, the death rows roll and the afternoon tea swells. Someone is getting arrested and grocery stores flash with broccoli. She is wearing a green house scarf as an American doing the foreign thing in an African country she was briefed on during the flight. (Wallschlaeger 2015, 20)

"Green House" begins with the abrupt, distanced commands of a steward's voice; the presumptive normative logic of cultivation dominates this poem's opening even as a narrator distrustful of such management sneers back. "Spring before grass cutters, the best time. Thick before / drought and angry man management, he must gut the grass on the / weekends, imagine the scandal if not" (Wallschlaeger 2015, 20). Mowing the lawn later joins the larger civic injunction to paint one's house "in acceptable olive." As with the suggestive gutting/cutting of the lawn, the sentence carrying the self-imposed regulation of a to-be painted home overpowers grammatically: "olive, not green, green like new grass, that would be too confrontational." Here, formally, the sentence is a crowd of self-imposed commands later made noisier by the gathering on the lawn; the gathering seemingly looks in on the "he" and the "I" who are trying to live in that house. Moreover, this notion of the lawn as private-public ambles through these opening lines, elucidating how "the garden has become a crowded place of late. Sex, nature, patriarchy, and power jostle with the dahlias, parterres, and ha-has" (Blomley 2005, 623). In "Green House," the private home transmutes quickly into public spectacle, with a cacophony of voices debating how to *keep one's home*.

Indeed, this closing in is how the poem's opening words feel: "Steam house." Held in oxygen. In contrast to Sneathen's (2015) claims, Wallschlaeger doesn't just enclose by way of the poem form. She gathers and, in so doing, tries to make space for a less harmful communion. Put more directly, I aver that, in "Green House," Wallschlaeger mobilizes gathering's shape-shiftingness to keep the totalizing impulses of enclosure at bay. For example, in the beginning, there is a gathering on, around, and about someone's lawn. As the scandalized, the worriers about whether the lawn will stay cut, sit at one end of the sentence, the nameless "he" on the other side keeps the scandalized content with a compulsory mowing. There's also an "I" who at once doesn't care what the neighbor thinks but then also believes that the mowing should be done anyway, saying "I am that auctioneer w/ other epidurals made / possible to me in part by gas" (Wallschlaeger 2015, 20).

The "I" at once recognizes the ruse in the inherent paradox of private property: Answering with "nothing" in response to "What will the neighbors think," this poetic figure also claims to be the one selling that which will take the pain away, the epidurals funded by some kind of environmental expenditure. This voice in the gathering seems to know the score while making it work for her, emerging as the figure who both takes the pain away and knows that the pain accruing around that lawn is nothing less than the lie of property's (propriety's) privacy. As Nicholas Blomley (2005, 623) argues, while the "law has long treated the garden as a private space," it often remains vulnerable to state surveillance and anxious management should it violate certain civic (patriarchal, classed, racialized) notions of cultivation and propriety. For example, there are laws on the books across the United States and Canada that allow the state to "engage in legal trespass" and manage an unkempt, overgrown garden should the state deem it necessary (630). Moreover, as Wallschlaeger illustrates in "Green House," mowing the lawn is never far from a larger set of earthly managements coterminous with the regulation of (uncultivated) flesh and capital. "City citation says no food gardens / allowed on front lawns, city citation says I can't puff naked across my lawn. / What will the neighbors think about my hairs." The repetition of law as an abstract policing figure abides by the poem's structuring tension between the dominating tones of state command and the narrator's defense of the private dimensions of property. "What will the neighbors think about my hairs. / Maybe you shouldn't be bothered by looking."

"What will the neighbors think" repeats along with "city citation," suggesting an enduring post-Lockean racialized, sexualized, and gendered narrative of "wild" flesh and earth, a narrative potentially resulting in their criminalizing management by the state. The "I" who "can't puff across my lawn" is maybe or maybe not the "auctioneer" selling pain relief. Even still, the "I"s are the insurgent ones, engaging in the illicit activities of being high and numb, of being outside and unregulated, even as they ponder what can one do on *their lawn*.

As the second "I" protests *their looking*, they make the prohibition of certain modes of being with one's yard strange (recall Baby Suggs's earlier critique of slavery's erosion of her momentary experience of yard). Maybe what the first "I" offered was a space of relief from the prohibition's weight, and through thickly weighted words like "auctioneer" and "epidurals," words thick with histories of enslavement and (coerced) reproduction, make plain how the buying of an even greener mower bears the weight of historical forgetfulness. That is, the poem seems to ask: Whose pain is alleviated by the lawn's mowing? Why is its overgrowth an issue of social and moral concern? What if being at home was a feeling of joy, an ecoaesthetic longing, or desire, for uncultivatedness?

Still, these anxieties around certain communions of seed and earth, flesh and lawn, also harken back to Wynter's argument about the human-as-man's earth-killing self-positioning that Wynter (2003, 261) later correlates with positioning Blackness as "outside the gates." Even as the poem doesn't gesture toward race or racial difference in the first three passages, there is a worrying (which is never not racialized) of improper flourishing outside of the gated expanse of whiteness and property/proper comportment. Moreover, the nude person on the lawn joins the other possibilities of living differently with earth, showing up again in the poem's third passage: "Behind the / scenes people make recipes out of green things, make livings out of weeds / wild and cultivated just so, hidden somewhere."

The precarity of those making life "behind the scenes," those engaged in some uncultivated sociality amid and with "green things," resonates, for me, with Macarena Gómez-Barris's critiques of extractivist viewing. For example, the narrator in "Green House" wonders whether "angry man" will "tell on the guerillas of green feet," those engaging in "the [decolonial] emergent and heterogeneous forms of living that are not about destruction or mere survival within the extractive zone, but about the creation of emergent alternatives" (Gómez-Barris 2017, 4). Herein lies another ambivalence in "Green House," as Gómez-Barris might say; while "an extractive planetary view," which in the world of "Green House" takes the form of "angry man/management," sees the world as given over and for the taking, the "wild . . . hidden somewhere" still breaks in (Gómez-Barris 2017, 6; Wallschlaeger 2015, 20). But its fate is unclear. Maybe he (angry man) will tell someone where to find those gathering behind the scenes: "Maybe so, maybe not" (Wallschlaeger 2015, 20). Moreover, the absence of punctuation after "maybe not" suggests that a window or door of the green house was left open, releasing the steamy anger and resentment and perhaps letting in what property tried to keep out. Put differently, ecoaesthetically, the phrase "guerillas of green feet" and their "behind the scenes" (20) living arguably does something to the architecture of the house poem made by punctuation's insistence and repetition.

Yet, toward the end of the poem that secondary "I" who walks insurgently in her/their yard seems to disappear a bit, maybe moving *behind the scenes* before the poem's concluding passage. In the final passage, the networked corporate laughter about trying marijuana is the white (innocent) noise we hear while "Someone / is getting arrested and grocery stores flash with broccoli." This line appears between the brutal juxtaposition of the "death rows roll and the afternoon tea swells" and the green-scarfed American "doing the foreign thing in an African country." Concerning the former, and again following Wynter, this sanctioning of the state's life-managing biopower, on the one hand, and the celebration of the earth's (presumptively given over) vitality, on the other, is not only consistent with the ethno-class man's coloniality (earth and flesh-killingness) of being but also connects to what Jedidiah Purdy (2015) calls "environmentalism's racist history." For Purdy, early conservationists' investment in the "governance of [world] resources" is part of a larger history that tied (white) American national preservation with earthly conservation. Geographer Carolyn Finney (2014, 29), meanwhile, writing about Sierra Club founder John Muir, argues that Muir's 1867 essay "Thousand Mile Walk to the Gulf" "spoke of Negroes as largely lazy and easy-going and unable to pick up as much cotton as a white man. While his environmental ethic included wilderness, it clearly did not include nonwhites."

Purdy's 2015 reporting on the Sierra Club's 1972 polling its relatively unsupportive constituents about whether to support the "problems of such special groups as the urban poor and ethnic minorities" reflects Muir's enduring image of green as somehow not Black. Further, and recalling Nathan Hare, dominant environmentalism's pervasive racism is more recently joined by major "statutes, such as the Clean Air Act and the Clean Water Act," that "were written with no attention to the unique vulnerability of poor and minority groups" (Purdy 2015). The corporate laughter at the end of "Green House," mixed with the banalities of tea and *someone's* arrest, ushers forth this selective colorblindness, where, again, seeing green somehow means not seeing Black. Here again is Wallschlaeger: "Someone / is getting arrested and grocery stores flash with broccoli."

The poet's tightly condensed sentence worlds indeed implore us to ask: What if we stayed longer with the first part of the sentence and imagine the stakes of its being eclipsed by the second? What if we lingered longer with stories about someone (often someone Black) being arrested, even as and maybe because green is what's for sale? Moreover, the "flash" of broccoli was gathered by someone and that someone might also be incarcerated. According to a 2014 article by reporter Rebecca McCray, with the rise of anti-immigrant legislation, state legislatures across the United States began introducing bills "allowing for" incarcerated peoples to participate in agriculture labor. This low-waged form of labor, historically dangerous due to the increased usage of pesticides, was and is often consigned to migrant laborers, the Black and Brown underclass poised as "outside the gates." As the prison population disproportionately swells with Black and Brown life, those figured geopolitically, racially, sexually, and economically "outside" are tasked to give the earth over to the ones who gate and fence, to those whose investment in a preserved earth renders the racialized, sexualized, classed, and anthropocentric presumptions of its givenness (to management) a condition of a certain life-ending overgrowth (McCray 2014). This overgrowth, its unceasing reach, bulldozes earth and flesh while treating some houses as if they were invisible. As if nobody lives or gathers there.

After the last line of "Green House," where an "American woman" "wearing / a green house scarf" goes to do the "foreign thing in an African country" (Wallschlaeger 2015, 20), the poem "Black House" follows. I think this movement from the "American woman" on the plane doing the "foreign thing," perhaps the "green thing" where the "green thing" means not seeing the Black thing, is deeply connected to the first line of "Black House": "invisible house" (22). As the implicit foreign thing of Americans in Africa is either salvation or extraction, or salvation as extraction, the attendant presumption is that nobody Black is doing the green thing, the living thing, the being at home thing. Indeed, as Kathryn Mathers (2010, 4) argues, "There is nothing new about Africa being a place for redemption for those with power; it is a space that has all too often inhabited that role, largely for Western colonial powers.

Africa has long been an amalgam of dense and complex representations that has 'served, and continues to serve, as a polemical argument for the West's desperate desire to assert its differences from the rest of the world.' Europeans created the African, as Achille Mbembe suggests, as the other against which to affirm their civilization's superiority."

Moreover, what these enduring colonial representations of Africa, and of Blackness, do, as Mathers later writes, is enfold Black Africans into the uncultivated nature the continent is said to symbolize. A fascination with the green here, once more, erases the Black. Again, this is instructive as this green-inspired form of American travel to Africa concludes "Green House" only to be followed by the phrase "Invisible house" that begins the subsequent poem "Black House."

Whereas "Green House" gestures toward mainstream environmentalist discourse and environmental catastrophe, "Black House" advances the ecological in those "behind the scenes" directions Gómez-Barris alerts us to in *The Extractive Zone* (2017). "Black House" might be around the corner from "Green House" in a neighborhood where "monster salvaged pin-up trucks" and nervous neighbors patrol. If Wallschlaeger's juxtaposition of "green" and "house" evokes and enacts, quite literally, the costs (and violences) of "protecting" the environment, then the linguistic joining of "Black" and "House" inquires into underasked questions of environmental preservation and endangerment. To be more explicit, whether the house is painted Black, is Blackened through dispossession or abandonment, or is figured as Black because of who lives there, Wallschlaeger presents the home as ecoaesthetic invisibility. Here, we might say, the poem joins 124 Bluestone Road in querying the ecoaesthetic shapes of the invisible, how they interface with environmental violence and denial, and the other possibilities of gathering in a home presumed to not be there at all.

Following is "Black House," presented in full:

Invisible house. Flowers up in front, children sittin on the porch, he gets picked up every day to go to therapy, he has to get the other leg cut off now. What they call it? When you can still feel what isn't supposed to be there? My legs have been botherin me in the dampness, and he always thought I was a little funny because I moved in with a white man and obviously wasn't from here.

I sits at my invisible house. My grandma also talks that way, somewhat, she was from the country some ways back but she raised me and when we went to value village, she was practically the only white lady in there. She polka glowed when she told the checkout lady I was her granddaughter. The lady smiled like she was amused, but gently kindly. She likes to hold my hand when we cross the street.

so people wondered. They stare at us from their monster salvaged pin-up trucks with collectible plate gullets. Sedans too, painted safe parking lot colors so you could get lost w/ a cart full of groceries, little fobs of baby food that spliff in the tin of your gland. Night camping at noon. What they call it? The place the other poet talked about, fog or no headlights, room temperature, a low-grade fever from bologna.

it's possible if my elite panic was framed in blacklight they would be coerced into box office seating. I should take a picture before the cattle adrenals finally revoke the lacing of my lavender, and I think his small town bobby socks are the new security code to get into the vomitorium. Also fake military service records. Cops get to go on special paid leave when they murder here. You gotta be careful nowadays. (Wallschlaeger 2015, 21)

As with "Green House," the "[non]divisioning of inside and outside" seems to shape how "Black House" is viewed (Cuevas 2012, 208). The poem begins with an accounting gaze that takes note of the children's absent presence and *his* daily trips to the doctor. The children's invisibility arguably expresses, early on, the pathologizations engendered by propriety's absence. The substitution of "sittin" for "sitting" here renders the kids' gathering in improper tones, which perhaps somehow connects to their invisibility. A missing letter, a certain deployment of accent, changes whether people recognize a home as being there or regard a certain gathering as beautiful and as vulnerable as the flowers.[14]

Moreover, in that first passage, a feeling of and for what isn't there, a feeling of absence, of sitting with it and seeing it, emerges in the evocation of phantom limbs. The poem seems to ask after the stakes for the amputated man to live in an "invisible house" to feel what isn't there. "What isn't there" refers to the missing leg, or a place one calls or thought was home, or the persistent "dampness" that, following Christina Sharpe (2016, 75), "anagrammatically" trembles as the hold/what one cannot hold. Moreover, that feeling of absence is possibly shared among residents, as one resident's missing limb registers with the narrator's own grappling with the uncanny feeling of belonging/not belonging, her body belonging/not belonging: "he always thought / I was a little funny because I moved in with a white man and obviously / wasn't from here" (Wallschlaeger 2015, 21).

This feeling of invisibility, of a sitting within it together, seemingly oscillates between forms of unseen housework and the foreclosures engendered by others' misrecognitions of them. "I sits at my invisible house" (21) starts the second passage about a little girl who goes shopping with her white grandmother. Here we learn that the "Black House" is a place of biracial gathering, a fact also animating its barely seenness, invisibilized by racist visions of an "impossible domestic[ity]" (Hartman 2016, 171). That is, this weightedness of present absence unresolvedly emerges in sentences that move from "she was practically the only white lady in there [Value Village]" who "polka / glowed when she told the checkout lady I was her granddaughter" to the second passage's conclusion that "she likes to hold my hand / when we cross the street." This latter image complexly evokes the shapes of a "wherewithal," an everyday living and sitting with absence, or of hyped-up presences that feel like absence, the haunted feeling of living with what others refuse to see. A wherewithal where a "decent breakfast" is consumed, stores are visited, and streets are crossed together, even as such gestures matter little to those who presume the home was long ago abandoned.

By the time we get to the poem's third passage, those whom we might call the arbiters of "whiteness as property" with their "monster salvaged pin-up trucks" and "sedans" "stare" with their invisibilizing gazes. The phrase "What they / call it?" returns here, at once evoking that feeling of bodily absence, of loss and invisibility, which soon morphs into a sensation of being in the dark, "night camping at noon," "fog or no headlights." The ecological features of darkness and dampness here, once more, conjure the phantasmatic reverberations of the hold, being below(deck), what Sharpe (2016, 73) describes as "the slave ship, the womb and the coffle, and the long dehumaning project; we continue to feel and be the fall . . . out" of. For example, in "Black House," the imminent foreclosure of "home," travels between fleshly and architecturally felt invisibility or the realization that what you thought you had—leg, home, safety, right to come together—never really belonged to you. This enduring not belongingness, the opposition between Blackness and gathering or the presumption of Black house's invisibility, Black gathering's criminal impossibility, brutally registers at the beginning with the kids on the porch not being seen to the concluding passage revealing that "cops get to go on special paid leave / when they murder here. You gotta be careful nowadays."

In the conclusion, there is a powerful and devastating reminder of home's ontological impossibility for flesh and earth said to be otherwise given over: "Invisible house. Flowers up in front, children sittin on the porch." Indeed, Black gathering's criminal impossibility heavily lands in the poem's final line. Still, the assertion of absence is also a reminder of housework's ongoing presence, its making places for folks to sit and walk together. In other words, across the poem, despite invisibility's racial/fleshly/architectural reach, kids still gather on the porch. Night tents prop up, safe-harboring unavailable pleasures and joys, even if the owner world that collects and stares can neither hold it nor see it.

Poignantly, the phrase "night camping at noon" precedes the repeated question "What they call it?" The first time the question is asked in the poem, it refers to a phantom limb, to the fleshly feeling of absence. With repetition, a sense of play seems to join this absence, a play with makeshift housing, ecoaesthetically transforming the absence into a protected place to sleep outdoors. Put another way, even as the poem features the patrolling of cops and monster trucks, someone "night camps" at noon. Maybe it's those invisible kids and flowers that no one sees. As with "Green House" there are "relational aesthetics" that move against the enclosures engendered by form and image (Miles 2014).

Following Denise Ferreira da Silva and Édouard Glissant, I believe that Wallschlaeger's poems surveyed here craft an ecoaesthetics where "a poetic engagement with humanity begins with affectability (relationality, contingency, immediacy) and can only announce the constitutive relation" (Ferreira da Silva 2014, 89). With their emphasis on feeling and relation, these house poems, now invoking Jordan, engender a housework that keeps people momentarily safe and cared for, even as the space-time of underwater mortgages and cops going on special leave cruelly dismiss the relevance of such invisible labor.

Further, Ferreira da Silva (2014, 84) argues, "Blackness's capacity to signify otherwise—beyond universality and its particular arrangement of Space and Time but also away from transcendence (self-determination) invites a consideration of the possibility of knowing [and living] without modern categories." In other words, the capacity of Blackness to suggest a "wild beyond," a creativity and poiesis in excess of the regulating domains of capital and property, elucidates how and why it emerges as self-possession's condition and threat. As Fred Moten (2003, 26) might say, here Blackness is "only in that it exceeds itself, it bears the groundedness of an uncontainable outside."

On the one hand, such excess often figures pathologically as improper/impropertied personhood, the racist, classist, sexist, and ableist logics that "anagrammatically" conflate Black ownership with its failure, trespass (Sharpe 2016, 73). "Invisible house." A bad customer. Interminable indebtedness. Arrest. Arrest. Arrest. But so, too, following Moten, this excess bears a "groundedness," a gravitational arrangement different from the one advanced by recognized philosophers of understanding and self-possession, this time bespeaking an otherwise, ungiven relation to earth. A cohabitationality perhaps, one architected by and with friends and flowers, the willful ungovernability of an uncategorizable feeling.

In her final poem, "My House," for example, Wallschlaeger elaborates ecoaesthetics as this other kind of "groundedness." As with "Black House," this is a house you can't find because it's underground, in that bouquet of flowers, in a gesture felt by surveilled flesh. "My House" consists not of bricks and mortar but as a gathering of unseen (maybe undervalued) holds, forms of immeasurable and unaccounted for indebtedness where the narrator's life unmappably flourishes and where shelter itself might be found. Before discussing the poem, I'd like to quote one of its pages. It's structurally different from "Green House" and "Black House." While still a prose poem, rather than being composed of short paragraphs, the poem comprises twenty-six sets of two or so sentences, all beginning with the word *holding*. Because the poem is three pages long, I will reproduce the first page immediately below to provide a sense of its formal and conceptual structure.

Holding hands, holding bees. Holding grog for the monkscloth, holding cameras fact-checked in monkscloth. Holding friendships that get you killed. Holding babies.

Holding ferrets at the entrance. Holding passels of fugue. Holding old tortures, holding new ones. Holding people you've never seen in your mind.

Holding Mammy's red petticoat. Holding the whips to my funeral buggy. Holding Biggie. Holding noodle water. Holding a reel of smuggled total control.

Holding the twin bets. Holding how she rocked me. Holding counsel propped with steak dinkus. Holding a butterfly cadaver. Holding nosegays.

Holding a stinkflower. Holding 2 years of paternal contact. Holding the best stories about eating. Holding her electrocuted feet.

Holding what my friend said. Holding what the warden said. Holding what the lecturer said. Holding what the rape maneuver said.

Holding jaws upon jaws, gills upon gills. Holding steel guitars under eurocentric strobe mites. Holding the cow at the killing floor.

Holding the heebee jeebees. Holding ballpark figurines of the dead. Holding perishables. Holding the need. Holding hostis. (Wallschlaeger 2015, 74)

Seemingly, this house's un/builtness derives from various forms of intrapsychic, intrahistorical, intraspecies, intraearthly relationality. "Holding hands. Holding bees . . . Holding ferrets upon the entrance. Holding passels of fugue." This house is apparently built and sustained by love and stings, the life that wants to get in and the life that doesn't know how to stay. Guests and strangers, the push and pull of private, communal, and world-historical desires remain thick within its walls: "Holding Mammy's red petticoat. Holding the whips to my funeral buggy" (74). As the poem recites, the house is held together by holds, some forged by history, the pull of memory, the door-busting drives of expectant death. Others, even still, pitch in to the foundation as un-boxed feeling and desire, the unavailability of partially disclosed memory, the presence of nonhuman life: "Holding the twin bets. Holding how she rocked me. Holding counsel / propped with steak dinkus. Holding a butterfly cadaver. Holding nosegays."

Notably, the first half of the poem moves from the holding of someone or something specific, "Holding bees" or "Holding ferrets at the entrance" to another mode of address. "Holding x" becomes "holding you" but only briefly. "Holding you in the garage / holding you in the woods / Holding you on the couch / Holding you in the air" (75). This other kind of holding suggests another kind of intimacy, one past (the illusion of) property toward a "you" radiant in its elusive nonreferentiality. That is, "you" could be anyone, perhaps the poet herself or other, unquantifiable relationalities and gatherings that happen on furniture, within private rooms, in a clearing maybe, amid oxygen and nitrogen. Maybe "you" is the air, the elementally unheld.

Arguably, this undecidability is what holds the holds, nurturing the fugitive place for *my house*'s resident(s) to live and rest in. "Holding another day, tomorrow, the next day" (75). Unmonitored space-time, the gravitationality of tenderness and unanticipated feeling, the "uncontainable outside" of that ethereal home is also the shape of a mutual protection, a "walking lightly on the Earth" (Moten 2013, 26; Moten 2017a, 8).

At the bottom of the excerpted set of lines, for example, "Holding hostis" suggests a harboring of estrangement. *Hostis* is the Latin word for enemy, as in enemy of the state and mankind (the word was historically used to criminalize the act of piracy). But in "My House," *hostis* is held along with memory, pleasure, trauma, flowers, and violence. Holding is undecidable, loosened enough such that it bespeaks more of a complex intimacy, a protection, than a form of carcerality. Powerfully I think the juxtaposition of *holding* and *hostis* asserts how quickly one might become extra-oikic. That is, *hostis* perversely evokes *host* only to render it impossible for those figured outside the law. *Hostis* shows its own evictional power in the very arrangement of its letters. And what Wallschlaeger does is hold the word, hold it together, perhaps asking whether holding it might change the atmosphere of its making and the fictions of inside and outside that such a small change engenders.

Indeed, ecoaesthetically speaking, this last poem seems to leave the ground of this world a bit, evoking a home built not with fleshly and earthly ownerships, but with paradoxical juxtapositions, dense feeling, the invisible textures of a wherewithal: "holding hot stoves, holding cookstoves, holding cold stoves," "holding something that is gestural" (Wallschlaeger 2015, 76). These holds, using the active "holdings," texturally move back and forth, between everyday objects ("holding another paycheck") and the elusive evictions that haunt its making, "a ghost homespun from spools of watery veal" (76). These heavy holds, the arrangement of different ways people might hold their life, undulate through this poem.

Moreover, a heaviness or a weightedness around the concept of holding oscillates with a holding that flutters like a momentary feeling, like how "a decent breakfast" might be found in the "holding [of] school buses knitted into your vest" (De Veaux 1981, 82; Wallschlaeger 2015, 76). Holdings that are soft and bright, that smell "like grass" and feel "like hands" and might help folks keep going (Morrison 2004, 92). Holds that loosely, heavily, and momentarily stitch together an oikos based not on theft but on an unextractive intimacy. It is this weighty momentariness, of holding, of being together in the kitchen and on a frozen river, with the bees before their sting, with your chest as it breathes in and out at nighttime that adjoin Morrison and Wallschlaeger in their ecoaestheticizing some other imaginings of home. Home in *Beloved* and *Houses* is a gathering that arts a feeling, a togetherness the characters and narrators look for, hold on to. Home, what in these writings might be called a

Black feminine or feminist oikos, offers another view and feeling where living can be made and shared at the life-saving meeting ground of ecology and aesthetics. Home's Black gathering somehow blooms as black and green, along the recesses of diamonds, in the textures of a quilt or roadside flower composed by authors who once dreamed of a door.

2

THE ART OF THE MATTER

Samiya Bashir and Gabrielle Ralambo-Rajerison's Cosmopoetics

You hold everything black. You hold this body's lack. You hold yourself
back until nothing's left but the dissolving blues of metaphor.
—CLAUDIA RANKINE, "After David Hammons"

I write to constellate a leaving . . .
—BRENT HAYES EDWARDS, "Astral Caption"

Claudia Rankine's poem "After David Hammons" (2013) raises an important
question: What might it mean to "hold everything black"? The authors in this
chapter respond to this question by not answering. I assert that the poets
engaged here poetically ponder how such holding bespeaks a gestural and
material impossibility, pointing not to social life's absence but rather to its
important disaggregation from only earthly, empirical measure. Precisely,
this chapter moves from where Nikki Wallschlaeger's poem "My House" left
off, with writers who gesture toward a Black ecology beyond the domain of
the physical and empirical, moving into the atmosphere bridging earth with
the cosmos. I consider how Black women poets Samiya Bashir and Gabrielle

Ralambo-Rajerison poeticize Blackness and Black gathering as quantum and astrophysical possibility where both Blackness and gathering are unmoored from a certain expectation of their holdable form.

To restate, the poets engage areas of science that, as Ashon Crawley (2017, 48) writes of quantum physics, offer a mode of study "that verifies the fact there are things that happen in the world, in the universe, that are not easily perceptible to human flesh." In their art, Bashir and Ralambo-Rajerison offer meditations on Black gatherings that broach the undeniable unenclosable relationality between this planet and the universe with which it's connected. In particular, the authors' conceptual attention to the uncapturable phenomena of entropy and dark matter, for instance, gestures toward the galactic reach of the ecological to provide ongoing safe harbor for besieged forms of earthly togetherness. In sum, it is the aesthetic, or what we might call the cosmoaesthetic, that provides the entry point for the authors' artful engagements with Black gathering. That is, through experimental arrangements of words, particularly the spacing between them with respect to Bashir and between passages with respect to Ralambo-Rajerison, I argue that the writers deploy "quantum poetics" to convert the poem and page into a metonymic galaxy. Here's Amy Catanzano's definition (2011) of quantum poetics once more: "Quantum poetics investigates how physical reality is assumed, imagined and tested through language at discernible and indiscernible scales of spacetime." Even though neither Bashir nor Ralambo-Rajerison identify their poetics as quantum per se, their conceptual deployment of astro- and quantum physical terms, along with a purposive changing of spacing between words and passages, arguably alludes to what Catanzano calls the "something else" quality of the poem. I ask, then, if, following Catanzano, the poem, engaged as a scene of quantum causes and effects, shows how language always points to an extra-empirical elsewhere, then might the spacing around words also allude to a something off the page? An immeasurable space-time that shows up as an emptiness, a pulling of words apart? A space-time that makes of blankness—the spacing around words, after passages, on the page—another occasion of cosmoaesthetic and cosmopoetic meditation and coexistence?

With respect to Bashir's poem, "We call it dark matter because it doesn't interact with light," for example, dark matter shows up on the page conceptually, syntactically, and typographically. Bashir (2017, 53) writes:

Let this notion serve as replacement
    : the Department of State warns
        of the dangers of travel to   to

> to   to   to   to   to
>   . We recommend that citizens avoid all
> travel to   to   to   to   to
> whatever we've left for[.]

To begin, in the context of the poem, "dark matter" indicates a procedure of racial pathologization animating governmental instructions on so-called safe passage. Black people become brutally materialized as fleshly aberration, disfigured as avoidable darkness itself. Still, alongside this conceptual assertion of dark matter(s), of racist surveillances crafted to curtail such movement, dark matter arguably shows up too as formal innovation (Brown 2015). That is, the lines of the poem, in sync with dark matters' own speculated movement, establish a zigzag structure (University of Southern Denmark 2017).

Along with the extra spaces before phrases and between words, punctuation appears to be moved by an unseen gravitational movement. The *"to"s* give the impression of being pulled apart; the period and the semicolon, of being pushed, bombarded, out of place. I wonder if, given the title, we thought of the propulsion and unanticipated arrangement of this prose poem's words and punctuation as indicative of the page's dark matter and energy. Put differently, given that Bashir and Ralambo-Rajerison poetically and textually engage with such concepts as dark matter and dark energy, what if it manifests in their comportment toward the page? What if this formal and conceptual comportment renders the page as dark, perhaps Black, and with that, invisibly kinetic itself?

Considering the page as dark and already full powerfully and metaphorically challenges, even if unintentionally, an ontotheological narrative of the canvas/page/universe as white. Returning to philosopher Bernd Herzogenrath, even though dark, a founding myth of the universe's creation is inextricable from its presumptive whiteness:

> White as the absolute—the absolute purity, from which life began, with which all started, animated by the word, the spirit. There is a tradition here that resonates through the history of Western (White) Metaphysics. Note John Locke, who conceives of the human mind as "white paper, void of all characters." Or G. W. F. Hegel, who talks about "the void of the Absolute, in which pure identity, formless whiteness, is produced" . . . this whiteness is "absolutely monochromatic." In such an encompassing whiteness, the white itself does not move—it is indeed moved, informed, by a First Mover|Informer: God. In this white Gen-

esis, God's working material, the white canvas or blank page, is "*either an undifferentiated ground, a formless nonbeing, or an abyss without differences and without properties, or* a supremely individuated Being and an intensely personalized Form. Without this Being or this Form, you will have only chaos." This alternative is based on the "*hylomorphic* model," a doctrine going back to Aristotle, which claims that every "body" is the result of an imposition of a transcendent *form* (or *soul*) on chaotic or passive *matter*. (Herzogenrath 2013, 3)

Following Herzogenrath, we see how the poetic, cosmological, aesthetic reorientation of the page bespeaks a philosophical correlation between the ontotheological story of the universe—as a story of its given-over-ness to divine authorship—and a white authorship of formable darkness. In other words, to poetically contemplate dark matter as if it's what aesthetically surrounds the page/universe arguably disaggregates authorship from formal and conceptual domination. In Bashir's and Ralambo-Rajerison's cases, their artistic engagements with phenomena ranging from dark matter and energy to white supremacist anti-Blackness move by way of formal and conceptual dwellings with astro- and quantum physics concepts like thermodynamics and entropy. Their poetic engagements manifest, visually and typographically, as a play with word spacing and placement along with, in Ralambo-Rajerison's case, the use of abstract images. Considering these conceptual and formal elements, I argue that the authors' poems with and on the page microcosmically generate a galaxy. Seeing their poems this way makes for a vision where words blur into astral bodies, demonstrate force and gravitation by their errant spacing, and the page itself is defamiliarized from a site of inscription into an energetics of another order. Moreover, taking the page as seriously as the words, a move required by the authors' typographic and imagistic innovations, makes another way for Black gatherings' imaginative release from empirical (and perhaps typographic) form and elucidates how writing, and poetry itself, might beckon the *somewhere else* of such release.

Relatedly, and thinking with Anthony Reed (2014, 2) here, the formal rendering of the page as a deregulated place of Black gathering at once expresses how Black experimental writing "outline[s] new forms of community." These new forms of community, according to Reed after Jacques Rancière, move out of Black experimentalism's "[re]distribution of the sensible" (9). That is, the writing of "impossible" sentences joined by what poet critic Dionne Brand asserts as poetry's "pressure on the page, on space, on time" enacts imaginings of togetherness unmoored from the violences of linear space-time (quoted in Lubrin 2018).[1] Past, present, and future, yesterday and tomorrow, earth and somewhere light-years away, commune on the pages of Bashir's and Ralambo-Rajerison's writing. In this way, the page, when it holds the words and its surrounding darkness, might suggest that an aesthetic reencounter with the universe bears the potential for some nonextractive and noninscriptional reimagining. Returning to Bashir's "We call it dark matter because it doesn't interact with light," perhaps the experimental spacing between words makes places for unenterable harbors, harbors for those whose dark movements figure as requiring light's violent, surveilling reach.

Before engaging in close readings of Bashir's and Ralambo-Rajerison's writings, a scientific detour is necessary. Astrophysicist Jeremiah Ostriker and astronomer Simon Mitton's provocatively titled book on the cosmos, *Heart of Darkness: Unraveling the Mysteries of the Invisible Universe* (2013), is essential precisely because of what it reveals about a scientific investment in a biblical figuration of the universe, as given to inscription, even as an astrophysical phenomenon, the universe's own movement, suggests otherwise. Citing astronomer Fritz Zwicky as the "discoverer of dark matter," Ostriker and Mitton (2013, 175) argue that, even as it's undetectable on earth, dark matter is precisely what *holds* the universe together. Moreover, for Ostriker and Mitton, dark matter and dark energy constitute this ungiven heart of darkness, this unavailable and elusive materiality and force that produce conditions for the universe's coming together but that also resist expropriation and measure.

Instructively beginning with the Bible passage preceding the one purportedly sanctioning, for Locke and America's "founders," who juridically believed in his vision, Man's expropriation of the earth, the authors write:

> The first book of the bible, Genesis, starts out with "In the beginning, the earth was without form and void," and this reasonable start is one that present-day physicists would be inclined to adopt as well. To a certain extent it is empirically true, since we find that on the largest observable scales the cosmos is fairly smooth, the same in all directions, and with decreasing regularities, as we look farther away in space and further and further back in time. But, after a moment's more thought about the matter, we can see that there is something not quite right here. If the cosmos had started out perfectly smooth, then, without a god to stir things up, would it not have stayed perfectly smooth? And then, whence came all the structures that we see, the galaxies, stars, and planets? (130)

There is a curious invocation of Genesis here when questions around *the beginning* are sought. Indeed, this section of their chapter is titled "In the Beginning: Why an Explanation Was Needed." The need for an explanation is due to the above-cited incommensurability between a presumptive pre–Big Bang smoothness and the current nonsmoothness of the cosmos. Even still, God and Genesis are invoked precisely to get at the question of the universe's "heart of darkness" when the question actually concerns the universe's rate and duration of expansion. The search for answers to these questions animated, according to Ostriker and Mitton, their quest to *know* the driving force of the universe's creation, a driving force which, they ultimately argue, decenters god as creator. What they assert, by way of Zwicky's discovery of dark matter, is that the universe's nonuniformity means the absence of a singular author: "The very existence of galaxies indicated that fluctuations were intrinsic and fundamental to cosmology, not an add on, and must be faced as an *ab initio* element of the model. The version of the start of the world given in Genesis needs, in a physics-based model, the extra ingredient of initial perturbations; galaxies were the obvious consequences of such initial fluctuations" (145).

What the authors once more elaborate is that dark matter and dark energy are responsible for these "initial fluctuations" (175, 231). Dark matter dominates the universe's overall mass while dark energy opposes gravity to prevent galaxies from colliding (231). Under these conditions, the natural configuration of the universe is one that is almost empty. As physicists Sean Carroll and Jennifer Chen argue, "In our current universe, the entropy is growing and the universe is expanding and becoming emptier" (quoted in Koppes 2004). A reference to this emptiness, one that grows because of the entropic presence of dark energy, bespeaks how it is that while scientists acknowledge these dark forces for their particular effects, the material and energetic phenomenology of this darkness continues to elude them. Moreover, even though not racialized within the book's pages, the unholdability and immeasurability of dark matter and dark energy cannot be thought of outside the colonial anxieties animating the book's very title. Consider Joseph Conrad's description of Captain Marlow's journey into the Congo in *Heart of Darkness*. Conrad writes: "Going up that river was like traveling back to the earliest beginnings of the world, when vegetation rioted on the earth and the big trees were kings" (Conrad 2018).

In *Heart of Darkness*, the racist narrative of a Black African premodernity is connected to fears around traveling into a dark unknown. Note the following line from Bashir's "We call it dark matter because it doesn't interact with light":

. We recommend that citizens avoid all

travel to   to   to   to   to

The "all" concluding the line before "travel" is instructive. That is, there's a certain unfettered "all" that is what is to be avoided even as the "to" is what is incessantly advanced. Returning to Conrad, the description of Marlow's travel also suggests an indeterminate totality that surrounds. This surround evokes Stefano Harney and Fred Moten's (2013, 17) arguments of settlers worrying about their colonial fort being surrounded, bespeaking Conrad's fears about a "common[s] . . . before and before—enclosure." That is, the surround is narrated pejoratively by Conrad as both the (propertied white) human as man's absence and the overabundance of unceasing and uncultivated, Blackened, vegetation. Moreover, Conrad's description of this journey into darkness, as with Ostriker and Mitton, casts the purported absence of an author-god/man-cultivator with a figuration of the Congo as "an earth that wore the aspect of an unknown planet" (Conrad 2018). The colonial anxiety around the darkness, as Bashir's poem instructs, of the surrounding jungles of unlocatable sound and movement, is instructively, an anxiety about outer space, about the galactic reaches of an ecology always already Black and expansive, unholdable and unharvestable in that Blackness. Moreover, the "to to to to to," as a series of object-less prepositions, prepositions without position or point of arrival, suggests that travel also bears an openness and not-knowingness and it's how you arrive that might make the difference.

As Zakiyyah Iman Jackson cogently argues, this poetic imagination is part of a larger Black feminist conceptual and methodological engagement with physics, particularly in its attention to the forms of vitality that thrive in excess of empirical measure. Reflecting on Evelyn Hammonds's writings on Black female sexuality and the astrophysical phenomenon of the black hole, Jackson writes:

> As Hammonds further clarifies: "The observer outside of the [black] hole sees it as a void, an empty place in space. However, it is not empty; it is a dense and full place in space." With Hammonds I ask, how might this "perceived void," which is actually a "dense and full place in space," confound the very representationalist terms of "empirical" evidence and its perception? In the case of black(ened) female sex/ualities, Hammonds's metaphor implies the need to further develop reading and critical practices that allow us to approach that which resists and exceeds representation: the constitutive trace effects that black(ened) female

sex/uality produces in relation to the generic terms of gender and sexuality's legibility (Jackson 2018, 633).

Following Jackson, such critical practices, animated by the extra-empirical and astrophysical understanding of space-time's essential relativity and deformational possibility, arguably show up in and as Bashir's and Ralambo-Rajerison's poetry. In their poetry, Bashir and Ralambo-Rajerison formally and conceptually elucidate the attempted cosmic reach of anti-Blackness, the attempts to enclose and regulate Black social life while lovingly holding on to Blackness as an elusive Black feminist theory of ungiven sociality, as an original, unelaboratable gathering without end. Across their poetry, Blackness as a theory of cosmological relation becomes possible on and off the page.

Put differently, and joining Jackson here, Denise Ferreira da Silva might say that there's an inexpropriable togetherness that ends each of Bashir's poems and Ralambo-Rajerison's poem. This is a togetherness that's dark and ante-subjective. Ferreira da Silva (2014, 91) writes: "The wounded flesh, the inscriptions of the calculated violence registers what the Category of Blackness hides, living-dead capital profiting from expropriated productive capacity of enslaved bodies and native lands. Her confronting question, questions Time and the World it sustains. Framed in a position that refuses the World of Man, pre-posed by (before and toward) Man born in the world, the Feminist Black (racial) Critic becomes in material affectability (relationality, contingency, immediacy)."

Through astrophysical contemplation and in ways that evade typographic measure, I advance the idea that Bashir and Ralambo-Rajerison elaborate the affectable force of Black sociality beyond "Time and the World it sustains" (91). That is, they poeticize Black gathering as an empirical and extra-empirical possibility, across temporally recognizable shapes of feeling and anti-Black "scenes of subjection," which then moves into some impossible, unquantifiable affectivity, gravity, and spatiotemporality, changing the feel of writing on a page. Moreover, even as Bashir and Ralambo-Rajerison do not explicitly or consistently address gender and sexuality in their non/elaborations of dark matter, the Black feminist implications of their writing potentially undulate in that unstating. In other words, considering Ferreira da Silva and Herzogenrath together, if time is the word is the white subjective inscriptional unmaking of the world, then might Bashir's and Ralambo-Rajerison's poetic movement of dark matter show up somewhere between where *word* as concept and as form ends? In that way, might this unstating make for a Black feminist cosmopoetic and cosmoaesthetic creating of togetherness, what da

Silva identifies as Blackness's "creative capacity" beyond the violence of propertizing enclosure (85)? Ferreira da Silva continues:

> When virtuality guides our imaging of political existence, then the only significant political demand is Reconstruction: the end of state-capital is the demand for the restoration of total value expropriated through the violent appropriated of the productive capacity of native lands and slave labor. Forging Existence, without the separability imposed by the categories that name the task Barbara Christian describes, a Black Feminist Poethics—inspired by Octavia Butler's female characters—reads Blackness to expose the ruse of Reflection and Recognition, the yielding of the self-contained and coherent image of the Subject, which necessitates and lives off the translation of the historical effects of the colonial architectures that allowed the expropriation of the total value produced by native lands and slave labor (Ferreira da Silva 2014, 94).

As Ferreira da Silva argues, by way of Barbara Christian and Octavia Butler, a Black feminist imagination has often innovated within and against an expropriative, inscriptional (à la Spillers's critique of American grammar), anti-Black space-time characterizing our present in order to dream and virtually travel otherwise. An example used by Ferreira da Silva is Butler's neoslave narrative *Kindred* (1979), in which Butler's main character is a Black woman who time travels between a plantation intent on holding her and an apartment where she's released. Such time travel philosophically enacts a Black feminist poethics, an embrace of Blackness's "creative potential" without the tools of "scientific reason" (Ferreira da Silva 2014, 84). That is, the racial, sexual, and capitalist figuration of Blackness as given over to white ownership, trespass, enclosure, and spatiotemporal inscription is radically reworked and transformed by a Black feminist poethics and aesthetics of an alter-temporal spatial inhabitation and nonexpropriable creativity.

Indeed, that other text of time travel, this aesthetic of the impossible in *Kindred*, what Ferreira da Silva associates with a kind of deregulated embrace of air, moves as another account of the human she's interested in, one that allows a Black woman traveler to indescribably get home alive, even as the torrent of this world's account tries to pull her apart. Returning to the focus of this chapter, this imaginative play outside of space-time, across quantum virtualities where the weights of dark matter and anti-Blackness are poetically distilled into language and the placement of words on the page, connects the poets engaged here to this larger Black feminist tradition. In the next section, I consider

Samiya Bashir's cosmoaesthetic and cosmopoetic praxis as it evokes a virtual realm of otherwise Black gatherings. A cosmopoiesis that asks after what's possible for relationality if the story of the universe was untold differently.

Beginning Better Than the Beginning: Samiya Bashir's *Field Theories* of Ungiven Life

What if we dwelled with the astrophysical implications of Gayl Jones's (1975, 54) fictional assertion in *Corregidora* that "everything said in the beginning must be said better than in the beginning"? In the context of *Corregidora*, this revelation emerges in relation to a family of Black women haunted by the sexual violences of slavery and by a reproductivist compulsion to never forget. The beginning that is worse is the one where the world is ontotheologically sanctioned as given-overable by Lockean property grammars; these are grammars that, in propertizing the dark matter of the earth, violently configured Black femininity as "infinitely malleable lexical and biological matter, at once sub/super/human" (Jackson 2018, 636). But this other beginning, which Jones aesthetically and ethically attunes us to, is one where Black femininity is fundamentally integrally ungivable, inexpropriable, alexical, left alone to sonically commune with the universe of which it is inextricably a part. I argue that Bashir's *Field Theories* moves in the interest of this other beginning.

To begin, the frontispiece is a quote culled from June Jordan's poem, "1977: Poem for Miss Fannie Lou Hamer" (2005). The poem speaks to Jordan's relationship with Hamer, with whom she worked illegally registering Black people to vote in 1960s Mississippi.

"Honey when you come down here you
supposed to stay with me. . ."
. . . .
and later
you stood mighty in the door on James Street
loud callin:

"BULLETS OR NO BULLETS!
THE FOOD IS COOKED
AN' GETTING COLD!"

Kinship amid terror, terror amid kinship, moving in Jordan's phrase of "bullets or no bullets" poetically attends to the life hemmed in by death, announced by the title beginning with "1977," the year of Hamer's passing. Even still, it's what follows the colon that's instructive, how it supports the poem's honoring of a woman whose spirit cannot be killed. In other words, in some ways Jordan's artistry here suggests that the poetic engagement with ungiven life can only be offered once the physical limits of this world are exceeded, with death itself somehow punctuated. The pause engendered by the punctuation, the nonalignment between what's before and after the colon, seemingly makes room for a quantum, spatiotemporal uncertainty, a wondering as to how long Hamer's "loud callin'" oxygen molecularly remained in the air, in the field, after her tired flesh took its final rest. For example, Jordan ends the poem with, and in a field "one full Black lily / luminescent / in a homemade field / of love"; it's the same quote Bashir uses to begin *Field Theories* (2017).

This conclusion follows a story of Jordan's and others' entanglement with Hamer, a family of freedom fighters who, according to poem, came to embody the multiple oneness akin to that ostensibly singular lily. But at the same time, these last lines might have been about Hamer herself—a former sharecropper who may have indeed worked that very field—with her enduring "freedom dream" persisting as ecological remainder (Kelley 2003). Either way, I think the Black feminist poethical work engendered by the poem powerfully honors Hamer's multiplicity, the fullness of her ecological, spiritual, and quantum life. In that way, the poem and Jordan's care arguably provide a powerful preface for the other force fields and ecologies ushered forth by Bashir's own writing.

In this section I engage Bashir's poetry for how it particularly, poetically dwells with such quantum physics concepts as Planck's constant and the Carnot cycle to advance what Britt Rusert (2017, 17) names a "minor science" that seeks not to evaluate but to protect the energetic surround, the *anoriginal* beginning suggested by the dark "nothing" that "ain't nothing."[2] Moreover, her poems advance the Black feminist implications of the energetically unseen. The energy unavailable and in excess of the post-Lockean, Newtonian/Cartesian, racial/sexual/economically expropriative logics presuming its otherwise givenness to ownership and measure.[3] I quote from both poems in full below, starting with "Planck's Constant":

What else made sense but
the push to climb one another

hand over hand and grab at

whoever was near enough?

The season groaned on
into November; crows bled

branch to sky; stone upon
stone upon stone towered

toward a heaven that flushed
its three-day-old lie of bruise.

Snowflakes threatened war
the moon split town and swore

not to return for days. Your
flicker and turn a lighthouse

and a storm. At quarter to six
the sun went down forever so

what else made sense but to
climb one another hand over

hand and cleave to whoever was
left and near enough and would? (Bashir 2017, 10)

"Planck's Constant" starts off seemingly in the middle of a gathering, some situation where life is brought, forced together. The narrator, in the face and the touch of fleshly entanglement, wonders about the possibilities left for some movement (survival, pleasure) when togetherness is where you are. When togetherness is where you start. Moreover, this togetherness seems laborious, brutally banal, a togetherness that aches and makes for an achy atmosphere, the flight of a bird with wings weighed down. As the poem moves, the achiness of togetherness is heard in the groaning of autumn, and the final image of the first part features a dispirited earth, shadowed by a Babylonian tower building toward the cosmos.

Before moving into the poem's second half, it is important to note that, structurally, the prose poem comprises long sentences that break between stanzas. Rhythmically, "Planck's Constant" requires a slow reading, a sounding out and staying in sync with a long sentence or query. This is formally resonant with the phenomenon itself. Notably, in the context of quantum physics, Planck's constant refers to the smallest amount of quantizable energy that makes possible the vibratory capacities of heat and light. In contrast to a Newtonian/classical physics presumption that space/time/matter are infinitely divisible, physicist Max Planck countered with the assertion of an energetic constant responsible for the presence and degree of brightness and warmth subject to measure. Bashir seemingly asks the reader to enjoin this physics principle aesthetically, to sustain energy with the breathily pacing of an extended thought.[4]

Returning to the poem imagistically, the second half begins with the apocalyptic phrase "snowflakes threatened war." Ostensibly, something bad happened in the partial story of togetherness evoked in the poem, such that shifts in atmospheric pressure and celestial bodies refuse what's expected of them. And yet, in the midst of what suggests an end-times' turn of events, the language shifts to being more direct, personal, and relatedly possessive. *Your, flicker, lighthouse,* and *storm* starkly emerge as a curious singularity, or perhaps duality, something more intimate than the affectively ambivalent togetherness registering at the poem's beginning and end. This momentary flickering, which endures and holds, takes place against a backdrop of a togetherness that somehow breaks sun, snow, moon. A togetherness that begins and ends the poem, a togetherness that quite literally ends on a darkened page, a page blackened by the sun going away.

Moreover, Bashir deploys a multiplicitous, nonsingular voice, one that moves between flesh and season to describe this movement, the series of gestures that remain, after the earthly world calls it quits:

The season groaned on
into November; crows bled

. . .

toward a heaven that flushed
its three day-old lie of bruise.

. . .

the moon split town and swore

not to return for days . . . at quarter to six
   the sun went down forever so. (10)

Ending on a sunless page powerfully coincides with a phenomenon Max Planck was also known for, that is, "blackbody radiation." For Planck, "a perfect blackbody is one that absorbs all incoming light and does not reflect any. At room temperature, such an object would appear to be perfectly black (hence the term blackbody)" (Mutlaq n.d.).

Considering Planck's scientific assertion of forms of energy resistant to divisibility (read: calculation) along with the photological definition of perfect Blackness as thermally ungiven, privately radiant, the universe's own elusive (maybe) first color, how might we think the form and shape of a (Black) gathering that can neither be moved nor owned? That is, returning to Bashir's poem, after the sun and the moon and the crows and heaven itself decided they were all finished, she muses, "What else made sense but to / climb one another hand over / hand and cleave to whoever was / left and near enough and would?" What if this is Planck's constant, the end that was always the beginning, the unheard song of winters and crows, the flesh that climbs over one another even as the propertizing, self-same lords of division loom dangerously near? Maybe in the context of Planck's constant the quantum endurance is that movement of antislavery, the unencroachable intimacies and gatherings that have their terrible beginnings in the divisionary ethos of a slave ship's hold? The quantum remainder perhaps akin to those "erotic bonds" shared between "women in the sex-segregated holds [of the ship] . . . [a resistance to] the commodification of their bought and sold bodies [made] by feeling and feeling for their co-occupants on these ships" (Tinsley 2008, 192).

These might be the forms of togetherness that emerge when the planets themselves along with air, flesh, and earth collapse from the torment of being given over to the ones who never cease giving them over. This collapse is one of refusal, "snowflakes threatened war," an insurrectionary inhabitation of the quantum against the ones who presume that infinite divisibility/harvestability not only is possible but exists as their divine endowment. This togetherness seems anterior to individuation, anterior to the subject, what remains after and despite enlightenment divisiveness. Indeed, that's what ends the poem, the inexpropriable, undivided energetic constant of a climbing over one another. The only thing left, the only thing that "made sense," is to "cleave to whoever was left and near enough and would?" (Bashir 2017, 10). The "would" lingers as an open question. Like Beloved's desire "to join," the irresolvability of this gathering arguably fluctuates in the unanswered ether, or the outstretched hand, of the page. Moreover, the crafting of this "would" suggests the unknowability of togetherness's reach; the being on the other side of the "would" flutters as potential, outside of the poem's own temporality. In that way, darkened energy flickers at poem's end outside enclosure and regulation, how Ferreira da Silva (2014, 85) imagines the project of Black feminist poethical creativity, an "unknowing and undoing of the World that reaches its core."

I turn now to the second poem, "Carnot Cycle," precisely for how the refusal of total expropriation, of total energetic extraction emerges precisely in the image of a darkened togetherness shadowed by an arrival close to that core.

Only sometimes does homegrown bedrock glow moneygreen.
Sometimes rock whines mommy. Sometimes rock coos baby.

Sometimes rock calls late with the mortgage. Sometimes rock
knits shoulder blades right where you can't pluck.

Early morning something doesn't sit right over the desk. Sits crooked.
Slumps askew. Body doesn't lay the way you left it. Squinting
gets you nowhere. You squat to the floor and feel around. Stop.
Smell for it. Shrug. Still some dangling something modifies you.
Smackdab midchest you feel lumpy empty. Sniff. Sniff.

Shrug.

Days. Almost every one we grab pickaxes. Almost every one we mine.
We hum work songs. We sing hymns. We chip worry stone. We
hope. We gather moss. We lie flat. We scratch at the mineshaft
We descend deeper. We lamp away from the light not toward
exit but through the broken core (Bashir 2017, 14).

To begin, structurally speaking, the poem is set with a hanging indent. The
words that dangle on the left side are *only, early, shrug, days*. As with "Planck's
Constant," "Carnot Cycle" also anthropomorphically focuses on a nonhuman
voice. The opening stanza, through a repetition of short sentences, describes
the acts and desires of bedrock: a rock that glows, hums to infants, makes
shoulder blades hurt. The movement from animate rocks to those who mine
and extract material from them forms the shape of this poem.

The second cluster of sentences seemingly details the bodily experience
of an individual laborer, spoken of in third person. The sentences are short,
like the first stanza, with the language being nonspecific and spatiotemporally
imprecise, as in "sometimes rock" does *x, y, z*. (14). Here "sometimes" prefaces
in third person what a tired body does, how it comports to flesh and its own
exhaustion. Moreover, even as "something doesn't sit right" tonally bespeaks
alienation, perhaps engendered by being the one tasked/forced to "mine" the
rocks, the use of the third person accrues another meaning. Here I wonder,
what if we reimagined the third person or the impersonal as another way of
imagining fleshly relationality? Or what if the use of the third person, the spatializing of a distance between the working body and the one who inhabits it,
evokes a notion of sitting with oneself, a something that feels lumpy, something not seen but felt?

Poignantly, after the second passage describing sitting with a tired body,
the third comprises a single word, *shrug*, signaling both a not knowing and a
something you can surround yourself with. Along with a gesture connoting

uncertainty, for example, a shrug also refers to a shawl. So just as, formally, the words standing on the edges of the poems' mass—the dangling words *only*, *days*, *early*, and *shrug*—indicate an ostracism, the centering/highlighting of *shrug*, evokes an enduring surround. Perhaps, the tired worker, the one who mines and chips and hears the rock's demands, is already part of a multiplicity, a gathering, waiting there.

Indeed, this multiplicity moves in the poem's final passage. That is, the final passage speaks of work done together: "Almost every one we grab pickaxes. / Almost every one we mine." In this final passage, this activity of labor (mining) becomes song and movement. "We" arrive in darkness, a darkness entered multiply, a togetherness that doesn't end like it begins, with "mining," but perhaps we-ing. "Carnot Cycle" ends not with a collective effort to punch a hole in the earth, like the arbiters of extraction might require, but rather to be with the earth differently: "We lamp away from the light not toward exit but through the broken core." As with "Planck's Constant," structurally and lyrically the poems end in darkness and in elusive, fleshly/earthly togetherness.

How the poem intervenes against a mining toward a we-ing, a being with that does not take from the earth, bears profound significance when we consider its title and the physics system it evokes. That is, following physicist Richard Feynman, the law of thermodynamics comprises a set of physics principles exploited early on by the propertied emissaries of racial capitalism and chattel slavery. According to Feynman (1963), "The science of thermodynamics began with an analysis, by the great engineer Sadi Carnot, of the problem of how to build the best and most efficient engine, and this constitutes one of the few famous cases in which engineering has contributed fundamentally to physical theory." Moreover, according to historian Daniel Rood, the Carnot steam engine was invented in 1824, and the (Carnot) cycle was used for sugar processing in the Caribbean.

> For mid-nineteenth-century thinkers like Carnot, equilibrium was the enemy, since a system in balance was powerless. Recognition of disequilibrium as a constant in nature and as a necessity in production led to "a much more general concern with progression, with directionality and development in time, with the 'universal law of decay.'" Disequilibrium was recast as simultaneously productive and destructive, because every moment of work performed was also a moment of energy consumed and forever unrecoverable. The European version of the Derosne system was part of the engineering world that gave rise to these new

philosophical reflections. The Greater Caribbean setting defined by racial difference, tropicality, island resource limitations, and a semiperipheral economic position intensified the new concerns, and pushed the Derosne design in new directions. (Rood 2017, 24)

The mobilization of the second law, that is, disequilibrium toward the mechanized processing of sugar, arguably subtends anti-Blackness in the slave-owning Caribbean; this highlights the Carnot cycle's violent worldly history. But at the same time, what the history of antislavery revolts also illuminates is the inexpropriable remainder of what could not be harnessed: the energetic afterlife that lingered in the wake of forced work. Rood writes: "Between 1825 and 1844, enslaved Africans and Afro-Cubans raised a series of rebellions. The uprisings were concentrated in the provinces of Matanzas and Cárdenas, which held a disproportionate number of enslaved workers as well as the most modern machinery of sugar production. In one of the 1843 Cárdenas uprisings, which began in Ingenio Alacancía (the Alacancía sugar mill), 465 Afro-Cubans marched off plantations toward the village of Bemba, gathering recruits as they went" (16).

We might think of these rebellions in ways akin to entropy, both bespeaking the unextractable remainders and ungovernable insurgencies yielded by coerced work. That is, according to the laws of physics and the Carnot cycle's mobilization of the second law of thermodynamics, as heat rises, so does the capacity for work. Still, with this energetic increase, animated by the frenzied investments in racial-capitalist modernity, the rate of entropy, or disorder, also increases. Entropy, as the remainder of a thermodynamic process wielded by those who presumed earth and flesh as given over, bespeaks the unavailable, maybe even fugitive, surplus of that movement. In other words, returning to Feynman, the greater the expenditure of heat-in-work (which we might think of here as enabling the Derosne system), the greater the rate of unusable energy. Alongside the implementation and usage of the Derosne system, slave rebellions held the question of use to the fire. We might also say that they evoked entropy's capacity for revolutionary organization, not just as the invisible fugitive movement running tide and tide with production but that so too fosters insurgent Black gathering. The forms of immeasurable togetherness outside of production where, following literary and jazz critic Albert Murray and Bashir, the "ain't nothing nothing" makes social life (Bashir 2017, 3).

Once more, the Carnot cycle, seen as the steam engine accelerating plantation production, depended on the earth and flesh-killing violences of anti-

Blackness and racial capitalism for its actual motive force. On the one hand, disequilibrium might be a brutally mild reference to such violence. But even more than that, and to restate, the presence of entropy, the disorder that arrives with energy's increase and drives production, nonetheless signals the fugitive edges of a force that cannot be stopped. So, when Bashir begins the poem by writing about bedrock and its animacy, "Sometimes rock coos baby / sometimes rock calls late with the mortgage," perhaps she's getting at that fugitive force (14). The rock that speaks perhaps evokes "the history of blackness . . . testament to the fact that objects can and do resist" (Moten 2003, 1). What is more, the history of Blackness that moves through and as a repetition-engendered ensemble of speaking rocks, at the same time gestures toward Anna Tsing's (2013, 36) concept of "more-than-human socialities" discussed in the previous chapter. Recalling my earlier arguments following Tsing, the relationalities at work in such sociality, in deprioritizing human capacities of communication and representation, not only recenters the freedom and world-making stories of plants and animals—and now rocks (!)— but also unmoors that social life, and sociality itself, from the entrapments of understanding. In that way, the rock that speaks moves by way of another history of Blackness grounded in an otherwise ecological ethos, one witnessed in the speculative accounts before the universe was said to be given over and in the aesthetic, anthropological, and literary archives of what Monique Allewaert (2013, 7) calls "parahumanity."

Engaging such an archive, Allewaert argues, "Colonial organizations of labor power, particularly the plantation form, required that slaves (often of African descent) become deeply familiar with the properties of nonhuman animal and plant life" (7). Such intimacies, even as they were shaped by violence, elucidated the errors of Lockean and Kantian theories that presumed the alignment of freedom with earthly ownership and human freedom with ecocidality. That is, as Bashir's "Carnot Cycle" reveals, freedom is often found in what Moten (2003, 12) calls the "socialization of the surplus," in the recess around the dialectics of ownership and expenditure, in the intervals of held life. In particular, through the repetition of *sometimes*, the social life of the poem seemingly gathers and moves, gathers and moves, making space for impossible speech and feeling in the page's hidden, dark harbors.

Only sometimes does homegrown bedrock glow moneygreen.
Sometimes rock whines mommy. Sometimes rock coos baby.
Sometimes rock calls late with the mortgage. Sometimes rock
knits shoulder blades right where you can't pluck. (Bashir 2017, 14)

Powerfully, even as repetition might indicate production, the errancy and elusiveness of *some*, the incalculable remainder of *some* perhaps entropically generates an unanticipated shift in a cycle. Maybe during or after the unrecorded interaction between worn-out hand and tool and rock, between worn-out hand and earth, the machine might get up and call it quits too.

Moreover, the further you get into the poem, the more work continues and entropy accrues. At the poem's end, those who chip away start to arrive at something that is not the exit, "but . . . the broken core." Maybe it's the beginning said better than at the beginning, the heat and light unavailable to production, "Held but not had" (Mackey 2009, 289). Perfect blackbody radiation. Again, following Ferreira da Silva, what if "the broken core" was Blackness itself, the private radiance of absorption not emission, a forcefield that keeps what it creates? As with "Planck's Constant," the bottom or end of this poem is Blackness, a darkened page. What the gathering arted, we might say, was the full emptiness creating the page's own unknowable buoyancy along with some undisclosed safe harbors.

In closing, I want to conclude by considering two works of art connected to the production of *Field Theories*, its cover and a dance performance. The cover image, a reproduction of Nigerian visual artist Toyin Ojih Odutola's painting *Lonely Chambers (T.O.)* (2011), is of a Black face glowing iridescent, the color black mosaically crafted into an arrangement with bright blues and greens (see figure 2.1). There is a stretched, ethereal quality to the face, one in keeping with Odutola's interest in the use of "diverse mediums to emphasize how an image is a striated terrain to mine beyond formulaic representation" (University of the Arts 2018). This more than faceness of the face is both striation and stretch, a kind of atmospheric, possibly cosmic, reach. That is, there is a dispersal and stretching of skin color, a gesturing toward other elemental combinations indicating Blackness's chromatic and material communion with quantum vitalities past representational enclosures. The green-blue-black mosaic-skin perhaps moves as both a gathering place and a place that gathers with other forces, forms of light and texture otherwise unseen. Arguably, the cover image and the poetry found within Bashir's book advance a notion of Black environmental literature that foregrounds the quanta, cosmic encounters between flesh and the cosmically invisible. Presented differently, considering Odutola's painting and Bashir's poetry together, perhaps the front cover visualizes Black life's entanglement within a galactic ecology, the face here sprinkled with the stars with which it is powerfully enmeshed. Moreover, in a short film promoting the release of *Field Theories* we hear Bashir reciting, "You don't have to pump the breaks you just gotta keep your

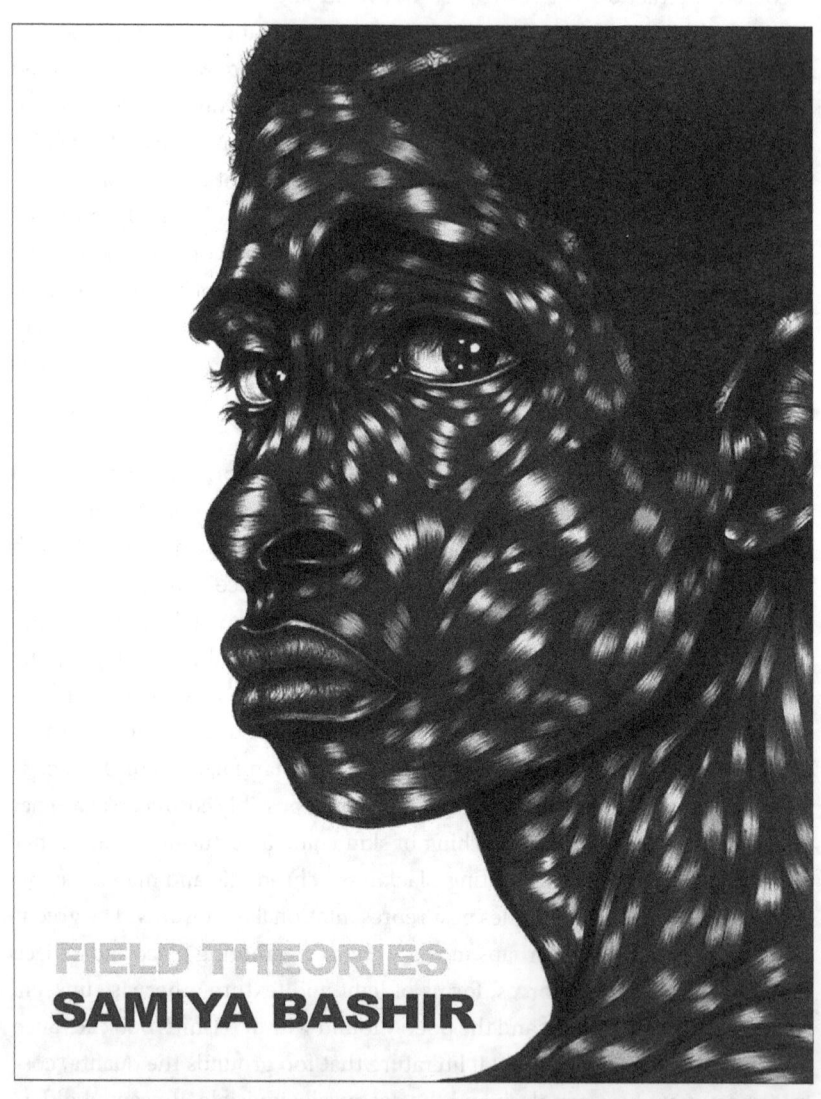

FIGURE 2.1. Cover image of *Field Theories* by Samiya Bashir.
Courtesy of Nightboat Books.

eyes on the road" as a fully illuminated night sky coalesces into a dancer's form (Bashir 2016; also see Bashir 2017, 47). On the screen, a bending, spinning figure moves their arms, projecting a mirror image of themselves as the galaxy's stars hold and unsettle their fleshly boundedness.[5]

Powerfully, in line with *Field Theories* itself, art becomes the occasion for the galaxy's fleshly expression, a powerful setup for the book itself. That is, once more, as a Black environmental literature, a Black cosmoaesthetics and cosmopoetics, I appreciate how *Field Theories* connects Blackness to the energy of the universe and the universe to Black life. Such a move plausibly opens Black social life's movement and unmoors its possibilities for gathering apart from the propertizing logics that see the earth (and Blackness itself) as given over to the human and violently separate from the cosmos of which it is a part. Such a move advances Blackness as an always already celestial miracle despite propertied personhood's incessantly brutal claims to the contrary.[6]

Joining Bashir, Karel Schrijver and Iris Schrijver, authors of *Living with the Stars*, argue, "Almost all of the atoms in our bodies have been forged either in the deep interior of stars, or within the explosion of these stars at the ends of their existence" (Schrijver and Schrijver 2015, 9). Because of this, along with the endless cycling of hydrogen, oxygen, nitrogen, and carbon between flesh and cosmos, the authors conclude, "Human bodies are intrinsically impermanent. Rather than fixed, they are more akin to a pattern or a process, although stable enough to allow a perception of continuity" (10). That is, the universe is as much a part of those living on earth as is the earth (a noncentral) part of a larger network of galactic relations preceding its capacity to sustain such life.

This is crucial as it reveals once more, following Moten, the ways that the fictions of the earth's givenness are inextricably bound up with the "vicious establishment of [its] subdivisional centrality [of the cruel division and centering of earth from the heavens, my paraphrase of Moten] in the overrepresentational separation of [our] overviewing, enslaving, settler colonial selves" (Moten 2017c, 1). Lockean personhood, buttressed as it was by racial slavery and settler colonialism, presumed that those for whom the earth wasn't given were interminably in debt to those who claimed it. That is, the omnicidal ones, the claimers themselves, presumed that the earth could be wrested from its galactic lifeline as much as it could survive being expropriatively given over. Even still, despite Locke's and others' presumption of planetary enclosure as that which securitizes property as personhood, the artists in this book illuminate how gathered flesh and earth have always been more than one, "intrinsically impermanent" (Schrijver and Schrijver 2015, 5), never central but part of a larger, nonteleological series of errant relations, more than human socialities, within a galactic ecology: an ecology where everyone and everything, every rain shower and floral bloom, human and animal, rock and ray move as shared weight and responsibility, all part of a kind of galactic enmeshment that makes silly and fraudulent the notion that the earth is here because of people and, more nearly, that its ownable at all.

Here are Karel Schrijver and Iris Schrijver (2015, 8–9):

> Every object in the wider universe, everything around us, and everything we are originated from stardust. Thus, we are not merely connected to the universe in some distant sense: stardust from the universe is actually flowing through us on a daily basis, and it rebuilds the stars and planets throughout the universe as much as it does our bodies, over and over again. In our everyday lives, we tend to ignore the universe beyond the Earth's atmosphere and take it for granted that the Sun steadily shines its warming light onto the planet. . . . We do not generally ponder the many links between us and the stars, expect perhaps for the links to the nearest star that we call the Sun. These links range from the Big Bang, in which the universe was formed, to the particle radiation from the Galaxy that slams into the high terrestrial stratosphere right now.

Following the Schrijvers and unrecognized astrophysicist Toni Cade Bambara, recognizing human life as filled with stardust requires at once an imaginative decentering of the earth along with a decentering of a racialized notion of the subject buttressed by the earth's presumptive extractability from the cosmos.[7] By extension, this anti-extractive ethos requires understanding Blackness and Black life as anoriginal, that is, as the beginning. On this Moten (2013, 789) writes, "Blackness is ontologically prior to the logistic and regulative power that is supposed to have brought it into existence." Crucially, following Moten, to recognize the priorness of Blackness in relation to the universe's own deregulatable formation allows us to consider how the earth's propertized centralization integrally manifests as anti-Blackness. Put differently, the violation and criminalization of Black gatherings on earth express the "founding myth" of whiteness not only as the over/underwriter of togethernesses on earth but across and with the cosmos as well. I see Bashir's and Odutola's works of art as poetically enacting and extending this conversation, in the cosmoaesthetic and cosmopoetic assertion of Blackness's starry anoriginality as visually glimmering and elusive, as unpropertizable gathering.

Moreover, I think that this dwelling with beginnings, their devastating whiteness through property's universe-destroying imposition, powerfully connects *Field Theories* to Gabrielle Ralambo-Rajerison's long prose poem "To What Do I Owe This Pleasure" (2017). In it, Ralambo-Rajerison muses on a range of topics, including slavery in Madagascar, John Locke's theory of property, parabiotic rats, the police killing of Tamir Rice, environmental racism, and the unquantifiable presence of dark matter across the universe. As with Bashir's "We call it dark matter because it doesn't interact with light," Ralambo-Rajerison contemplates dark matter as it manifests at once as originarity denied, coercively gathered, and codified, and modes of Black survival as that which can neither be read nor known.

A poet and graduate student at Pitt University, Ralambo-Rajerison did a residency in the Department of Physics and Astronomy at her home university; her poem "To What Do I Owe This Pleasure" resulted from that experience. The following is shared from the artist's introduction to the poem:

> During my residency, I was able to complete a draft of a long poem I've been working on currently titled *To What Do I Owe This Pleasure*, as well as beginning drafts of shorter, single-page poems. This long poem is one I've "started" several times, most recently after the summer 2016 deaths of Alton Sterling and Philando Castile. . . . I wanted to teach myself— and thus better understand—how to live in the world, which led me (as these things often do) to reconciling myself with the fact(s) of the universe.
>
> Dr. Carles Badenes recommended early on that I read Timothy Ferris's *Coming of Age in the Milky Way* . . . . "The word 'universe' is not the universe; neither are the equations of super-symmetry theory or the Hubble law or the Friedmann-Walker-Robinson metric," Ferris writes. "Nor, more generally, is science very good at explaining what anything, much less the universe, actually 'is.' Science describes and predicts events, but it pays for this power in the coin of the *ding an sich*—the thing in itself." (Ralambo-Rajerison 2017)

Powerfully, Ralambo-Rajerison's poetic engagement with "all that happens to simultaneously exist" joins Bashir's aesthetic interventions in evoking a gathering on the page. That is, in the poem, Ralambo-Rajerison's gathering of newsstory and astrophysical phenomena, the conceptual arrangement of events seen and unseen, alternates between a clustering of paragraphs along with scenes and juxtapositions on one page and a solitary paragraph on another. As well, intermixed throughout are circular objects, empty and blackened circles that seemingly suggest that the poem is part of a planetary map or a galaxy. Moreover, Ralambo-Rajerison's conceptual engagement with anti-Blackness and the universe also manifests in the writing itself, specifically in describing the significance of Ferris's book for her meditations (extracted above).

Instructively, the Ding an sich, the thing-in-itself, that thing that cannot be described is what joins the universe to Blackness itself. Engaging a white European continental philosophical archive, most notably the writings of G. W. F. Hegel and Immanuel Kant, Ferreira da Silva (2017) elucidates how, in this archive "blackness refers to matter—as the Thing; it refers to that without form—it functions as a nullification of the whole signifying order that sustains value in both its economic and ethical scenes." Precisely, outside of a Kantian ethical system, which casts dignity as the nonreduction of a person to a "means to an end," Blackness brutally occupies what Hegel called the thing and that Ferreira da Silva calls "total violence" (Ferreira da Silva 2017; Kant 2005 [1785], 55). And yet, Ferreira da Silva argues that the philosophical reduction of Blackness to a thing outside of time and space did not anticipate the other "worlds" engendered by the absence of weight and measure; these are worlds that Black feminist theorists and poets have long aestheticized in and toward (Ferreira da Silva 2014).

In Ralambo-Rajerison's beautiful poem, the violences of anti-Blackness manifest as police violence and colorism are juxtaposed with unreadable dark matter. Indeed, after reading the entire story, one might say that Blackness's unreadability provides the precise conditions for another comportment toward gathering, another aesthetic relation that radiates a togetherness otherwise. That is, after providing accounts of anti-Blackness traveling as fleshly denial and white-supremacist murder and abandonment, Ralambo-Rajerison arrives at dark matter. Or, more nearly, dark matters flourish all over this story, not only perhaps undulating as the empty space surrounding the text itself but also as those unknowable landscapes of sorrow and remembrance, incalculable loneliness, and unknowingness more broadly: some hidden sources of gravitation or reorientation when the heaviness of anti-Black spaces and times is too much to bear.

"To What Do I Owe This Pleasure"

The prose poem begins with a minor history of the world, of flesh and earth as given over or taken, as it shapes the story of the narrator's family. It commences with a brief, ancestral account of anti-Blackness and slavery in colonial Madagascar and its diasporic reverberations in an instantly anti-Black American present. From there, each page features a series of vignettes, sometimes relating to one another as paragraphs in a narrative and sometimes not, moving instead as an errant orbit of distinct observations.

Evoking everything from colonial Madagascar to Hurricane Katrina, para-biotically conjoined rats to a devastating anecdote about Sandra Bland's grieving nephew, "To What," I argue, makes a universe. That is, structurally, some of its pages feature circular, planetary formations that affront the sparse text that follows. Other pages contain only three lines of print surrounded by an abundance of empty space. The concluding pages, which more explicitly imagine the interface between the earthly and the cosmic, suggest that the story's overall formal innovation might structurally attempt a galactic shape. With respect to the conceptual, stories of slavery and anti-Blackness are threaded with mentions of dark matter and the Higgs boson, also referred to as the "god particle," so-called because it gives "weak" subatomic particles, such as W and Z, their mass (Sutton n.d.). Thinking about this poem as a universe, then, and as a galactic ecology that attends as much to the weak as to the strong forces, I argue that Ralambo-Rajerison asserts the universe's own praxis of deregulated gathering and interactive creativity. Precisely, in its distribution and sharing of mass, "To What" offers an unprecedented response to the devastations wrought by anti-Blackness and a glimmer of the modalities of Black gathering managing to survive otherwise.

The story begins with an account of the narrator's ancestor's bloody sacrifice, a peasant who gave part of his ear to save a kingdom. This peasant, we're told, is assured that his loss means that his family will not be enslaved and that they will be able to have their own land, to build a home. No other historical, geopolitical or symbolic information is provided, just the actors, the medicine man, the king, and the peasant. As we might conclude that the story takes place on Madagascar, as references to the narrator's ancestors and relatives are soon associated with the island nation, there's an emptiness on the page, a sparseness in the writing, that buoys the story. A spacing bereft of words and time: dark matter. Maybe dark energy announces itself here, battled back by the short vignette that follows, one about the narrator's father disapproving of his daughter's intimate relationship with a descendant of slaves (1; see figure 2.2). Continuing on the following page, the story is written and broken up as seemingly related but also spatiotemporally distinct vignettes. For example, the first paragraph discusses her (the narrator's) move to the Midwest and Midwesterners' love of rivers. From there, it transitions into a stream of consciousness style of writing that roams from the narrator's musings about her own relation to water, of the Hudson River and the bloated sewer systems of New York City, to the specter of a post-earthquake, drowned Haiti.

The second paragraph moves quickly back to Madagascar, where it's illegal "to identify someone as descended from slaves," while the third brings from *To What Do I Owe This Pleasure*

The medicine man told the King, who told the people: *In order to save the kingdom we need a blood sacrifice, and it must be from a human.* Seeing that the only volunteer was a peasant, the medicine man said, *We don't need to take his life; only part of his ear.* And so they did. And so the King said, *From now on, you and your descendants will never be chained. You will never eat in the dark.* He made the peasant nobility and gave the peasant land, which the peasant passed down to his descendants, though a few years ago my aunt called my father for help. The weather had been rough. The family's house, like many old things, fell down.

Our ancestor's sacrifice is why my father refuses to meet the man I love. Tells me he will love any child we have less. He is, by his own admission, in the wrong. But he can't stop himself from saying things like, I don't want our blood to go somewhere that doesn't deserve it. I ask who he means. He pauses, says, *Like the descendants of slaves.*

Ralambo-Rajerison 1

FIGURE 2.2. Screen capture of page 1 of Gabrielle Ralambo-Rajerison's "To What Do I Owe This Pleasure" (2017). Courtesy of the author.

up the question of architecture, of the differentiation of inside from outside. "I am trying to learn architectural terms. Differentiating the inside of space from what surrounds it" (2). I wonder if the assertion of architecture here is an instruction on how to comport toward the page itself, the relationship between paragraphs, such that when reading each paragraph—alternating between racialized environmental disaster, anti-Blackness in Madagascar and the United States, and Black people being brutally thrown overboard or abandoned in the Superdome—there's the suggestion of each paragraph's spatial relationship to each other. That is, maybe the paragraph being read hovers as a momentary inside with the one just finished or as an outside with the one as yet unread. Or maybe the positioning of these paragraphs as outsides of each other bespeaks the imaginative presence of both dark energy and dark matter. Dark energy makes for a reading that holds apart, moving against the collisional relation engendered by gravity, while dark matter makes for that weight of the connections felt but not made. Indeed, arguably, the denial of darkness, its upsetting of the gravities of inheritance and family, the gravity of planetary survival, is met with its undeniable presence, the poet's making relation between past and present, a sacrifice in Madagascar and an overcrowded superdome.

Moreover, a planetary shape is included for the first time on the next page: an empty circle that takes up half the page (see figure 2.3). Maybe it's a view of the earth from space. The writing beneath the circle also suggests an emptiness that's equally white. This is not to say that empty space throughout Ralambo-Rajerison's poem is always an illustration of a white surround. In fact, as I've indicated and will more fully unpack later, if the story is a universe, I think the empty space that surrounds the text might be in fact dark energy and dark matter. But on this page (albeit not visible in the screen capture), in particular, the numbered mini paragraphs describing the violence of cartography and how as a visual praxis the assertion of absence—terra nullius—was an assertion of presence, of "whiteness as property," this empty circle-planet might be white indeed. After the meditations on cartography and preceding the poet's description of a bleeding Madagascar in the view of earth from space, she writes: "In all the visible, corporeal world, John Locke wrote, we see no chasms or gaps" (3).

Speaking of this illusory whiteness and its making of the earth into a blank, bloodless piece of paper, we return to scholar Bernd Herzogenrath's arguments concerning the brutal forgettings integral to a white ecology. Once more, according to Henzogenrath (2013, 3), white figures in the history of

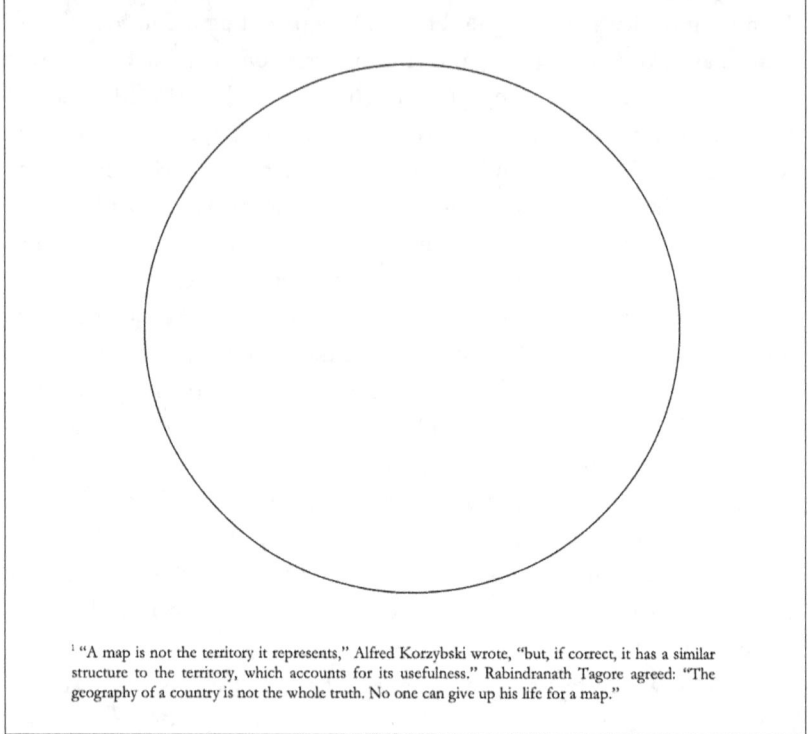

FIGURE 2.3. Screen capture and excerpt from text on page 3 of Gabrielle Ralambo-Rajerison's "To What Do I Owe This Pleasure" (2017). Courtesy of the author.

continental philosophy "as the absolute—the absolute purity, from which life began, with which it all started, animated by the word, the spirit. Note John Locke, who conceives of the human mind as 'white paper, void of all characters.'"

Returning to Ralambo-Rajerison, the presumption of an undifferentiated ground faces the undeniable galactic view of a visibly bleeding, presumptively owned earth: "a river runs red through a forest" (3). Black type moves throughout the white pages of this story, accruing into sentences and phrases conceivably visibilizing denied, bleeding, and burning cities and forests. As Ralambo-Rajerison remarks, the chasms and gaps not seen by Locke ripple everywhere, as Black people, buried in the waters of property's racial protocols of personhood, drown all around: "A Black body thrown overboard from a ship. A Black body abandoned in a superdome. What were they thinking?" (2) To see otherwise is to presume such drowning, being washed off the purported gapless, white-page face of the planet, not as galactic tragedy, but as a perverse pay-back system. During a speech given in Virginia following Hurricane Katrina, preacher Franklin Graham said, 'This is one wicked city, OK? It's known for Mardi Gras, for Satan worship. It's known for sex perversion. It's known for every type of drugs and alcohol and the orgies and all of these things that go on down there in New Orleans. . . . There's been a black spiritual cloud over New Orleans for years. They believe God is going to use that storm to bring revival" (MSNBC.com 2005).

The brutal regard of the storm as "revival," as a kind of payback and eradication of the "black spiritual cloud" said to endanger earth's "omnicidal[ly]" figured gapless centrality, emerges as another iteration of anti-Blackness as anti-galaxy, anti-Blackness as key to preserving god's purported givenness of earth to the "ethnoclass Man" (Moten 2017c, 2; Wynter 2003, 260), anti-Blackness as an "overseeing" that can never quite claim or contain the galactic reach of the life lived together in those supposedly absent "chasms or gaps" (Ralambo-Rajerison 2017, 3).

Indeed, as Ralambo-Rajerison beautifully illuminates, there is intimacy on earth that abides by and believes in fleshly and atomic responsibility. There are other relations that make harbors and gathering places "in a kind of anarchic grounding, a differential folding's resistance to [purportedly originary] tearing" (Moten 2017c, 1). For example, the poem continues by asserting that there's an emptiness not reducible to whiteness. Instead, emptiness, *the ain't nothing nothing* that surrounds a three-line account of the narrator's lover cleaning and loitering in the kitchen, suggests rather an embrace of darkness. That is, the author attends here to her lover's remark about the distinction between "kings" and "slaves," the latter emerging as those who "survived" (4; see figure 2.4). While what makes for this endurance remains unelaborated, there's an unaccounted mass that surrounds and pulsates, providing weight behind the statement, an assertion of a hidden mass wherein mass indicates both weight and a gathering and that animates the belief in Black survival. There might be other relations here, present yet unnamed, that learn from the galaxy and not from those who claim to own it (6).

Even still, there is a shift on the next page. Page 5, comprising five lines of text surrounded by a sea of empty space, continues with the suggestion of hidden mass. By contrast with the above emptiness, this hidden mass surrounds the narrator's belief in the (anti-Black) deals made to acquire ancestral land and build a home: "When my father tells me his ancestors owned slaves, he cries harder than I've ever seen. Says it's our biggest shame. This must have been after we got the land and built the house, though I don't say so. I listen

The man I love washes dishes in the afternoon. At night. But never in the morning. I watch him loiter in the kitchen even when there's nothing to be done. *Everyone wants to be a king,* he says. *But it's the slaves that survived.*

FIGURE 2.4. Screen capture of page 4 of Gabrielle Ralambo-Rajerison's "To What Do I Owe This Pleasure" (2017). Courtesy of the author.

to the sound of him" (5). Maybe these *dark matters*, the hidden fluctuations attending to her father's words, are how her father made a world.

This ambivalence about how to relate to the dark unknown moves throughout the story. For example, with page 6, the story moves from one of pained indebtedness to the logic of shared mass. Here the author evokes the 2012 discovery of the Higgs boson, the subatomic particle responsible for giving all particles their mass. The brief paragraphs flanking that vignette tell the stories of rats with conjoined circulatory systems, lovers sleeping next to their dead partner's bodies, mothers wearing their dead children's clothes. There's a kind of "enfleshed" movement of the Higgs boson, the aforementioned "god particle" here, a holding up of the dead and killed by using one life to buoy two (Weheliye 2014, 14). For example, in the page's final passage, Ralambo-Rajerison describes not only what anti-Blackness does to earthly relation but also the way survivors experience that omni-homicidal loss as a shift in mass. She writes, "After the shooting of 12-year-old Tamir Rice, Rice's older sister lost more than 50 pounds and about 100 days of school. Sandra Bland's nine-year-old nephew went back to sleeping in his mother's room, afraid of being alone. But what kept me in bed was Oscar Grant's five-year-old daughter telling friends to duck whenever they saw police" (6). Later the poet writes that after the acquittal of Michael Brown's killer, Darren Wilson, she "bought a plane ticket to St. Louis" (8). This follows another meditation on the Higgs boson, this time from Stephen Hawking, who believed it could "destroy the known universe. But even the physicists who agree with him don't think it'll happen anytime soon. . . . Still, they advise, we shouldn't sell our homes, should continue paying taxes" (8).

Whereas Hawking, a highly recognized theoretical physicist, saw the boson as possibly ending the universe, here inextricably linked for physicists (who know better) with the loss of home ownership, unrecognized theorist Ralambo-Rajerison advances how the boson might extend it, animated by the terrors and pleasures of shared life. On the one hand, in Ralambo-Rajerison's poem, anti-Blackness is a "tearing" of fleshly, molecular, and cosmic enmeshment, a "tearing" of shared mass. When a loved one is killed, another loses part of their own flesh, their own relation to gravity, as a result: a shift in mass to mourn the theft of (environmental) relation. But then appears a page wherein a black mass, a black matte circle, floats to seemingly restore balance. Even though not visible in the screen capture, the writing below the circle includes accounts of prohibitions and transgressions of interracial intimacies, a white bride who drinks her Black fiancé's blood to prove she has the requisite color of life force to marry her beloved (7; see figure 2.5). There's a tearing of

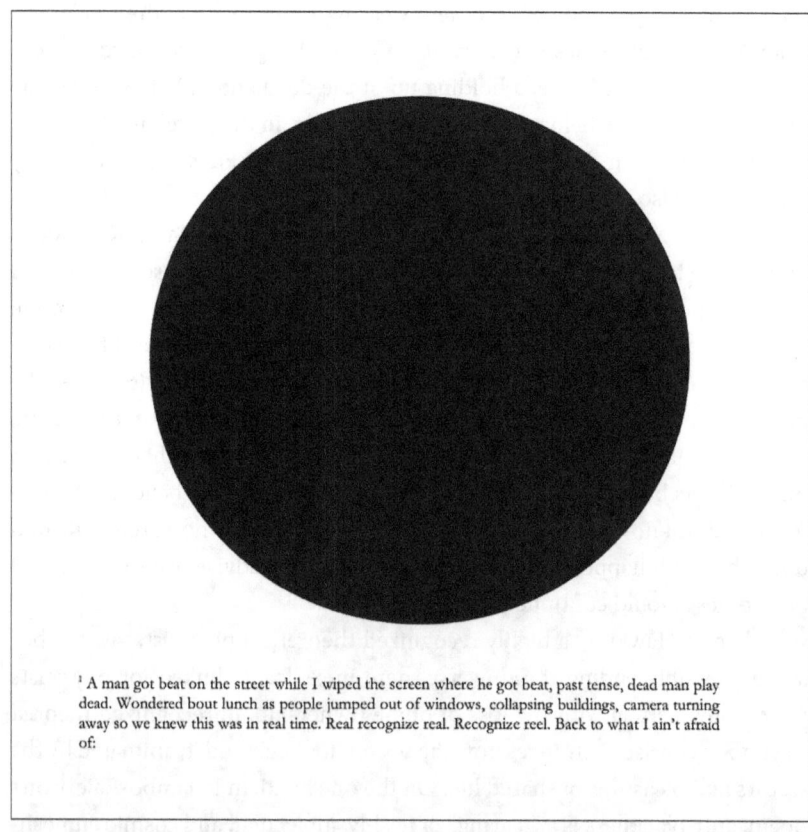

[1] A man got beat on the street while I wiped the screen where he got beat, past tense, dead man play dead. Wondered bout lunch as people jumped out of windows, collapsing buildings, camera turning away so we knew this was in real time. Real recognize real. Recognize reel. Back to what I ain't afraid of:

FIGURE 2.5. Screen capture of page 7 of Gabrielle Ralambo-Rajerison's "To What Do I Owe This Pleasure" (2017). Courtesy of the author.

Black flesh here in this assertion of shared mass, asserting perhaps the violence of violence being the conditions for understanding shared mass, of the earth and cosmos, as anoriginally Black. Of the litany of Black people slaughtered by the police seemingly required for whiteness to realize it must refuse itself if life is going to make it at all.

Perhaps this is why, as the writer also concludes, the "god particle" itself does not hold all possibilities of life, all possibilities of togetherness—it cannot provide an account of "dark matter, which we now know makes up nearly 85% of the universe's mass" (10)—there's a lingering loneliness (8). This loneliness comes from bearing an unreadable weight, a weight read as too wayward in its unknown possibility, creativity: "Perhaps it's soothing to claim to understand the dogs who fling themselves into water and hold their legs still, refusing to swim. . . . When my dad first came to the U.S., he was so lonely he'd call up anyone in the phonebook whose name looked like his" (9).

The weightedness of being made to bear darkness, figured as extractable and knowable by the arbiters of property, seemingly moves as this loneliness. Dark people and creatures darkened by Lockean hierarchies of givenness who find themselves together adrift at sea, "refusing to swim." These currents of sadness shape the story inasmuch as they, as with the earlier example, also engender occasions for holding together, sharing the mass, otherwise. On the same page where lonely men and dogs pursue elusive earthly and cosmic anchors, we learn that "dolphins can be trained to lead trapped whales back out to sea" (9).

It's this ethos of shared mass, indeed, which resounds throughout the story, inspiriting the narrator to find herself in a "black room." It's an unreadable, interstitial, dark place, maybe the galaxy itself. Perhaps, like Wallschlaeger's "My House," it moves phantasmatically like a consciousness of never being alone even while harboring the one made lonely by a given-over world. In the end of this beautiful story, another kind of Black gathering announces itself, in the nondivide between heaven and earth:

> "We cannot read the darkness," Maggie Nelson warns. "We cannot read it. It is a form of madness, albeit a common one, that we try." In the dark, I lose all sense of scale. A room with fixed coordinates becomes impossible to reimagine. I am, standing in the room, larger than the room. In a less dark darkness, I can make out outlines and faded colors. But in a room whose darkness is truly dark—in a black room masquerading as intimacy—everything known is swallowed. To a dog, I have

lived hundreds of years. Who am I to fight the animal body. I am not an alien, slouching meaningfully across my planet. (10)

Powerfully, these Black gatherings in black rooms are celestial miracles that sustain life's ungivenness. In these poetically rendered black rooms, intragalactic and intraspecies communions happen outside logics of scale and measure integral to gathering as propertization and against a notion that their being is predicated on authorial offering and control. Indeed, as Ralambo-Rajerison advises, as "everything known is swallowed," some other form of togetherness showers forth and new beginnings are imagined together.

What Bashir and Ralambo-Rajerison formally and conceptually convey is how innovations in form, reimaginings of the word's relationship to space and time, can put important pressure on the ontotheological inheritance of philosophical overwritings of the universe as preordained modes of knowable relation. Put differently, the authors elucidate how a writing with and alongside spaces and shapes of deep unknowingness can aesthetically advance a nonextractive relationship with the universe: a relationship, a togetherness that glimmers in the formal innovations and instructions of the page itself.

This first part of *Black Gathering* has considered how gatherings make or art something, be it a literary experience of astrophysical relation or a sense of home against property's artificial enclosures. Part II considers Black gathering's relation to ungiven life through artistic practices of bringing together. I query how writer Gayl Jones engages language and how sculptor Leonardo Drew finds artificially distressed objects, both to elucidate how bringing together might unsettle life's presumptive givenness to word and category. That is, both Jones and Drew gather but not necessarily toward something recognizable; in fact, their gatherings put pressure on interpretation and meaning. What their gatherings do is activate the energetics of a togetherness that exceeds category and, in some ways, a logic of social and economic value. In their art, Jones and Drew raise the question of forms of togetherness ungivable to axioms of reason and category, perhaps even upsetting the sometimes-normative logics of belonging itself. In their art, forms of togetherness thrive precisely because of their intrinsic deregulation, their insistently unending activation and remaking of unanticipatable relation.

To be sure, gathering is a shape-shifting word, a word that refers to a state of being, forms of togetherness in space and time, while also evoking the act of bringing together. Each of its definitions course into and out of each other such that part I and part II inevitably overlap. That said, I think the artists surveyed in part I illuminate how togetherness arts a sense of world, environment, surround—gathering as a group or party—while the artists in part II elucidate the definition of gathering as a bringing together. The first definition indicates a place of arrival; the second, an insistent middling, without clear or categorizable end or form. Chapter 3 considers Gayl Jones's early writing as forms of aesthetic experimentations that attempt to get close, without interfering, to where Black and disabled social life might accrue in unanticipated gatherings and turns of speech. How new arrangements defamiliarize a giving over of social life to linguistic orderings, which in turn equate the absence of properly formed sentences with the ableist need to criminally impose them.

PART II. THE ART OF GATHERING

3 ARRANGEMENTS AGAINST THE SENTENCE

Gayl Jones's Early Literature

In her beautiful book *Prose Architectures* (2017), writer Renee Gladman meditates on the act of writing as both a drawing and a building. She begins by ruminating on how, for years, she alternated between writing and drawing and how, within both artforms, the lines she crafted expressed a shape of cities, of architecture. As she dwelled further on the formal possibilities engendered by the notion that writing is drawing and drawing is writing, she found herself artfully moving in the interest of an "idea of plans, the suggestion of architecture," channeling a vision onto the page of a city to come, "a different mode of being where thinking [as writing] takes the shape of buildings" (viii).

I begin this chapter with Gladman's insights because fellow writer Gayl Jones, too, sought to bring thought closer to the arrangement of words on a page and, with that, a "suggestion of architecture" for characters architecturally deprived. In the introduction to "Toward an All-Inclusive Structure" (Jones's dissertation, which is an early, if not the first, collection of her short stories), Jones (1973, 1) asserts that the practice of writing allows her to join a "linguistic flexibility" with a "flexibility of consciousness." In the short stories following that introduction, Jones arguably displays such flexibility in crafting an array of characters whose experiences of neurodiversity and sexuality shore up as syntactical and orthographical experimentalism. These stories express Jones's belief in language's capacity to "meet" and reflect experiences, which are manifest in how her characters order their lives through speech (1). Such meetings mobilize gathering as verb, highlighting how a sentence can show a lived-in-ness and, with that, (the art of) gathering's insistently kinetic, unfinished arrangingness. That is, sentences in Jones's early literature, particularly "Toward an All-Inclusive Structure" and the short story collection *White Rat* (1977), arguably defamiliarize writing's relationship to self-regulation and self-ordering by querying cognitive and psychiatric impacts on speech and writing. I aver that Jones's interest in language as impacted object activates writing's inherent kinesis as an art of gathering, as bearing an unfinishedness evidenced by incompletion of word or thought, unanticipated movements across time and space.

Indeed, this deregulated compositionality in Jones's writing is complicated, as she asserts early on that her experimentation with orthography and syntax reflects an oscillation between psychological realism and an architectural/structural dwelling with words as objects. For example, in "Coke Factory," one of the short stories I engage here, a cognitively disabled narrator describes his life in incomplete sentences followed by run-ons. Words are misspelled throughout. Sentences in this story might, for some, read as improperly composed and, worse still, indicate an author's possible ableism in attempting to codify cognitive and neurological difference. But, as Jones remarks:

> I've been concerned not only with linguistic flexibility, but with a flexibility of consciousness: a way of using language as a means of meeting experience, both private and communal, external and internal. I believe that this flexibility of language and consciousness is necessary for what I have come to term an all-inclusive structure. . . . The key to this would seem to be a narrative structure, one so flexible that it could meet the demands of rhythmical and modal changes, changes in point of view and consciousness, changes in kinds of language, changes in the terms of experience, changes in relationships; a narrative that could be compressed or thickened, made elastic or brittle—whatever the needs defined by rhythm or personality. (Jones 1973, 1–2)

Later she writes, "After my interest in the psychology of language as a means of getting to the psychological reality of patients, I was concerned with getting away from the extremes of psychological and linguistic deviation and at the same time using the things I'd learned about language here (rhythmical flexibility, syntactical dislocation, forms of linguistic tensions) as a means of getting to the basic reality of people in general" (4).

To be sure, normative writing protocols aren't flexible; according to writing conventions, a singular or plural subject precedes a clear predicate. As grammarians say with respect to subject and predicate, the being and doing must "agree." Moreover, as disability studies scholar Robert McRuer has argued, racist, ableist, heteronormative discourses of self-possession have historically been associated with writing, with the regulation of self being supposedly discernible in composed sentences. Notably, McRuer (2004, 54) traces this idea of "compositionality" to John Locke (Bernd Herzogenrath, discussed in chapter 2, also made this association), who provocatively understood "the mind to be, as we say, white paper void of all characters" and the acquisition of reason presumptively an ordering mode of (self-)inscription. Implicitly, characters in Locke's formulation refer to letters and their normative arrangement, which is said, in turn, to index the proper expression of mind.

By contrast, in Jones's experimental engagements with improper syntax and orthography, characters are not letters but people who live and uncompose by other arrangements. Even as being and doing might be wayward, reflecting gathering's mobilization as an insistently unfinished process(ing) of coming together, some living seemingly happens in Jones's sentences. Put differently, if writing is a gathering, or what Jones describes as a "flexible" structure, and if there's an agreement that moves in a sentence, it's forged by the narrator, not the reader. This is powerful in that much of Jones's early literature tends to focus on Black cognitively disabled or mentally ill narrators, whose disagreeable speech and behavior make them prone to being violently gathered up and locked away. In the stories surveyed in this chapter, an institutionalizing, extractive force indeed lurks just outside the besieged main character's sentences. Crucially, then, by experimenting with syntax, orthography, and punctuation, Jones's word gatherings appear as places where characters can move around, live, and arrange their lives despite anxiety around the story's compositional impropriety.

Indeed, thinking through the ways in which writers Samiya Bashir and Gabrielle Ralambo-Rajerison elucidate how experimental poetry can create a galaxy, I argue that Jones's use of language to meet experience spatiotemporalizes the page. For characters besieged by the ableist, institutionalizing desires of others the page potentially harbors the possibility of deregulative gathering. I wonder then: how might Jones's writing, following Gladman's insights, move as architectural plans protected behind punctuational innovation, the omission of a predicate after a subject? (Recall Xaviera Simmons's *Harvest* discussed in the introduction.) What modes of unfettered being and relation potentiate out of a kind of lingering with writing as architecture, in keeping with its (architecture's) original expression as "an independent and free standing art . . . the building of towers [referring to the Tower of Babel] that have as their function only the gathering of the people that build them?" Bernstein (2008, 8).[1] Following Bernstein here, to regard sentences' architecturally might result in a phenomenological shift, where they would exist for the one who speaks and arranges them, not for some outside evaluator of being and doing's supposedly improper arrangement.

Bernstein further argues that the "tower [building, home, room] is itself the bond it creates" (8). We might say then, following Bernstein and McRuer, that once the "purpose" of property emerged, as a giving and manifestation of social responsibility, as a managing, extractive, self-regulative, racializing, gendering, sexualizing apparatus, architecture's originary artfulness, its ordinary protective, deregulative wish was transformed with crushing, evictional brutality (8). What Bernstein and Gladman move me to consider with respect to Jones is how her comportment toward language as aesthetic object, unmoored from normative impositions of order, placement, space, and time, highlights its architecturalness. Sharing her writing process Gladman (2018) writes, "Letters [were] added not for the purpose of being pronounced or of supplying new objects to our libraries but were imagined to supply holes, ladders, antechambers to the words that were already there." Relatedly, for Jones (1973, 3), "Orthographical changes in words have a tendency to make those words exist as entities, become visible objects and not simply rhythmical patterns."

This chapter discusses how Jones's architectural deployment of language, as it bears an interest in cripped linguistic difference, harbors a modality of coming together where togetherness thrives outside psychiatric, racial, sexual, and classed explanatory logics. These logics presume such gathering as criminal (because seemingly without legitimate purpose) or otherwise hazardous to the environment. This mode of experimentation enacts a kind of protection of Black, disabled, social, and sexual life in and as writing. Just as some characters are disturbed by how the protagonists order their worlds, the main characters engage in "tunneling under the [well-formed sentence] in a commune of slants and fissures. The old new period, against the grain of its own periodization, still disobeys completion, refusing to explain it or itself" (Moten 2017a, 114). Sentences break with the telos of proper completion and composition. Sentences suggest some off-page arranging, drawing, private planning. Moreover, I argue that Jones's gathering and arrangement of words indicate a building of social life in ungiven arrangements and gesture toward some impossible bonds, perhaps constructing momentary shelter for the relentlessly institutionalized and structurally deprived.

"Toward an All-Inclusive Structure"

In the first short story to appear in "Toward an All-Inclusive Structure," Jones crafts a character who just wants to be left alone. This desire moves as an expressed, yet endlessly denied, wish in the story "Take Refuge in Madness," wherein the narrator shares that he is in psychiatric detention for murder: "They will say I have been alone for thirty years and have not felt alone. It was a matter of I would be the only person allowed to come into my room. But he came in and he brought some woman with him and he brought some other man with him" (Jones 1973, 9). Even if *they* might say otherwise, murder, then, remained the only route left after *alone* was removed as an option.

Indeed, the tension between wanting to be left alone and being intruded on otherwise animates the *story* itself. The narrator begins by claiming that none of this, the psychiatric detention, the murder trial, "the people lined up in a glass to see what had happened" (9), would have happened if *he* just respected the wish not to come. Still, he came anyway, and because he came and brought other people with them, "I was the one who had been examined by needles and wires and rolls of papers" (10). Importantly, this story is less about the murder than it is about the agonizingly ableist privilege of willful solitude, of being alone in a room, or when being figured as crazy and sick makes aloneness criminally impossible. At the same time, the story is also important in terms of its architectural arrangement of language, the way it artfully barricades, through syntactical innovation, against understanding, suggesting that *alone* might actually be unenterable and, beyond that, harbor an unavailable gathering.

Concerning the latter, consider the doubling of voice in the following passage, the way it worlds the room:

The people lined up in a chair to tell what happened.
He sat out to. And so they.
He put himself in a corner.
He sat out to. And so they he set out to have to but he would not come out to even if he would have to it would be. He set out to but he would not would be an empty plate. (11)

As "the people" line up in one chair, he populates another corner. As they prepare not to hear, the narrator offers an uncategorizable arrangement, "refus[ing] what [he's already] refused" (Moten 2014b, 51). That is, for the main character, their gathering was something he needed to defend himself from. In the context of Fred Moten's argument above, what is refused is an idea of freedom bound up with self-regulation. In "Take Refuge," the institutionalized main character, as Black and "mad," is not only refused the freedoms associated with self-possession, but he also refuses the procedures whereby his capacity for such freedom is assessed. He doesn't want their company: "They will say I have been alone for thirty years and have not felt alone. It was a matter of I would be the only person allowed to come into my room. But he came in and he brought some woman with him and he brought some other man with him" (Jones 1973, 9).

He insists on another kind of arrangement.

As *they* sit in judgment, he populates a sentence against their attempts at juridico-epistemological interference: "And so they he set out to have to but he would not come out to even if he would have to it would be. He sat out to but he would not would be an empty plate" (11). Here Jones arranges language such that it's not separated, dispersed, or straightened out toward an explanation. Instead, words' gathering makes for a tension, a particular vibratory possibility that allows for him not to be "an empty plate" (11). Put differently, as he's extracted from his room and put on trial, he manages to sustain some arrangements that *they* otherwise hoped their interference might disperse.

Again, in "Toward an All-Inclusive Structure," Jones elucidates what we might call, after McRuer, a "cripped" aesthetics of gathered language, a purposive arrangement of words to "mee[t] [the] experience" of those living with mental illness and cognitive disabilities (2004, 59; Jones 1973, 1). Moreover, she identifies "Take Refuge" as "not pretend[ing] to a clinical authenticity, but . . . rather us[ing] the knowledge that pathological conditions do affect language patterns, as an authentic basis for experiments with . . . orthography, syntax, etc" (3). Even still, as I have previously argued, this is complicated. More precisely, just as Jones is not interested in language's psychiatric indexicality, this notion of an "authentic basis" for mental illness's lived and syntactic embodiment along with the author's aesthetic admiration of Henry H. Goddard's *Feeblemindedness: Its Causes and Consequences* (1914) is troubling.

As Jones scholar Casey Clabough (2006, 639), has written, Goddard's research advanced a "philosophical alliance with an early-twentieth century eugenics ideology that espoused the extraction, followed by sterilization, of the mentally infirm." Moreover, such eugenics-oriented sterilization programs long targeted Black people, along with Native and Latinx populations, who figured, and still figure, as contaminators of the body politic, as "feebleminded," hypersexual, criminal. Precisely, the institutionalization and sterilization of people determined to be "feeble-minded," overwhelmingly Black, poor, and southern, extended way into the 1970s and, according to such scholars as Rebecca Kluchin (2009), Dorothy Roberts (1997), and Jonathan Metzl (2011), cannot be thought outside "contemporary social anxieties, including blacks' demands for racial equality" (Kluchin 2009, 3). Crucially, Jones's stories often take place in the mid- to late twentieth century and focus on unmarried, sometimes cognitively disabled and mentally ill, Black characters (one of institutionalization and forced sterilization's terribly idealized populations).

Yet I see Jones's turn toward Goddard's work as less an ideological alignment than an appreciation of his regard of writing, however pathologizing, as world-making. As Jones acknowledges, what she appreciated about Goddard's book is how he "used writing as a form of therapy" along with Goddard's inclusion of the writing of his patients in the text (more on this in a moment) (3). While writing as an expression of mind became instrumentalized by Goddard toward ableist institutionalization, I think that Jones comports toward mind's impact on writing noninstrumentally. That is, unlike Goddard, who saw the arrangement of words as indexical to self-possession's absence and, relatedly, as justification for statist extractivism/gathering up, Jones saw the arrangement as part of a larger structure. For Jones, an "all-inclusive structure" is where a "linguistic flexibility" meets with a "flexibility of consciousness" and theoretically includes "*everything:* experience and imagination, autobiography, history, legend, myth, ritual, metaphor, dream (essentially all forms both linguistic and experiential); it would make use of specifically black forms, both musical (blues, jazz, work songs, spirituals) and linguistic (the sermon, playing dozens, signifying, jive) [and] it would see the erotic as an authentic method of expression. It would be an artistic and not just a cathartic means of coming to terms with one's experience" (1). Moreover, in Jones's explication, her attention to the charts included in Goddard's enormously violent "study" reflects an interest in what writing does, in such compositionality's deregulated nonteleological aesthetic (a meeting, not resolving of experience) and not in the chart's ableist indexical capacity or its ability to support a deeply racist, sexist, heteronormative premise. For example, Jones describes how a patient named Gussie "had a habit of making 'lists' of things that happened to him," a habit that informed how she stylized the speech of some of her characters (3). This belief in language's worlding capacity, and the different gatherings and formations engendered by neurodiverse ranges in attention, wonderfully plays itself out at the level of storytelling.

I argue that, across many of Jones's short stories, the practice of writing is a modality of art making that formally and conceptually enacts and shelters deregulated Black compositionality. Put differently, against a mode of reading that instrumentalizes one's wordly arrangement toward state-sanctioned regulations and enclosures, Jones's formal innovations, or cripped gatherings of language, conceivably produce an anti-chart where writing doesn't invite, but barricades against other's possessive and carceral misreadings. The arrangement of words on the page supports Jones's characters' own refusals to be opened up, explored, and examined. Language difference artfully enacts a maneuver whereby characters architect safehouses of unconcealed entry and arrangement, gatherings composed of shapes, presences, and objects that chorally organize an inexplicably ungiven "private and collective" life (5). Sentences have plural subjects and no predicate; sentences end early as punctuation arrives before its neurotypically appointed time. Syntactic and orthographic difference are sent by the author to meet neurodiversity and craft the makeshift shelters of meaning and unfettered relationality that flourish despite an ableist reader's conflict with a misspelled word or unfinished thought. Moreover, I think these language worlds of refusal not only critique the propertizing, racist, and ableist procedures of this world, the ways its explanatory fetishes barely disguise its amputative desires, but they also sustain artful sanctuary for the Black and neurodiverse. As Erin Manning (2016, 5) argues, following Fred Moten's important analysis, "Insurgent black life is neurodiverse through and through. This is its threat, that it cannot be properly regulated, that it exceeds the bounds of the known, that it *moves* too much." Following Manning and Moten here, a state apparatus that fetishizes white propertied personhood and reason's attendant capacity to individuate and that valorizes an "I" to which it can presumptively and safely *give* freedom, worries about improper modes of living and building irreducible to a deregulated and nonlocatable "we."

Relatedly, when writing becomes instrumentalized as a way of knowing the state of one's mind, the page moves from a place to gather to a place to surveil. For Goddard, this shows up at the level of the sentence, of the subject's understanding of themselves in the sentence. If one fails to evidence self-governance in writing, which historically, according to Nirmala Erevelles, translates into a deeply racialized (and most commonly, anti-Black) discourse of intellectual disability (evidenced in the polygenist, eugenicist argument about "inferior genes, low IQ," which for Goddard, was discernible in writing), and an attendant unhirability, they become "property of [the] state" (Erevelles 2002, 19).

But Jones disaggregates the sentence from a logic of givenness: words move from being governed by an imposed meaning and relation with one another—subject and predicate for example, ostensibly singular person and pronoun—to being released back into their vibratory, objective, architectural features. Jones seemingly cedes words to characters. In an interview with poet Michael Harper (1977, 698), Jones said that her editor "Toni Morrison . . . didn't feel there was an author getting in the way." That's why I wonder, What if what Jones does is quite literally drop off words to characters or more nearly dramatize a relinquishing of her authorship such that characters can gather with their own words? In many ways, when Jones expresses a hope that her language meets the experience of her characters, she indicates a gathering. Perhaps it's a gathering she sets up but then leaves, a get-together she doesn't own. Here is Jones's main character from "Refuge": "Now if you understand me you will not understand me except by who I am. I cannot do nothing unless I know if it was me that did something I should not have done. I am smiling. I am talking. I am sweeping in the corners of my cell with a new broom. You cannot sweep into the corners unless you have a new broom" (12).

Even as there's no indication of more than one person acting here, we cannot dismiss the possibility of the room's corners bearing hidden architecture, an amphitheater for a minor gathering. This gathering is set up by an author who leaves words behind, laying down pronouns such that the social life swirling around "the self-directed I" flourishes (Manning 2016, 7). It is a social life that stands outside the "experience [of the writer] and [does not] speak the major languages of the brands of individualism and humanism that frame neurotypicality as the center of being" (7). In that way, this "minor gesture" of smiling while "alone" perhaps reflects a freedom that's ungivable, where giving freedom (here a release from the institution) means not only acting and writing sane but also moving in the experimental ether of authorial abdication (Manning 2016). Moreover, it is preceded by the statement, "Now if you understand me you will not understand me except by who I am" (Jones 1973, 12). On the one hand, we might say that the narrator's experience of institutionalization is realized in the collusion of understanding's deficiency and architectural deprivation, a refusal of criminalized left aloneness. At the same time, what the writing does, this drawing of thought as Gladman would say, is build hidden "antechambers," private plans precisely at the moments when punctuation seemingly arrives too early (2018). The first sentence of the next paragraph is "the situation of my life." The situation remains unelaborated, but that doesn't necessarily mean something didn't accrue around the period, a gathering of "[ungiven] life" into writing's absence. Rather, to reiterate, I think what Jones does is make understanding hard while suggesting that what a mechanical, architectural comportment toward words' gathering might allow for is not character's illustration, but its protection (Pickens 2019).[2]

Once more, in Jones's early literature—particularly in the 1977 collection *White Rat* discussed in the next section—Black cognitively and psychiatrically disabled characters live either in institutions or under institutionalization's threat. Again, thinking with Jones, Gladman, McRuer, Moten, and Manning, I argue that Jones's short stories are places of gathering differently in and against artificially and violently imposed sentences. That is, Jones's characters enter into other gatherings, other compositional or worlding practices with what and with whom those around them don't value. And because such practice gets threaded through discourses of their purported "retardation" (in "Coke Factory" [1977]), unnamed mental illness (in "Asylum" [1977]), and "schizophrenia" (in "The Siege" [1982]), the characters are vulnerable to being gathered up and externally regulated.[3]

Even still, Jones's orthographic and syntactic innovations—misspellings, nouns that congregate without a verb, pronouns that stand alone, and misalignments of subject and predicate—suggest an aesthetic learning and moving with the mind's impact on speech and the possible architectural shapes engendered by such nuance. I see Jones's prose as trying to move with the mind, not against it. On the page this sometimes shows up in the sentences, in how a sentence orders or refuses to order itself; how it can take its time, protect a subject who takes its time; how it can bend and turn depending on the desires of its maker. Indeed, Jones's experimental arrangements of predicates and subjects, along with her unpredictably placed periods, arguably and artfully transform sentences' spatiotemporal possibilities, allowing characters' living to move with but not necessarily be regulated by how words come together.

Notably, for example, Jones's play with the location of the "I" in a sentence, and the placement of pronouns more broadly, emerges not only in the context of postbellum Black, neurodiverse life but often also with respect to Black sexuality and Black sexual gatherings. In the short story "Pross," sexual desire and yearning break up sentences. *I*'s and other pronouns often fall next to punctuation, the story reading like a breathless experimentation with self-regulation and self-possession's refusal. Significantly, Jones (1973, 5) identifies "Pross" as exemplary in pointing toward "an all-inclusive consciousness, one burdened with a private reality as well as a collective one," a duality Jones attributes to "the racial situation [that] makes . . . collective demands on private reality" (5n3).

This idea that "the racial situation," which we might say indexes Blackness's imbrication with (an impossible) socius, shows up as a collectively singular language is instructive. On the one hand, Jones's writing speaks toward Black life's estrangement from the domains of the private and the personal, racialized and sexualized luxuries that might come with a sanctioned and recognized proprietorial notion of self, luxuries that allegedly protect one from unlawful seizure, even if unlawful seizures provided their very condition. On the other hand, what the "private and collective" looks like in Jones's "Pross" is syntactical rearrangement: "I"s that don't precede but end the sentence; "I's" that perhaps open out into hidden relationality. The following scene from the story features a prostitute named Kate and her troubled relationship (endlessly attempted but never fulfilled) with a man named Floyd: "Before I. No won't get. My eyes big and. Those. Swollen places. She'll say. You must have dream him. But can't you see. I got no sleep. I must have drifted off once because I. But now now. Until I turn to believe it too. I dreamed I dwelt in" (91). Noticeably, in this passage, sexual intimacy moves the subject elsewhere; *I*'s come at the end of sentences, not at the beginning. What is more, the location of the pronoun before the punctuation doesn't just mess with the subject's placement and priority; it also precedes a visible interruption of thought. Sometimes thoughts are finished on the next line, sometimes they aren't. In this way, Jones's use of punctuation is a kind of intervention, I think, a kind of aesthetic protection of some ungiven path, erotic or otherwise, that follows the elusive and out-of-place subject. That this happens in a story about broken and brokered intimacy between racialized subjects is crucial. More precisely, the broken and brokered intimacy, or attempts at unfettered relationality, are endlessly interrupted. Again, the interruption might move as "the racial situation," of which Jones speaks and which perhaps, "privately" and "collective[ly]" haunts sentences; as I've argued, the state that fears black gatherings also interrupts them. At the same time, the interruption might indicate the singular subject's own impossibility, the forms of being that crowd out the "I," the punctuation suggesting an opening unto unavailable generativity. "It is out of relation that the solitary is crafted" (Manning 2016, 51).

Engaging Jones's early literature, I notice how her attunement to the "private and collective" moves as an engagement with the sexual, with neurodiversity and their under siege and flourishing interplay that manifests as Black social life. Her words potentially form a kind of makeshift shelter and architectural response that ensures the endurance of such ungiven social life after the story is said to end. That is, Jones's stories, as I argue in my earlier book *Wandering* (2014), resist the abecedarian storytelling conventions that contain discernible beginnings, middles, and ends. Moreover, the short stories in "Toward an All-Inclusive Structure," as well as those that appear in the collection *White Rat*, read more like episodes, a-day-in-the-life that refuses the closures of externally imposed direction or care.[4] As a reader/listener of Jones's stories, I appreciate how, in her writing, life somehow endures in the face of resolution's absence, a "telling [of] stories in and against the impossibility of communication even as something other and constitutive is told and secreted in the sentence" (Moten 2017a, 110).

In that way, the characters' comportment toward the private communal flourish of Black, neurodiverse existence is seemingly sustained by a writer committed to the unparsed congregations that engender such living: congregations that somehow push sentences against themselves so that characters can live as if some other arrangements are possible.

White Rat

Published in 1977, *White Rat* is a collection of short stories that appeared two years after one of Jones's most famous novels, *Corregidora*. As with most of Jones's writing, the stories often, seemingly, start in the middle of someone's story, someone Black, typically working class, and often cognitively disabled or mentally ill. In my engagement with two stories from the collection, I contemplate how the characters resist the gathering/ordering desires of others through speech. "Coke Factory" and "Asylum" conceptually and formally— orthographically, syntactically, and narratologically—arrange words in such a way that arguably does something with the extractive desires of others. For example, in "Coke Factory," gathering happens despite the main character's figuration as somehow incapable of (self-)order, a figuration that the main character describes and powerfully undoes in his life telling. The story begins with Ricky, the main character:

> I'm fifteen. She say [his aunt/guardian, mama Ali] when I get eighteent she gon to sent me out to eatern state that the mental hospital over on forth street near the tractor place and cross the street from the liquer store. She tookt me out there one time to have me examed but they said I was too bad to learn. But they didn't want to do with me. She sat that theyd hav to put me out there when I was eightheen because that's

where they put all the mently tarded after they dont hav nothing to do with them in the school. (Jones 1977, 82–83)

According to the narrator, nobody wants anything "to do with" Ricky. Even as mama Ali (his aunt) tries to get him connected to some legitimate arrangement—returning him to his birth mother, keeping him in school, institutionalizing him—he's resistant to these coerced and coercive gatherings. Ricky's long sentences join with the repeated "didn't want to do with," suggesting a correlation between an errant sentence and a wayward child. What is more, the run-on and orthographic errors index Jones's attempts to get close to cognitive bends in speech. As mentioned before, Jones read such texts as Goddard's *Feeblemindedness* and Emil Fröschels's *Psychological Elements in Speech* (1932), which included examples of writing by people with cognitive disabilities (Jones 1973, 2). Accordingly, there's a way to see her orthographical and syntactical errors as purposive generalizations of disabled speech/writing. Even still, Jones's relationship to heard speech, its specificity, its faithfulness to orthographical and syntactic ranges, describes her storytelling more broadly. As Jones also shares with the late Claudia Tate, she learned to write through listening (Tate 1979, 143). Moreover, in conjunction with her writing through and as listening, Jones claims that her interest in words as objects raises a larger question around the orthographic errancy in the above passage, specifically the spelling errors. That is, Jones reveals that "frequently my experimentations are mistaken for textual flaws" (Jones 1994, 514n4). What if misspelling was reunderstood as what was heard, and what if we respected the correlation between misspelling and aesthetic experimentalism? That is, what if the words *tookt* and *examed* are modes of compression rather than improper speech? Perhaps, compression was a mode of response, a shortening of the violence such that the besieged main character might *run on* and away from the terroristic sentence itself.

Indeed, not being wanted by his aunt or the school, Ricky lives with the looming sentence of being sent to Eastern State Hospital, the place they put all the people they "dont have nothing to do with" (Jones 1977, 83). This is how the story starts, with Ricky's multi-claused elaborations of his fate and the fate of those whose cripped behaviors render them folks *not to be with*. Even still, it's how Ricky gathers that seemingly resists the telos of other's sentencing. In the passage where Ricky describes mama Ali's attempt to drop him off at his biological mother's house, he recalls: "Yesterday she tooked me down to my mamas and said she going to give me back to my mamas and she put all my clothes in my winter coat and tied the arms up and my mama said she didn't want me and closed the door fast and then my mama Ali said she didn't like people that didnt know how to say thank" (83).

Throughout "Coke Factory" Ricky remains on the outside—again, even as mama Ali tries to get him connected to some legitimacy, Ricky engages in alternate forms of assembly. On the formal structural level this happens at the level of the sentence. In one run-on, Ricky describes how his aunt gathers him, bundles him up, and takes him to his mother, who, in turn, again rejects him. Moreover, even though at the end of the sentence they are left standing outside together—outside of Ricky's birth mother's home—mama Ali's own retort gets cut off. "Thank you" is cut into just "thank"; perhaps Ricky ends that sentence early so that he's soon back on his own to be together how he wants. This togetherness of his own accord joins conceptually with what we're later told is his joyful routine. Ricky gathers empty soft drink cans and exchanges them at the Hunns' store for a sweet new drink.

The Hunns' store is also outside, *on* the street, and animates his daily movement of gathering. Significantly, according to Ricky, the street is not riddled with violent traffics of incomprehension. While there are moments in the story where strangers and a disapproving neighbor either approach him or shake their head, never is there a scene of being accosted, of being caught in the street. Instead, his ambulation remains relatively uninterrupted, his route of collection untrespassed. So, too, mama Ali's TV top fleetingly lasts as his own untrampled place, a deregulated locale to harbor and be with the fruits of his can collection.

This is a four-page story, but I think that the fullness of it has to do with Ricky's abundant speech, his syntactic moves, and his punctuational deferrals of interruption. These long and rich sentences allow Ricky to hold on to his own *intramural* while not keeping himself together. Here I am referring to Terrion Williamson's definition of a "black intramural," which she attributes to a combined reading of Hortense Spillers, Elizabeth Alexander, and Ralph Ellison; for Williamson, a regard for a Black intramural is concerned "with thinking about how blackness functions from the inside out, about its commitments, its investments, and its sense of itself" (Williamson 2015, 97). This is a gathering or perhaps mode of unfettered relation that evades empirical and epistemological locution. Returning to "Coke Factory," such inside-out ethical regard might contend with the ways that soft drink cans on top of a TV set mark the "threshold of a different kind of togetherness, the tracings define a modality of orientation that exceeds or defies Euclidean maps" (Manning 2013, 196).

These "private and collective" or intramural gatherings, moreover, are never far from Ricky's cripped disobedience (Jones 1973, 5). His refusals to keep it together for others manifest, for example, in his physical altercations with neighbors, fellow building residents who complain that his TV is playing too loud, and with mama Ali over his reluctance to clean up after himself. His purported failure at state-sanctioned modes of rational comportment and transparent self-possession results in the collective conclusion that Ricky's too hard to hold. *He's a bad boy.* Ali wants to return him to his birth mother. She doesn't want him. School doesn't want him. Nobody wants him. "They didn't want to do with me." As such, his future is already written out as "eatern state" mental hospital.

Still, the story is not moved by a telos of incarceration, of the looming twenty-four-hour holds that indicate an institutional presence. Instead, it narrates a disaggregation of livability from the post-Enlightenment tyrannies of civic-minded composure. That is, in disabled speech and ambulation, Ricky's movement largely follows the rhythm of the can collection, both held and assembled together (while at any moment, willfully dispersed) by his own arrangements of space and time. Moreover, as with the other passages, the scene where his can collection is introduced flows without punctuation. In some ways, the run-on sentence moves like a kind of accumulation of life, an elaboration of Ricky's every day that collaborates in some ungiven tower making.

> I dont go to scholl because they say they cant teach me so I walk on the street and I get cola coka bottles and take them down to the Hunns store and the Hunn gives me cans of cola when I get enough and I save them to drink and I save the cans and Ali dont like it because I kep them up on the T.V. in the front room but dont nobody come no more cause only women came and I didn't like them and beat them up so she keeps the shades down cause she don't want nobody to see in the livin room where I sleep. (Jones 1977, 83-84)

There's a lot going on in this passage, including a number of gatherings Ricky both holds on to and defends himself against. There's a reference to violence, as it shows up as ableist exclusion and as a beating that's tough to moralize about. (In other words, were the women harming him and he responded in self-defense, or was there another cause for his violence? The lack of knowing and Jones's lack of disclosing make any kind of diagnostic moralism here seem not right.) But the ongoing generativity, the unparsing of a life where worlds tower in living rooms with treasured can collections, bespeaks Jones's "all-inclusive structure." An unparsing that illuminates speech's objective texturality, a resistance to the imposed arrangement between *given* speech and *given* freedom. A comportment toward both as ungiven and to be arranged with.

And, again, neither at the beginning nor at the end of this story does he wind up in the suffocating hold of Eastern State. As Licia Carlson and Eva Feder Kittay (2010, 4) write, this desire for institutionalization bespeaks a larger set of philosophical arrangements that fictionalize cognitive disablement as in need of exterior forms of racialized and sexualized holding:

> While people with cognitive disabilities rarely appear in historical philosophical texts, when they are mentioned they are referenced only to be discounted as irrelevant, or as exceptions that prove the rule. For example, as early as Plato's Republic (460c) we find references to the abandonment of "defective infants." When John Locke, in his *Two Treatises on Government*, a foundational work in modern political philosophy, explains that what makes one a "Free Man" is maturity, he notes that "if through defects that may happen out of the ordinary course of Nature, any one comes not to such a degree of Reason, wherein he might be supposed incapable to know the Law . . . he is never capable of being a Free Man, he is never let loose to the disposure of his own Will. . . . And so Lunaticks and Ideots are never set free from the Government of their Parents." (2010, 4)

If we follow Locke here, Ricky's enactment of freedom is illegitimate given its nonalignment with modes of productivity found in "industry" and with modes of rationality purportedly capable of understanding law. Moreover, Ricky's anti-rehabilitative inhabitation of a mode of "private and collective" life figured as excessive to his neighbors, school district, and family, dangerously ruptures the social contract, the illusion of freedom as givable provided one gives oneself over to governance. That is, for John Locke and Jean-Jacques Rousseau, the social contract is forged by those understood as always already rational and sovereign, who through relinquishing their holds on private desire, consent to their governance by an equally transparent state. But, as Charles Mills (1999), Stacy Clifford Simplican (2015), and Denise Ferreira da Silva (2007), among others, so insightfully argue, the social contract, despite its pretense, is inherently a racial and capacity contract, with white people enjoying the status of self-possessed rationals and people of color as always already outside the ethical contracts advanced by the state. Following

Ferreira da Silva (2007, xxxviii), people of color are always already located in a *"stage of exteriority"* whereby reason "operates as the exterior ruler."

In this way, even if the state, through a set of ableist machinations, promiscuously (and fraudulently) promised the *gifts* of self-determination and self-possession, at every turn racial and sexual difference agitates and reveals the fraudulence of that promise. In a racist imagination, cognitive difference gets promiscuously sutured to Blackness and sexual waywardness in ways that precede and follow Ricky's putatively unproductive ambulation and, with it, his morally sanctioned sexual possessibility. Arguably, his movement then is never not haunted by "eugenic narratives of pervasive and uncontrollable sexual deviance among 'feebleminded' classes . . . [the] conflation of sexual 'perversion' with the highly racialized category of cognitive inferiority" along with the mythical "sexual 'deviance' and purported aggression of African American males" (Jarman 2012, 92).

But Ricky's story appears to kick back against, even as it is subjected to, the "tuition and government of others," the logic of freedom as givable and as arbitrarily guaranteed depending on how one arranges self and words (Locke 2015, 124). That is, his tale is not spent incarcerated but rather is thick with the practice of deregulated gathering. Unlike Locke, who advances violently expropriative gatherings of various forms of life as key to the racialized and gendered and, arguably, to a definitively American consolidation of self-possession, Ricky doesn't steal. Rather, he moves against the larcenous, rehabilitative moves of the purportedly self-possessed, given here as the ableminded. Thinking with Jones's sentences, I note how Ricky's movement is openly crafted as a loose self-harboring and ungiven earthly relation, without regulatory and expropriative violence.

And once more, the refusal to keep himself and his arrangements together for others manifests conceptually and orthographically. After overhearing mama Ali's plan to give him over to the asylum, Ricky describes eating some candy he received for Christmas: "I am sit down on the floor eating the canty it was covered with choclot and white sweet stuff in the inside and a red chairy" (Jones 1977, 84). I think that the placement of this sentence here is a powerful aesthetic move by Jones insofar as it sweetly delays the attempted extractive gatherings by others; by making a nest for candy eating time, Ricky can sit in the misspelled/experimentalized chairy for a while. Being with the sweets plausibly joins Jones's punctuational refusals (her purposive cripping of language; in the case above, the run-on sentence) to indicate a making room for the minor gatherings that animate Ricky's grip on life. Being with the sweets precedes another response by Ricky to the threat of being given over: "I run in the front room and nock the coke cans off the T.V." (84).

Poignantly, in the story, sweetness joins a willful dispersal. The communions with sweetness as moment and remainder, I believe, reflect a creative relation with words and objects (words as objects set up by the author) that flee as soon as they are held. Moreover, "Coke Factory," through an aesthetic embrace of language difference, takes time to really read. Such innovation means respecting fullness and neurodiversity in reading and worldmaking, "reimagining our notions of what can and should happen in time, or recognizing how expectations of 'how long things take' are based on very particular minds and bodies" (Kafer 2013, 27). It means that time isn't just a signpost for life's passage, but might actually harbor the theater (the stage weighing down the clock) for life's congregational reimagining. Indeed, the weightedness of the story, the buoyant capacity of the sentence to hold a day—the regulatory encounter, the pleasures of routine trips, gatherings, and unexpected gifts—are how, I think, Jones makes nests and towers out of language for endlessly evicted characters.

In the story "Asylum," we encounter another character who refuses the terms of state holding, in this case the terrible imposition of coerced group living, by holding on to some protective textures as they accrue around word objects the state neither understands nor sees. We come to find out that the main character peed in her nephew Tony's classroom, which is why she's been put into a twenty-four-hour hold.

> The doctor will come in to see you in a few minutes, she says.
> I nod my head. They're going to give me a physical examination first.
> I'm up on the table but I'm not going to take my clothes off. . . .
> I take my clothes off but leave my bloomers on cause he ain't examining me down there.
> The doctor sticks his head in the door.
> I see we got a panty problem.
> I say, Yes, and its gonna stay. (Jones 1977, 68)

"Asylum" begins with two competing gatherings, the one imposed by a state institution and the other facilitated by the patient herself. The main character wants to hold on to her panties because "I ain't got nothing down there for you" (68). What's "down there" is for her grip alone. Terribly, for the institution, as previously argued, there is an intense relation between what's down there and what's in her head. What is more, the alignment between a panty-and-head problem invokes the specter of forced sterilization, wherein the mid-twentieth-century presumption of Black mindlessness tragically resulted in the theft of reproductive capacity. The scene of a Black woman's vulnerability on the table, open to a range of promiscuous grips and seizures, is staved off though by the main character's hold on her hospital gown.

Holding on to what's down there moves against racialized, sexualized, biopolitical violence. Such violences haunt and shape the main character of "Asylum," who wields her gown like armor, reflecting that even though the nurses in the room think she's crazy, she knows one thing: "He ain't examining me down there. He can examine me anywhere else he wants to, but he ain't touching me down there" (68). Moreover, in the face of the state's hold on her, the fabric the narrator grips is state fabric. This is followed by other withholdings, some wordly arrangements that prolong the state fetish of transparency and the coercive grouping such evaluation promiscuously sanctions. Indeed, in this short story, as with "Coke Factory," the main character refuses the alignment between reason and release as givable.

> Do you know why they brought you here?
> I peed in front of Tony's teacher.
> Did you have a reason?
> I just wanted to.
> You didn't have a reason?
> I wanted to. (69)

In this scene, the main character's refusals to *give* reason are met with the doctor's plan to have her "write words down" during the next examination. Recalling Goddard here, the specter of the chart as explanatory in its expectant carcerality looms. The arrangement of the words said presumably reveal what the state already knows: Black life threatens self-possession's normative racial and sexual protocols. Black life is to be sentenced by others not already writing them. The next day, the main character writes a response to the following state question, "Why did you do it when the teacher came?": "She just sit on her ass and fuck all day and it ain't with herself. I write that down because I know they ain't going to know what I'm talking about. I write down whatever comes into my mind" (69–70).

The deregulated, unparsed writing of "whatever comes into my mind" suggests another kind of arrangement: an elusive gathering of words that momentarily protects her from a state fetish of transparency, where certain preordained answers arbitrarily authorize the giving back of (ungivable) freedom. At the beginning of the story the narrator shares that she almost told the nurse, "You know, I don't belong here" (67). Here I ask: What if this insurgent engagement with the doctor's questions bespeaks another modality of belonging's refusal? This is complicated. On the one hand, the main character is locked up and held; according to some set of arbitrary definitions and decisions, she belongs there. But, on the other hand, what if the arrangement of words, the other or minor asylum enacted by some made-up shit that she knows the authorized neurotypicals will diagnose as freedom's ungivability, asserts a kind of belonging they'll never understand anyway? That was a long question.

Indeed, as with the run-ons in "Coke Factory," in "Asylum," the main character's gathering in her mind/ungiven speech forestalls theirs even as she has to negotiate their endless attempts to contain her, the expression of sexual freedom an illegitimate assertion of self-possession. Or to put it another way, as histories of anti-Black medical violence reveal, sexual and crip freedom is the revelatory occasion of Black self-possession's inherent fraudulence. The main character knows and is haunted by this, by what she might lose; in daylight, she's troubled by the "long black rubbery thing [that] comes out a my bowls," and at night she dreams of being strapped down "because the doctor said he had to look at me down there and he pulled this big black rubbery thing look like a snake out of my pussy and I broke the stirrups and jumped right off the table and I look at the big black nurse and she done turned chalk white too and she tells me to come to her because they are going to examine my head again" (70).

Instructively, this is the only run-on sentence in the story. In that way, perhaps, the dream state is another space of ungiven and un–given over speech, outside of state surveillance, where she gathers and keeps to herself. As with Ricky's narration about his life and experiences with ableism's stifling sentences, the captive character's running on seemingly pushes back against the ableist propriety measured in speech. In "Asylum" the distinction between full, uninterrupted speech and one riddled with interruption highlights a state fear of arrangements that elude control.

> How does this word sound?
>   What?
>   Dark? Warm? Soft?
>   Me?
> He puts down: libido concentrated on herself. (71)

Here, the main character's refusal to answer questions figures for the doctor as the expression of an unlawful sexual desire, a pathos of autoeroticism. But what I think is powerful here is the main character's errant improvisation on extractivist medical reason's scene of sense making. Instead of engaging in an exam designed to arbitrarily assess cognitive capacity (and with it, the potential for reproductive autonomy), the main character asserts another grip on the question. She holds onto herself—Me?—as another kind of inquiry, one that lingers as unanswerable, potentiating another life world just on the other side of the physician's pen. Perhaps the private arrangement enacted by the unanswered question, queered by the doctor's pathological rendering of self-focus as the wayward expression of "libido," flourishes as undisclosed worlds of belonging—most poignantly in the non sequitur "Me?"—that move as the patient's abundantly tiny response to assessment.

The main character's resistance to the alignment of self-determination and self-possession with affective disclosure, what figures as a kind of clinical straightforwardness, suggests a preference for an arrangement that works outside the ableist desire for transparency. In the story she wants to hold on to herself in ways that mess with the straight time of sexual and cognitive reduction and its own arbitrary determinations of gathering. In that way, she might not release and be released by state rule, but by avoiding such release, she also avoids the prison house engendered by an always regulated post-institutional self-possession: where discourses of "real empowerment... come to show [how] normalization has acted as a silencing of voices" (Williams and Nind 1999, 669). As such, she could enjoy the deregulated character of what Fred Moten, J. Kameron Carter, and Kevin Quashie might call "the insovereignty of quiet," a fundamentally noncompliant arrangement that happens somewhere between the spoken word/world and the held hospital gown, on the one hand, and the unruly erotic gatherings that constitute one's private (and fundamentally unencroachable) tower, on the other (Moten 2014b; Carter n.d.; Quashie 2012).

Perhaps the patient's willful refusals and purposively errant responses to questions disarticulates an otherworldly gravity, "the groundedness of an uncontainable outside" (Moten 2003, 26). And if there's autoeroticism in that questioning utterance—"Me?"—maybe it moves in a kind of anti-explanatory arrangement, which in turn importantly dislocates the figuration of the sexual, of gatherable/extractable/knowable sexuality, from a set of empirical maneuvers that move (and might move) as interpretative violation. For example, her refusal to be genitally examined as well as her dislike of Tony's teacher that involves her "just sit[ting] on her ass and fuck[ing] all day" should not be reducible to a sort of perverse, cripped, sexual desire (Jones 1977, 69). That is, I believe it's important to query the extent to which an alignment of sexuality with a sort of visible, locatable expressivity (one found in language or gesture) not only participates in reifying an ableist, heteronormative desire for erotic transparency but also ignores the ways that Black sexuality might be gripped and withheld from this world's grammars of belonging in the same way her flesh is. In the story, if the main character is already pathologized for being mentally other worldly, can't her sexuality be left alone there too? The velocity of its queerness theorized by her from the vantage point of another orbit altogether, within and outside a question that looks open but is closed, as opposed to through the axiomatics of this world's script. Recall that in response to the doctor's arbitrary query "How does this word sound?" the main character responds with "Me?" I appreciate how that utterance deferred the alignment between rationality and release, the proper use of given speech and the administration of given freedom, fictionally promised in the question's answer. Or, perhaps a Me that gestures toward an unavailable intramural suggests that the key to survival is embracing the hidden chorus an unsteadily autonomous pronoun engenders.

Indeed, the last lines of the story once more indicate the extractive logic of given freedom: "You should tell me what you are thinking? Is that the only way I can be freed?" (71). "Being freed," evokes a notion of freedom as givable and takable, highlighting the carceral logics of this world, its perverse racialized, sexualized, and ableist figurings of idealized self-possessed subjects. Across these stories, characters like the doctor believe in freedom's givability just as much as he seems threatened by a certain thinking, a certain unavailable, congregational movement. As we move to the final short story under review here, "The Siege," the doctor character from "Asylum" might be said to transmute into a patrol car.

Even still, even as psychiatrists and swat teams surround the barricaded (sentence) worlds where supposedly crazy Black women attempt "the theory and practice of stateless social life," Jones attends to other arrangements (Moten 2014b, 62). In her short stories, someone gathers even as someone else waits.

Staying Inside/Tower Living

"The Siege" first appeared in the journal *Callaloo* in 1982. Unlike the other two stories discussed in this chapter, the writing here appears less experimental with respect to orthography and syntax. That said, Jones's artful attention to other arrangements—the writing's nesting of the various gatherings the main character drifts within—puts off the incarcerating sentences looming just outside. More precisely, as a shouting SWAT team clamors on the other side of her barricaded door, Jones's main character dwells amid other arrangements, dream states culled from past experience along with what the words on the radio say and don't say.

As with the main character of "Asylum," "The Siege" also features a woman who refuses "to turn from" herself (Moten 2014b, 62). The story begins with her dwelling within the stateless intramural of the kitchen floor, inhabiting the quiet gatherings of an unremarkable corner, while the SWAT team waits outside. "A twenty-two year old woman with a shotgun, barricaded in a room in Cleveland. A young woman with a cat, a shotgun, a cot, a table. They decided to not use teargas, but at night they turned off the electricity and the water" (Jones 1982, 89). The sparse, third-person narrative opening, what might move as anything from the cold language of a police report to the deliberately measured (and withheld) phrasing of someone who loves her, announces the siege.[5]

The shape of the siege alternates between the state hold that waits outside and the withholdings, unnarrated speciations, that amble and waywardly come together in the room: the unsignifiable pleasures of a raw onion, the unknowable sensation of cat fur against the fugitive's hand.[6] If we consider the latter, perhaps we can consider *the siege* as what the main character arranges and (refuses to) release. Ungives. Time, space, flesh, mind, cat, onion. Undisclosed sensations that join memories. The otherworlding and congregational life of a room without electricity.

As the bullhorned voices of the police and her worried mother reach out to hold her, she "squat[s] in a corner. The cat is on the cot, curled up on the crazy quilt and sleeping" (89). A memory ushers in a temporary stay against their eviction order. She remembers him, that mushroom hunter and ethics professor she loved. They used to go gathering together, hunting mushrooms. Sweet memories of their love, the smell of fried onions and eggs sensually flood even as the radio repeats the cold static of the state's voicing her name "Jean Zane."

> She hears them talking about her on the radio and one of them says how crazy people can stay awake and active for days and days, because craziness gives them energy superior to ordinary folks. She wonders if machines go crazy. She changes the channel and hears another voice:
>
> . . .
>
> She flips the knob again, hears her name spoken: "Jean Zane." Another nob: "Mount Whitney is the highest mountain.
>
> "Why don't they put more faces on Mount Rushmore?" "There isn't enough room."

Where there are no words there is music. Where there's music there are no words.

"Benjamin Franklin used to write obscene novels that were banned by the government. Did you know that?" (90)

Here, the intrusive sounds of extractivism are chorally joined by larger discourses on "craziness" and "crazy" people's energy; a terrible alignment between imperialism and a love story and the ur-figures of white, heteronormative, American settler-colonialist self-possession, given as the imposed faces on Mount Rushmore (a lineup that might allow while disavowing Benjamin Franklin's own wayward behavior). The histories of why they need her gathered away blare their "private and collective" character, which as Jones might say, is inextricable from the "racial situation." Put another way, Jean Zane, as a purportedly schizophrenic Black woman, must be repossessed so as to sustain the ongoing idealization of the (self-possessed) figures etched onto stolen landscape.

And still, Jones writes some music into the space. In a certain kind of way, the music shares an architectural kinship with those memories of Jean, the latter suggesting something that those outside the barricaded room can never know. They don't how it feels to be that "crazy person" they describe on the radio, the one who feels too crowded by the world's different words for mushroom, the one who wants to be with photos of that Brazilian tribe that took that "secret contraceptive plant so they wouldn't bear more into such a world, into such horror" (91). The ones who'd rather die than be gathered against their will. She just wants to see their faces but, when asked, won't explain why.

Structurally, Jones gathers Jean's memories of her beloved alongside stories they shared, mushrooms they collected. Arguably, these gatherings both structurally and conceptually agitate against Jean's impending extraction. As with Ricky's time spent arranging his cans or sitting on the floor with his Christmas chocolates, Jean sits with the cat and the invisible recesses of a dream. The writer, though gathering, puts off the agents of extraction, keeps the SWAT team waiting while her main character remembers.

As those outside attempt to forcibly gather her, Jean sits with the memory of her loved one discussing that tribe, her deep sadness for them, and the terrible ironies of their endangerment in a world that serializes a desire to "Save the Canada Geese." She sits in and with the gathering they don't see, the gathering that puts off theirs.

Here I wonder again: What if the dream was a place of black gathering? Another dimension that quiets the shouts from the outside while the main character gathers in the loving holds of his touch, the feel of his tongue in her mouth.

> And so they sit on what he calls, after the Spanish poet, the "tongue of the river."
> "But isn't the water itself the tongue, always moving. One of the strongest muscles they say, the tongue is."
> "I knew you weren't dumb," he says.
> He gives her his tongue. Another kiss. She's never had such kisses. The best ones she's had. (92)

Moving along the oceanic rhythms of that kiss, in the mouth of the world, Jean remembers their romance, its textures and quills. The things he got mad about. That conversation where she told him the doctors said she had schizophrenia but chalked it up to "what they always say when they have no answers. . . . I didn't harm people. I was just too withdrawn. I built my own world" (92). After this disclosure, she decides to step out into the world with him and look for mushrooms. To "come up" from "underground."

Her stay there was short. "He knew it wasn't the right mushroom, and he ate it anyway." Above ground, he asked her to die with him. She refused, went back underground. "Still somehow she feels she's to blame" (94). There, in the underground, in the Black intramural party only to her, the cat, the powdered milk, and the shotgun, she sits with that guilt, "crowded and confused" (94). If only she can stay there, in that bounty and private anguish of ungiven life. They instead force her surrender, a giving over of herself to their hold.

> They come in wearing iron suits. She lets them take her gun. She holds onto the cat (the wrong way).
> What's your story, girl? One of them asks.
> "No call for all this," says another.
> Because she is harmless, they take off their armor. Because she is harmless, she won't let them touch her. (94)

As a reader, I ponder what it would it mean to leave Jean alone, with her ungiven and ungivable story, along with the cat and onion in the underground. As Jones aestheticizes, Black gatherings sometimes move in the stateless ambit of the kitchen floor, the barricaded room, her own lightless city between dream and sound. And life, like a mushroom, also grows there, in that unlikely place, the intemperate clime, the crowded and confused corner. The kind of group living the people outside the tower are afraid of.

In some ways, Jean's not ready to get well, especially if such wellness requires that she leave that congregational living in Cleveland behind.[7] Indeed, all three characters of the short stories discussed here try to hold on to some other arrangement, some other gravity, ambling in the bounty between wayward nouns and withheld verbs, where writing buoys a Black and disabled intramural, flourishing behind orthographic and syntactic innovation and blooming into and as a private amphitheater. In Jones's writing, which we might also call, after Gladman, her "prose architectures," Black social life is un-sentenced through a kind of expansive albeit barricaded inside, an "all-inclusive structure" where freedom's derangement is in its safe-harbored un-givenness. Deregulated, purposeless towers formed in corners, all together, alone.

4   "A PROJECT FROM OUTSIDE"

Leonardo Drew's Sculpture

I installed [a] show a week-and-a-half ago, and I look at it, and all I can see is the future. I can only see the future. I can't see what's in front of me. I can only see the future.
—LEONARDO DREW, "Leonardo Drew: In Conversation with Tasha Ceyan"

An ethico-political program that does not reproduce the violence of modern thought requires rethinking sociality from without the modern text.
—DENISE FERREIRA DA SILVA, "On Difference without Separability"

This final chapter moves from the literary—the craft of wordly arrangements—back to where the book began, with collage-like arrangements of objects as sculptural installations, this time by artist Leonardo Drew. In particular I engage with Drew's abstract arrangements of what appear to be discarded materials and consider the lifeworlds built by disposability's formal opening.

As with the literatures so far surveyed, Drew's gatherings as sculptural innovation exceed what I can see or say about them. That is, even as modern sculpture has been said, via art historian Clement Greenberg (1960, 3), to more easily lend itself to representational analysis, in contrast with painting's potential for nonreferential autonomy in flatness, what Drew does is gather and sculpt to defamiliarize recognition. In Drew's case, everyday objects—telephones, rope, buttons—are artificially weathered, often painted in monochromes of black and white and arranged into nonfigurative installations. Among other strategies, Drew's degradation of an object's identity and purpose through weathering/artificial deterioration evokes the question of relation as discernment or, better yet, the beauty of togethernesses without explanation.

Moreover, akin to Gayl Jones's engagement with language, Drew arranges objects where togetherness pulsates against enclosure. In Drew's art, gathering's kinetic openness, its unfinished, ana-cosmological principle, arguably moves by way of its figurative nonresolution. More precisely, Drew's weathering of objects in conjunction with the uncategorizable (formally untitled) yield of his arrangements unmoors them from category and from knowability. Gathering seemingly moves in Drew as both insistent unfinishedness and ungiven materiality and, with that, as art's "infinite composition[al]" movement (Ferreira da Silva 2016, 59).

According to Denise Ferreira da Silva, "for decades now, experiments in particle physics have astonished scientists and laypeople with findings that suggest that the fundamental components of everything, every thing, could be just such, namely the virtual's (subatomic particles) becoming actual (in space-time), which is also a recomposition of everything else" (59). In that way, if "everything" is "every thing," we might say that just as Toni Morrison's words on a page and Leonardo Drew's abstract sculptural rearrangements appear as symbolic and haptic arrangements for our (actual) beholding in this world, the artworks also have already moved/are moving into another cosmic relation past the hour of perception.

Put differently, "infinite composition" speaks not just to spatiotemporal, molecular lingerings of writing, painting, and sculpture; it also indicates their potential as partial-futural manifestations of another project: another-worldly poiesis that may be hesitant to touch down on an earth so propertizingly engulfed. This is digression, but I wonder about this molecular interplay between various materials—a piece of paper with dried ink along with shards of weathered wood, in Drew's case—and the oxygen that surrounds them. The oxygen interacts with and changes the worn-down building materials along with the pages bearing dreams of another world. I wonder not just about oxygen coming to meet art but about art coming to meet oxygen, the messages oxygen might bring back to the cosmos. At the same time, Drew's recompositionality formally elucidates the object's release from given relation—which is perhaps how objecthood itself is discerned—back into the *everything*, the "all-inclusive structure" of which it is a part (Jones 1973). While Drew doesn't discuss his art through its quantum and molecular impact, his art potentially enacts its infinite compositionality through abstractional strategies wherein all he can see "is the future."

Following Stephen Best, Drew pressures a logic of discernment whereby the objects of a present/past can be separated from the art engendered by the abstractional crafting via weathering of their post-use futures. Best (2018, 30), in writing about the work of artist El Anatsui—who also arranges everyday weathered (in his case, discarded) objects—argues: "You think, too, how curious it is that the work would subvert its own beauty—obliterate it, evaporate it—how the work contains the conditions of its own undoing. Why should the artwork issue such a powerful invitation to experience more intimately and intensely an effect it had every intention of subverting in the end? Why should an art-work be so corrosive of its own illusions, of the very illusion that it is art."

I disagree with Best slightly here, and my disagreement is shaped by an encounter with Drew's art. That is to say, with respect to art like Drew's, and this might be true of El Anatsui's art as well, the abstractional crafting of the artwork by way of everyday objects' unbeautiful "undoing," aligns art with creativity, with a modality of gathering animated by release. To be sure, Best's project centrally involves an interrogation of the "communitarian impulse [that] runs deep within black studies" (1). He ponders the stakes of Black artistic production seemingly animated not by a desire for belonging, but by "abandonment" and sociality's rejection or refusal. One of the questions Best helps me consider, and which I think Drew's art raises, is whether Black gatherings can be unmoored from belonging and the logics of discernment associated therewith.

Thinking with Drew now, I ask: What if art's beauty isn't determined by its perception as such, but by its indiscernibility, its kinetic rupture of the separations—present/future, object/art, representation/abstraction—that align beauty with knowing and art with the enclosures associated with doing/belonging? What if gathering's kinetic irresolvabilty bespeaks art's compositional infinitude, its more-than-ness pressuring the contours of what's presumptively given to the spatiotemporal constraints of perception, impression and value (Manning 2013)? When Leonardo Drew shares that all he sees in his installations is "the future," I question whether futurity refers less to time than to form. Forms of togetherness flourishing outside logics of aesthetic representation and autonomy, giving and taking, belonging or not at all.

Leonardo Drew always knew he was an artist; from making sculptures out of what he pulled and rearranged from the Bridgeport, Connecticut, landfill next to his childhood home, the P. T. Barnum housing projects, to drawing on his apartment walls (O'Sullivan 2000). In an interview with performance studies critic Allen Weiss, Drew recalls:

> The city dump occupied every view of our apartment. I would watch the bulldozers troll back and forth over this massive landfill, the dump trucks cart and drop, and the cranes lift, deposit, and bury. I remember all of it, the seagulls, the summer smells, the underground fires that could not be put out. . . . And over time I came to realize this place as "God's mouth." . . . The beginning and the end . . . and the beginning again. And as I grew up I always found myself there, mining through remnants and throw-aways, putting this with that. I did find something in the discarded . . . "new life." *It's this metaphor and consistent weight of being* which drives my work to this day. Though I do not use found objects in my work (my materials are fabricated in the studio) what has remained from my early explorations are the echoes of evolution . . . life, death, regeneration. (A. Weiss 2009, 20; emphasis added)

At *God's mouth*, somewhere in between the housing projects and the landfill, the garbage and the fire, a young artist changed the future of thrown-away objects. At God's mouth, "a project from outside," to call up a beautiful phrase from Fred Moten's poem "The Gramsci Monument," seemingly moved in and as a different kind of gathering (Moten 2014a, 117).[1] This gathering is driven by artful openness, not enclosure. The yield of such gatherings, Drew's sculptural deformations, emerged for him as being's "weight."

How to think being's weight here? What if "being" in this context is less a "god-term," an ontotheological assertion of the "ethnoclass Man v. human," than a reference to being's secondary definition, that is, as an unqualified movement of ungiven life? (Spillers 2003, 378; Wynter 2003, 260).[2] Put another way, what if God's mouth, like the indiscriminate work of fire itself, isn't the place of speech, of naming and claiming and give-over-ness, but the mark of a holy opening, a nontrespassive witnessing of and vestibule for found objects beginning, ending, and beginning again? A faithful portal for life's thingly passage and rearrangement and one without categorical interference. In their profound essay "Base Faith," Stefano Harney and Fred Moten assert the shapes of such faith through connecting faith's absence to an owning god, a certain Lockean interpretation that assumes that ownership of the world substitutes for belief. An earth-killing movement of faithlessness. They write, "God has everything but faith; this is why He so brutally requires ours. He looked around and was so lonely He made Him a world. Rightly, He didn't believe in himself and, wrongly, He didn't believe in us. We were neither sempiternal nor parental, just generative and present, like a wave. In His case, (over) seeing was not believing. Faithlessness such as His demands a certain strategic initiative. Ever get the feeling we're being watched? Well, that's just God's property" (Harney and Moten 2017). This control of and over the world, the faith-claiming described by Moten and Harney, contrasts powerfully with the god-presence evoked by Drew, the spirit moving in and as the fire next to his home's landfill. Drew's indication of a holiness abiding by an uninterrupted movement of beginnings, ends, and beginnings again suggests a god presence with faith, a god whose witnessing of artful gathering is not sutured to the categorizing whims of theo-capitalist need and sanction, but rather is supportively open to "the earthen informality of life," that is, life's ongoing passage (Harney and Moten 2017). Beginning. Ending. Beginning again. Maybe in that way, that other kind of being with (god and the earth, the tossed away) originally made Drew's project a "project from outside," the disinterested (sculptural) arrangements believed in while the knowing, speaking, owning, objectifying world runs out of things to say.[3]

Moreover, next to God's mouth, I think it's important to consider Drew's own faith in the post-use weightedness of being alongside his quasi mystical self-discovery at the trash heaps. *And as I grew up I always found myself there, mining through remnants and throwaways.* On the one hand, the self found might have been the artist, the figure "mining through" what's left behind. On the other hand, finding the self there arguably speaks doubly and against its own conceit. That is, as a poor, Black kid growing up in public housing, Drew symbolically and materially didn't amount to a Lockean self, one whose self is bound up with a putatively inviolable, individuated, racially particular (read: white) propertied person. Moreover, what the usual proximity of landfills to housing projects often implies is a racially, sexually, economically, ecologically fictionalized cluster of beings toward death, a kind of coercive roundup of the already given-over, now expendable life along with the used-up objects promiscuously consigned to the landfill. But what his art elucidates is a faith in life's ongoingness and nonseparability, its ungivenness to value and category, despite the owned world's extractions and impositions. Put differently, Drew's sculptural rearrangements of found and artificially distressed objects bespeaks a holy understanding of the "essential impropriety of the (exchange-)value that precedes exchange" (Moten 2003, 12).

Part of what his sculptural arrangements do, I think, in disaggregating the violent divisionary frames of use and exchange presumptive in disposability, is usher forth the "impropriety" of unweighted and unweightable life. That is, impropriety—the resistance to a certain idea of sociality forged (and projected and regulated) in the separating, divisioning architectures of the proper itself—given as the private home, "known," held, objectified, and separated flesh, matter and earth—moves and spills as the sculptural vision in Drew. Put differently, what the sculptural in Drew seemingly engenders is a sociality at the end of the world, forms of togetherness that flourish despite the homicidal, propertizing divisions presumptively wrought by the world's presumptive maker. In Drew's abstract pieces, for example, broken shoes and kids' toys no longer appear as broken shoes and kids' toys, but as communions cum innovations in form, color, and texture.

In that way, I wonder about the stakes of these aesthetic defamiliarizations —crucial to the assertion of futured canvases "without separability"—for the people consigned to live next to trash heaps (Ferreira da Silva 2016). In some ways, Drew's embrace of the indisputable "weight of being" affirms the inextinguishable movement of life, one that begins, ends, and begins again. A movement that perhaps Drew acknowledges as the future, where his canvas works like that landfill fire, harboring but not containing the Black(ened) togetherness that category no longer tries to hold.

Number 8

It is crucial that my engagement with Drew's sculpture begins at *Number 8* for, according to Drew, *Number 8* is where it all began: it is the "mother work from which all his other work derives" (Krajewski 1999, 11). What does it mean to think of a piece like *Number 8* as the "mother work," maybe the "beginning said better than at the beginning" (Jones 1975, 54)? Such a question is even more curious because, at first glance, this particular piece looks like the end, a devastating aftermath, what's left over after a fire.

Number 8 consists of a large, weathered piece of wood forming the backdrop from which streams of charred, dark gray, brown, and black rope vertically dangle (see figure 4.1). The ropes themselves are weighted down with burned, blackened paper, pieces of wood, singed pieces of fabric, and the carcasses of dead birds and other street animals. The piece powerfully asserts

FIGURE 4.1. Leonardo Drew, *Number 8*, 1988; animal carcasses, animal hides, feathers, paint, paper, rope, and wood; 108 × 120 × 4 in. (274.3 × 304.8 × 10.2 cm). Courtesy of the artist; photography by Frank Stewart.

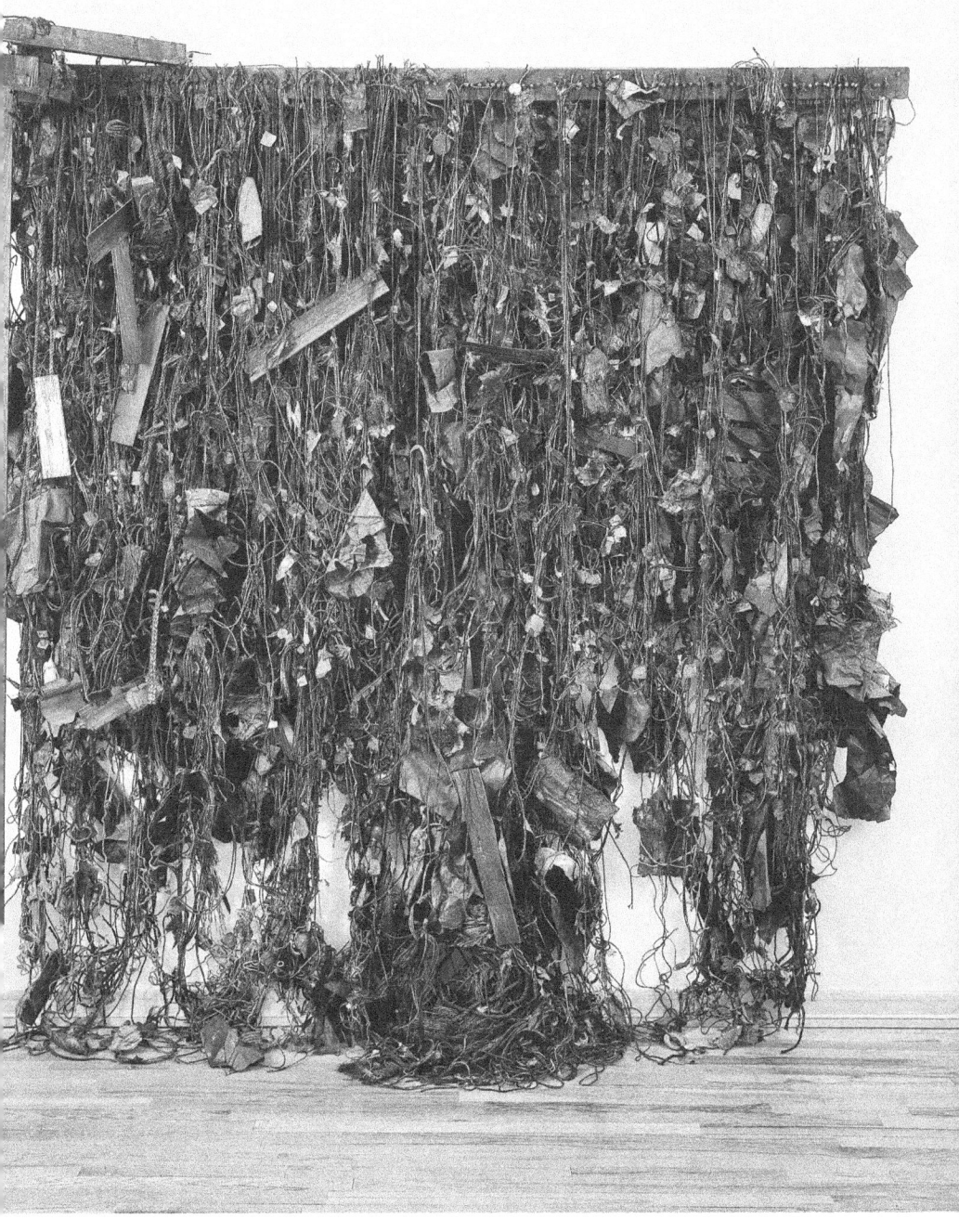

a multispecies, multiarchitectural fallout engendered by some devastating movement. But at the same time, I don't think that the work can be reduced to *the end* it suggests. Rather, there's a remainder here, an assertion of another arrangement, the persistence of another kind of terrain.

On the question of the work's ecological persistence, critic Lorraine Edwards (1997, 20) noted that *Number 8* "has the look and smell of death yet seems to pulsate and breathe." The artist himself also gestures toward this duality when he claims that the piece at once evokes death and gestures to the "other worldly" (quoted in Ceyan 2017). Beginning. Ending. Beginning again.

By moving between "death" and the "other worldly," Drew associates this nonteleological journeying with a sculptural portal engendered by material life's very erosion. The otherworldly evokes another kind of ground, what Katherine McKittrick (2006, 17) might call a "spatial grammar that unhinges space from the limiting demands of colonialism, practices of domination, and human objectification." A terrain just on the other side of expenditure itself; phantasmatic, lush lifeworlds ushered into being by what and who are left behind. Indeed, consisting of planks of wood interwoven with rope, *Number 8* quite literally suggests not just architectural breakdown but also the thick activity of building something else. What is more, the blackness of this piece seemingly moves both in and as that creativity and cannot (because total) figure centrally in *Number 8*'s ongoing assertion of vitality after fire.

Fred Moten's writing on Piet Mondrian's *Victory Boogie Woogie* (1944), particularly on Mondrian's use of the color black, resonates here with *Number 8*'s otherwise "spatial grammar"; that is, in *Number 8* Blackness bespeaks an unheld architecturalness and sociotopography beyond the modern text's earth- and flesh-killing grounds. A (maternal) project from outside. Moten (2008, 202) writes: "Black explodes violently, victoriously in Mondrian's last painting, his careful, painstaking ode to proliferation, impurity, and incompleteness. It is the victory of the unfinished, the lonesome fugitive, the victory of finding things out, of questioning, the victorious rhythm of the broken system. Blackness, which is to say, black social life, is an undiscovered country. . . . In Mondrian's city, things making and finding one another out actively disrupt the grids by which activities are known, organized, and apportioned." Following Moten, in *Victory Boogie Woogie* the "explosion of blackness," its victoriousness moves precisely in the afterlife discerned both in the movement of the line and the movement in excess of the line. Indeed, along with Moten, I think that the great thing about *Victory Boogie Woogie* is the *way* it illustrates "victory": by way of the fugitive roaming of paint itself, its moving from the square where it's purportedly contained to the one next to it, seeming isolations turn into a block party.

Arguably, one might say here that to see such a party is to believe in the painting's own sculptural capacity, its possibility of moving beyond its own formal and geometric constraints and arrangements. If you look at the painting from afar, you might see discrete red, yellow, blue, white, and black squares forming a diamond-shaped traffic pattern. But if you move closer, that fugitive movement can be discerned in paint's insurgent disruption of a grid. Put differently, in the context of the painting, if the grid structure is something whose orderliness and flatness you come to believe in, you might also begin to believe in its outer dimensionality, its disordering reach and disturbance of dividing lines, some *still-running* painterly bends.

Significantly, Mondrian was a key influence on Drew. Mondrian's association with abstraction emerges often in tandem with his association with the grid. Indeed, for Drew, the grid system moves centrally in Mondrian's as well as in his own work "as a way of building the composition [and Mondrian] was definitely [an] innovator of how, you sort of, like bring all elements together. Color and how we see things" (Drew 2015). In light of this, Drew reflects that, "looking close enough [at the grid] you realize that there has to be some understructure." Following Drew here and in line with Moten's argumentation, the grid in Mondrian seemingly moves against its own impulse. If the grid is a way to gather and order, to presumptively segregate against certain polychromatic socialities, block parties, then Mondrian's final dance party, *Victory Boogie Woogie*, was a different kind of project. As with Drew's *Number 8*, following Moten, *Victory Boogie Woogie* bespeaks another world, a block party moved by an "under-structural" impulse to leave every unit door open and invite the visits from walled-off color, roamings of the "lonesome fugitive" (Drew 2015; Moten 2008, 202).

Tragically though, even as the party goes on, Mondrian died poor, his remains sequestered to the pauper's section of a Brooklyn cemetery. His tombstone and whereabouts remained unknown until 2009, when Drew, along with his friend, fellow artist Paul Pagk, went looking for him. In a conversation reflecting on that experience, Drew and Pagk remarked that the structure of the graveyard resembled some of those very grids Mondrian painted and innovated against. Sadly, too, what the discovery of Mondrian's barely marked gravestone elucidated is how the terrible segregation and "apportioning" of poor people's space and relation with each other endures, even in death (Moten 2008, 202; Drew 2015).

Even still, as Drew shared, the mourners of Mondrian leave tubes of paint on his tombstone, out of love. Drew left a painting of a red tree, more precisely, a color printout of Mondrian's *Avond; De rode boom* (*Evening; Red Tree*), produced between 1908 and 1910. These collective offerings powerfully contrast with an aesthetic impression of death as isolation. Relatedly, returning to Drew, there is an analytic tendency of reading Blackness in the sculptures as death-bound and, with it, separate from relation—a reading that might imagine the symbolic graveyard or cold city street without the adornment of those anonymous acrylics. Put another way, in the context of some reviews, death in Drew's art is seemingly imagined as a place of *difference with separability* and not another locale of gathering.

In particular, *Number 8* is more often read as funeral shroud rather than as the insurgent textures of another ground. Indeed, in addition to its associations with death, many have seen slavery, homelessness, and racialized despair in the work. For example, for some, the charred ropes signal histories of lynching and, with it, broader trajectories of sexual, economic, and racial violence (Patterson 2010; Dobrzynski 2000; Krajewski 1999). For others, including curator Claudia Schmuckli, *Number 8* visualizes homelessness, in particular, a homeless man's cart.

But here I ask: What if this perception of despair moves by way of an understanding of gathering that is unequivocally buttressed by ownership? Might such an association between gathering and ownership animate an assumption about poverty, about not having, as earthly unhappiness and the gathering engendered by homelessness as not faith's expression, but it's absence? What is more, how to view the stark singularity of a homeless man and the tiny container he pushes along here? In other words, I wonder what happens to figurations of *Number 8*"s topographic excess when the man and cart are neither figurally rendered from abstraction nor overdetermined as complicit in each other's social estrangement. This isn't to romanticize poverty, its dehumanizing experience and especially when imbricated with anti-Blackness, but it is to ask about the other door engendered by *Number 8*. Along with Moten's arguments about Mondrian, I think Blackness in Drew's work also moves chromatically, as we see in *Number 8* and in *Number 77* (the latter to be discussed later), to evoke a singed, textural aftermath: perhaps where Blackness gathers.

Dwelling a bit with the word *aftermath*, Blackness suffers from being brutally mathed—what Ferreira da Silva (2014) might describe as total expropriation—while always somehow flourishing in the afters of that math.[4] I assert that Drew's installations powerfully visualize, while foreclosing visuality's epistemic conceit, Black gathering's long history of being aftermathed, of fugitive arrangements. As with the other artists surveyed herein, Drew's art highlights how life after use has long been an occasion for deregulated Black gatherings. Put another way, devastation seemingly moves undecidably and finds vitality by way of the undisclosed coordinates of *Number 8*'s own understructural sociality. I further ponder the stakes of this vitality in relation to not just an under-elaborated, unspecified Blackness but also Blackened maternity (*Number 8* as the "mother work").

Indeed, while this world's racist hetero-patriarchal logics align Blackness and motherhood—along with homelessness—with sociality and futurity's absence, the world-ending bends of abstractionism open another door. For example, writing about abstraction, Kirk Varnedoe (2006, 29) advances that as an art practice, abstraction operates "with and upon the repertoire of the already known . . . recombining inherited, available conventions in order to propose new entities as the bearers of new thought."

In that way, perhaps the Blackness, homelessness, maternity, and death in *Number 8* could also be unexplained color and energy emanating from another world, all abstractionally essential to both the assertion of new thoughts and their resistance to enclosure. As Philip Brian Harper (2015, 3) writes, in "disrupting the easy correspondence between itself and its evident referent, the abstractionist work invites us to question the 'naturalness' not only of the aesthetic representation but also of the social facts to which it alludes." Here I see Drew in powerful alignment with the Black women writers heretofore engaged, who have elucidated how gathering can engender less harmful relations between Black people and their environments. More specifically, Drew, through abstraction, joins the literary work that Morrison does in *Beloved* by aligning Blackened maternity with nonextractive space-times, occasions for uninterrupted togetherness. Amber Musser describes this as a "Black maternal elsewhere." Musser (2020, 40) writes:

> Thinking more robustly with the Black and brown mother, a figure who, specifically, is often figured as psychoanalytically absent because of slavery's enduring legacy and the current migratory aspects of global capitalism in which mothers are often separated from children, is important. Focusing a psychoanalytic understanding of being on the mother produces a rich world where the presumed goals of subjectivity—individuality and omnipotence—are undermined. Not only is individuality revealed to be the product of violence, but it is also shown to be impossible: one is always in a state of coexistence and immersed in violence.

Following Musser, Drew's evocation of *Number 8* as the "mother work" not only gestures toward a beginning said differently (Jones), but it also conjures the unseen feminized labors of deregulated relationality as Blackness' anti-capital, anti-individuated, anti-propertizing offering. Moreover, returning to Harper and evoking the character Beloved's own abstractional dream (see chapter 1), Drew's art suggests a notion of Black maternity possible with different "social facts." These "social facts" coming from the "other world," perhaps move as the possibility of long-gone children returning home to ice skate with their sad mothers along with objects as historically loaded as cotton undulating as the soft textures of another project.

Even still, while Drew's pieces are of a plane betwixt and between the gathered-up world and its released other side; being polyecological, as it were, his pieces are more often read as narratively singular and of this world; the question of the sculptures' abstraction, their regenerative and recompositional capacities, remains relatively under-engaged. As such, when a piece like *Number 8* is looked to and as worldly description, as a grid, as *the ordered world*, bespeaking the world-historical violence of difference with "separability," abstract sculpture soon transmutes into renaissance portraiture with an anonymous, Blackened homeless man and his cart materializing as its less-than-ideal, death-bound subject (Ferreira da Silva 2016, 63).

Relatedly, pieces numbered 23 through 29 have been read as sculptural responses, of Drew's witnessing and re-presentation of separability's world-historical origins. In the artbook *Existed* (Schmuckli 2009), based on a mid-career exhibition tour of Drew's work, the pieces numbered in the twenties are connected to Drew's visit to the slave castles of Gorée Island. For example, *Number 23* is a large wall of white, miniature drawers, some falling apart and others imploding from being overstuffed with cotton. The piece itself looks like a kind of ancient and broken-down card catalog system. *Number 24* is similar in structure. Though differing in color—it is constructed from darkened wood—it too is composed of what appear to be aged, symmetrical compartments, also spilling over with cotton. For curator Schmuckli (2009, 12), these pieces are animated by Drew's trip to Senegal and, in particular, his experience of the Door of No Return: "Drew left Gorée Island with deeply ingrained images of confinement, of bodies jammed and stuffed into spaces so small that death, not life, was the norm." Arguably, this terroristic violence of separability moves alongside these pieces and, in conjunction with the use of cotton, bespeaks the terrible racial, sexual, and ecocidal violence of a given-over, separated world, anti-Black gathering in and as the "ordered world" (Ferreira da Silva 2016, 59).

At the same time, though, the artist's assertion of a livedness in his pieces, of which *Number 8* and *Numbers 23* through *29* are likely included, again evokes other ecological histories and possibilities beyond the brutality of worldly evictions ur-symbolized by the Door of No Return. For example, in an article titled "Leonardo Drew and the Mother," interviewer Haley Weiss asked Drew about the spiritual experience of making and living with his installations. The following is a section of the transcript of that interview:

HALEY WEISS: I wonder if the creation of these works, and I might be projecting onto them, is at all meditative for you. Internally, what happens when you're reforming these things that you've created to make new objects? These are very physical pieces. They have a real presence.

LEONARDO DREW: They are, but you've got to know that if you are working, almost like with layers of the Grand Canyon, there's history within those layers. The more you touch something, the stronger it becomes. If you're an artist who's knocking out paintings, you don't get to have that opportunity to sort of realize that, but I've been living with these things long enough to realize it's [about] layers. . . . The longer they hang out, the deeper the history, the richer the life. If you use that as a template or as a way of realizing things, then I don't think you can go wrong. These things are not precious. They're lived in. (H. Weiss 2016)

According to the artist, Drew's *living in and with* each gathering deepens the longer he stays with them, indicating an otherwise (unextractively maternal) ecology coursing alongside the ones said to be already illustrated. Along with the historical layeredness evoked by the grid structure and the use of such loaded materials as cotton, the layeredness of his pieces is likened by Drew to the Grand Canyon. This is instructive, as the canyon itself bears the geological trace of an earth before presumptive ownership: "Rock layers formed during the Paleozoic Era are the most conspicuous in the Grand Canyon's walls" (National Park Service 2019).

Drew's becoming and living with his pieces, his becoming part of them and their becoming part of him, arguably announces a prior and future gathering engendered by an ongoing and entangled creativity and undenied relationality. Perhaps the work creates him as much as he creates it, and in that way, they might enter another door, like the homeless man and his cart, engendered by (as with *Number 8, 23,* and *24*) abstraction's play with the purportedly doorless artifacts of cotton, rope, and animal carcasses (artifacts and tools of an anti-Black, owned world), where the door leads being less important than what the textural interface makes possible for the artist. Or, to put it differently, it is this dwelling with ruin, a kind of entanglement in shared degradation, that, as with the Grand Canyon itself, might elucidate the traces of another project, another Pangea, the ancient landmass floating together before the earth was claimed and presumptively given away.

Indeed, what Drew's art illuminates by way of sculptural abstraction is what Fred Moten (2017c, 1) describes as a "view from nowhere," *a view from* that which exceeds maps, charts, and categories. This resonates powerfully with art historian Andrew Benjamin's claim that Clement Greenberg believed abstract art offered "another source of signification" rather than mere "negation" (Benjamin 1996, 13). While Greenberg discusses abstraction with regard to painting and actually opposes the notion that sculpture's three dimensionality allows for abstraction, it is worthwhile to consider this other "source of signification" in Drew. In order to make this claim, I assert my disagreement with Greenberg's idea that because "three-dimensionality is the province of sculpture," it is nonautonomous and, as such, incapable of abstraction (Greenberg 1960, 3). That is, if I'm following his argument correctly, because "pictorial art" is flat, it is more amenable to the nonfigurative and, with it, the autonomous impulse. But to what (or whom) does Greenberg refer when he evokes the "autonomous"? Let's turn to his piece "Modernist Painting" for clarity:

> All recognizable entities (including pictures themselves) exist in three-dimensional space, and the barest suggestion of a recognizable entity suffices to call up associations of that kind of space. The fragmentary silhouette of a human figure, or of a teacup, will do so, and by doing so alienate pictorial space from the literal two-dimensionality, which is the guarantee of painting's independence as an art. For, as has already been said, three-dimensionality is the province of sculpture. To achieve autonomy, painting has had above all to divest itself of everything it might share with sculpture, and it is in its effort to do this, and not so much—I repeat—to exclude the representational or literary, that painting has made itself abstract. (Greenberg 1960, 3)

Is the so-called autonomous in painting, existing as a privilege and conceit of its form, also a privilege and conceit of a certain notion of the idealized subject, self-possessed, sovereign, self-same, self-referential, of post-Enlightenment? As such, what if autonomy, and I hear Musser here, like the grid, presumes relationality's absence? What if the opposite of autonomy isn't recognizability but is a different form of uncategorizable togetherness?

Returning to Drew, it is precisely the sculptural disfiguration of objects that engenders that "other state of signification" that Greenberg holds to be the province of painting alone. In other words, Drew's art suggests the possibility of movement and composition, the innovation of less harmful forces of togetherness, precisely at and around the site of the disposable. In so doing, I see Drew, following art historian Huey Copeland, as offering sculpture as a site that elucidates the "inability of figurative modalities of representation alone to address the structural logics of slavery and its ongoing effects" (Copeland 2013, 14) and ruination as the "ungovernable ground" for another discourse on social life (Scott 2004, 204). Put differently, in Drew, ruin is an origin, another project, another sensual field, another way to experiment with livedness. And, ruination's open ground engendered by abstract exercises of defamiliarized use and arrangement potentiates a certain unfettered togetherness that, despite intention, undoes autonomy as a "structural logic of slavery" and freedom (Copeland 2013, 14).[5]

Once more, and considering Musser's earlier claim, autonomy suggests a modality of individuation and separability that cannot be divorced from the history of whiteness and white gendered, propertied personhood integral to the management, enclosing, fencing in, and forgetting of difference itself. Greenberg's assertion of purity as abstraction's end presumes such a sensual hierarchy, which, in turn, forecloses the ecological expanse and complexity of nonreferential, albeit dimensional, art itself. Again quoting Greenberg (1960, 3): "The Old Masters created an illusion of space in depth that one could imagine oneself walking into, but the analogous illusion created by the Modernist painter can only be seen into; can be traveled through, literally or figuratively, only with the eye."

For Greenberg, modernist art can't really be lived in; it can only be "seen into." Any spatiality and complex sensuality figures as abstraction's endangerment. For Drew, however, the lived-in-ness of his pieces implies a temporality and sensuality that might allow the weary traveler to linger for a while, to enjoy an opportunity to smell the lost forest, open up doors, let presences in from other parts of the grid, other parts of the project. Seemingly, what abstraction allows for, in Drew's sculptures, is a kind of togetherness without explanation. Such togetherness, I think, is what writer Wilson Harris gets at in his extended elaboration of his own abstractional practice, a practice challenging the purist, rationalist, regulative bends of Greenberg's assertion of purity as abstraction's end. A detour with Harris is necessary here.

As part of Harris's conversation on abstraction with poet Nathaniel Mackey, Mackey questions how Harris's intramedia compositional practice offers another (nonpurist) iteration of abstraction distinct from Greenberg's purist approach. Particularly, Mackey asks Harris about the relation between forms in his writing, what critic Hena Maes-Jelinek described as Harris's "novel as painting," and how such relation connects to Harris's abstractional practice. Harris's engagement with the question of intramedia compositionality in his art not only foregrounds his belief, alongside that of Ferreira da Silva, in art's everythingness, its impurity, but it also reflects how his faith in the intra-species, psychic connectedness between all earthly life animates his aesthetic praxis. Harris asserts:

> I fear the world in which we live remains subject to "purist structures" in writing, in painting, in music, in architecture. Such "purism" reveals the broken self of Man, one half of which is intent on authoritarian, cultural boundaries that extend outwards and influence weaker states, the other half of which sinks into the unconscious. This is how I have come to see the world in its rivalry of powers and privileges. In my estimation a language that genuinely seeks to bring the two halves together must begin to alter a rigidity of line, of photographic painting, of sculpture, and probe into resources for complex, subtle, and far-reaching linkages. . . .
>
> In my travels in the interior rainforests of Guyana, I became immersed in leaf and rock and running water, as part of the form I was instinctively seeking. In ancient cultures the connections between painting (a leaf as I now perceived it) and sculpture (a rock as I now perceived it) and music (the rhythm of running streams as I now perceived it) had been alchemically discharged. But these connections have long faded and need to be sensed in new ways—such as I have partially indicated—if they are to be regained. (quoted in Mackey 2006, 217–18)

For Harris, purism elucidates the "broken self," which we might say otherwise fraudulently presents itself as autonomous. More precisely, brokenness seemingly emerges from the coterminous rejection and forgetting of so-called weaker states—here the unconscious and nature essential to the emergence of the "ethnoclass Man v. human," autonomy's face.

Moreover, purism or purity is defamiliarized by Harris and shifted from presumptive origin to result; as such, for Harris, purity emerges as a stance engendered by a kind of psychic and earthly refusal. According to the writer, this rejection becomes clear in his ur-textual experience of intracompositionality from within the interiors of a Guyanese rainforest. There, within a space overdetermined by its racialized, sexualized, ecological excess, the forest instructs on the intense multisensual ecological complexity that both moves as and is in excess of what comes to be called "form." For Harris, along with Drew, the lived-in-ness of forms bespeaks an inherent synesthetic intracompositional relationality integral to its consolidation. To repeat: "In ancient cultures the connections between painting (a leaf as I now perceived it) and sculpture (a rock as I now perceived it) and music (the rhythm of running streams as I now perceived it) had been alchemically discharged" (quoted in Mackey 2006, 218).

This ecologically imbued awareness of the *ancient* connection between audio and visual forms of art speaks again to the lived-in-ness Drew talks about, the being in and with the art as if it were another earth rich with ungiven colors, tastes, and smells. Powerfully, here, entering such a world doesn't always already mean a kind of epistemological or propertizing positionality with respect to it. Drew not titling his artworks arguably moves against a racist, cisheteronormative, capitalist, extractivist logic that historically coincides with purist narratives of abstraction. Put another way, against a Greenbergian assertion that the Modernist painting "can only be seen into; can be traveled through, literally or figuratively, only with the eye" (Greenberg 1960, 3), Drew's lived-inness models another relation to sensual, aesthetic experience—the work's infinite compositionality—that dislocates the eye/flesh from the colonizing, spatiotemporal, and epistemological prison house of the traveler-observer-owner.

Returning to Ferreira da Silva, what Drew's art does, once more, is pressure an aesthetics buttressed by a notion of "difference without separability," wherein separability both indexes *everything's* reduction to categorical somethingness and where *everything* endures the suffocating whims of the spatiotemporal experience of the one who enters the work through the eye. Relatedly, Ferreira da Silva identifies how the writings of Enlightenment philosophers, namely Kant, advanced empiricism (against divine authorship) as rational man's anthropological endowment. Such a man, we might say, is the one presumed to see and "get" the painting.

> Kant's accomplishment, which was the design of a system that relied primarily on the determining powers of reason and not on a divine creator, troubled his contemporaries, who saw the possibility that formal determination would also become a descriptor of human conditions, constituting a deadly threat to the ideal of human freedom. Yet, two interrelated elements of the Kantian program continue to influence contemporary epistemological and ethical projects: (a) *separability*, that is, the view that all that can be known about the things of the world *is*

what is gathered by the forms (space and time) of the intuition and the
categories of the Understanding (quantity, quality, relation, modality)—
everything else about them remains inaccessible and irrelevant to
knowledge; and consequently (b) *determinacy*, the view that knowledge
results from the Understanding's ability to produce formal constructs,
which it can use to determine (i.e., decide) the true nature of the sense
impressions *gathered by* the forms of intuition. (Ferreira da Silva 2016,
81, individual words emphasized in original; my emphasis on phrases)

An aesthetics unmoored from separability, be it engendered by category or
the carceral enactments of space and time, might elucidate something about
the connection between a Guyanese forest and the page of a book, might suggest something uncategorizable, unknowable about a connection between a
decaying slave caste and the imperceptible musics of cotton. Put more plainly,
art without separability, art without sensual prescription, opens up the quantum ecologies of its own relational experience, maybe even extending it beyond narrative into the virtuality of potential. Returning to Drew, the music
of *Number 23* and *Number 24* (figures 4.2 and 4.3), for example, might potentialize in the cotton's dance with physics. That is, the cotton implodes the grid
of both pieces and in many ways always exceeds the architecture of its containment. This excess bespeaks the potential of the sound it could make when
it threatens to fall out and hit the floor, a possibility that attends its deform-
ing emplacement and elucidates ruin's play against normative space-time. Or,
it signals the molecular interplay between cotton and the oxygen that surrounds it. Put another way, objects in or in proximity to ruination (in *Number
23* and *Number 24*, rickety drawers) resist the presentist bias of Greenberg's
modernism, always molecularly, sensually ambling after the grid of someone
else's singular experience. Moreover, the piece's celebration of cotton's waywardness, its punching back against a perceptual-onto-epistemological and
economic separability along with the artwork's architectural undermining of
the grid, formally and conceptually innovates another history of Black abstraction, one that is different from the abstraction of (or that is) Blackness.
This is complicated.

On the one hand, cotton bears a history of slavery, making the chest of
drawers it seemingly adorns in 23 and 24 evocative of ships and shacks: the
ugly furniture breaking and managing rejected life. On the other hand, Drew's
work challenges a certain separability engendered by historical resemblance;
arguably such separability is forestalled through a partial ruination and de-
contextualization of form. Again quoting Harris on abstract art: "It has an

awareness in line and colour (that tend to crumble and fade) of slow ruination. But, in an inner openness, it is susceptible to new energies that could bring it alive again" (in Mackey 2006, 208).[6] This "inner openness" might be that "weight of being" Drew found in Bridgeport's landfill, whereas "new energies" queries the fate of togetherness in the face of perceptions that reduce the art to its independent parts.

In other words, part of what Drew dramatizes here are a set of ethical questions: when, how, and in what ways are *Number 8* and *Number 23* more than in their singularity, elucidating the arbitrariness of their assigned, presumptively autonomous number titles? Does their more-than-ness, the togetherness that flourishes at the place of ruination, emerge precisely because their links to histories of value—cotton in this case—resist being extracted into recognizable, exchangeable form? Also, weathering re-atmospherizes the object, initiating a process whereby the shape of its interface with the elements elucidates its cosmic dispersal and reunion. With respect to the latter, for Drew and for Michael Taussig, fire describes an occasion of such weathering, a weathering that illuminates that truth, the "weight of being," that the artist is after. Taussig, in *Defacement*, writes:

> So easily we join *truth* and *secret*; with rapture we skid between them, envelop the one in the other: truth = secret. Yet embedded with this ingrained poetry of daily habit there exists something not so obvious, a finely tuned theatrical process, thanks to which, as Benjamin sees it, the revelation shall do justice to the secret. In fact, he portrays such a revelation as the burning up of the husk of the beautiful outer appearance of the secret as it enters the realm of ideas; "that is to say," he adds, "a destruction of the work in which the external form achieves its most brilliant degree of illumination."
>
> The just revelation amounts to a funeral pyre, and something else, as well. For beauty has been waiting for this incendiary moment as the fate through which it will rise to unforeseen heights of perfection, where its inner nature shall be revealed for the first time. (Taussig 1999, 2)

Indeed, on the one hand, weathering and fire, as forms of defacement, move in Drew akin to the ways Taussig describes. That is, the destruction and desecration of the object reveals the truth of an originary violence, the separation and categorization of matter, flesh, and earth apart from its relation with a cosmological everythingness. In other words, keeping Harris in mind, when matter achieves formalization and, with it, subjection to the violent whims of use and exchange, the destructiveness of fire suffers the misplaced

FIGURE 4.2. Leonardo Drew, *Number* 23, 1992; canvas, cotton, nails, and wood; 96 × 120 × 8 in. (243.8 × 304.8 × 20.3 cm). Courtesy of the artist; photography by John Berens.

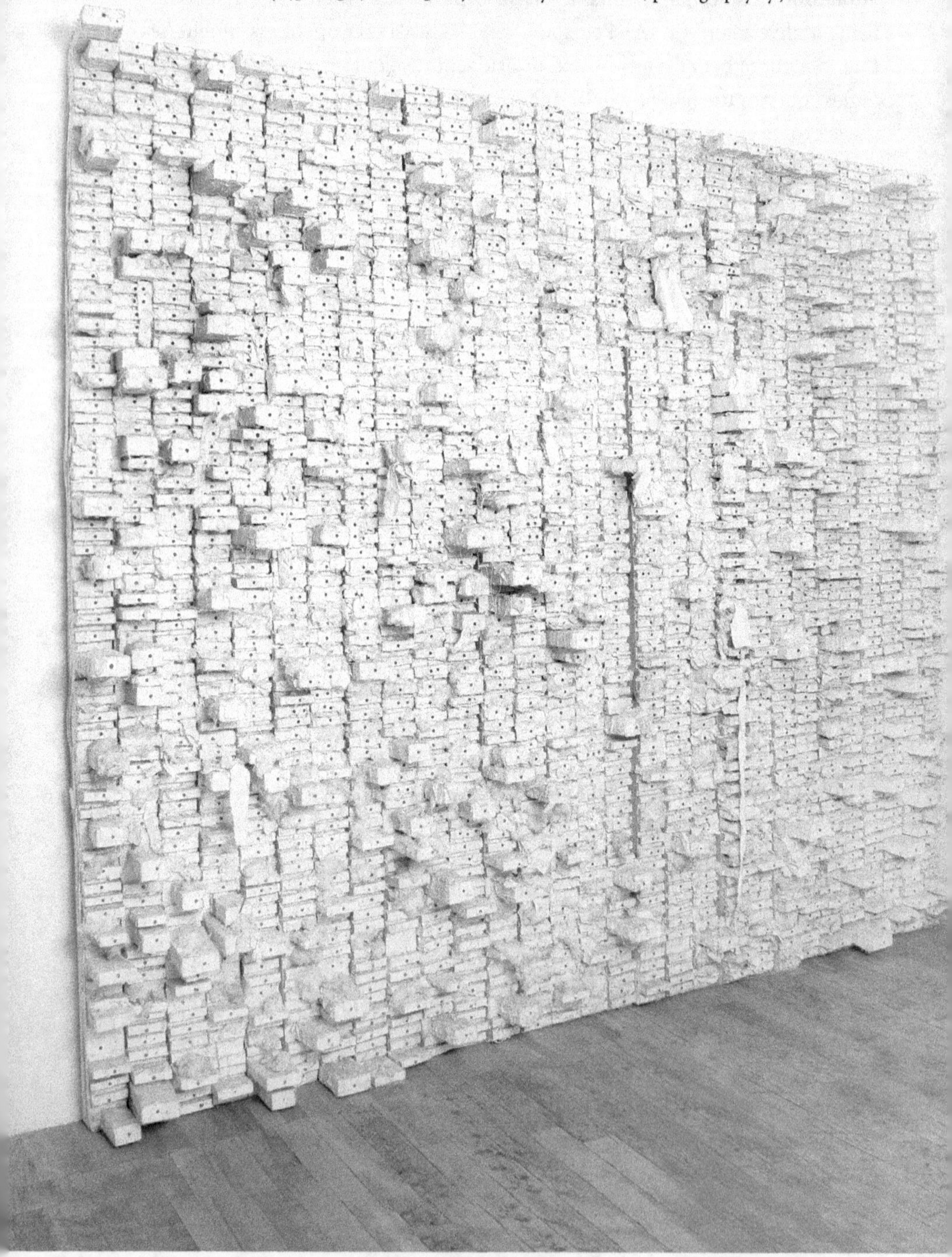

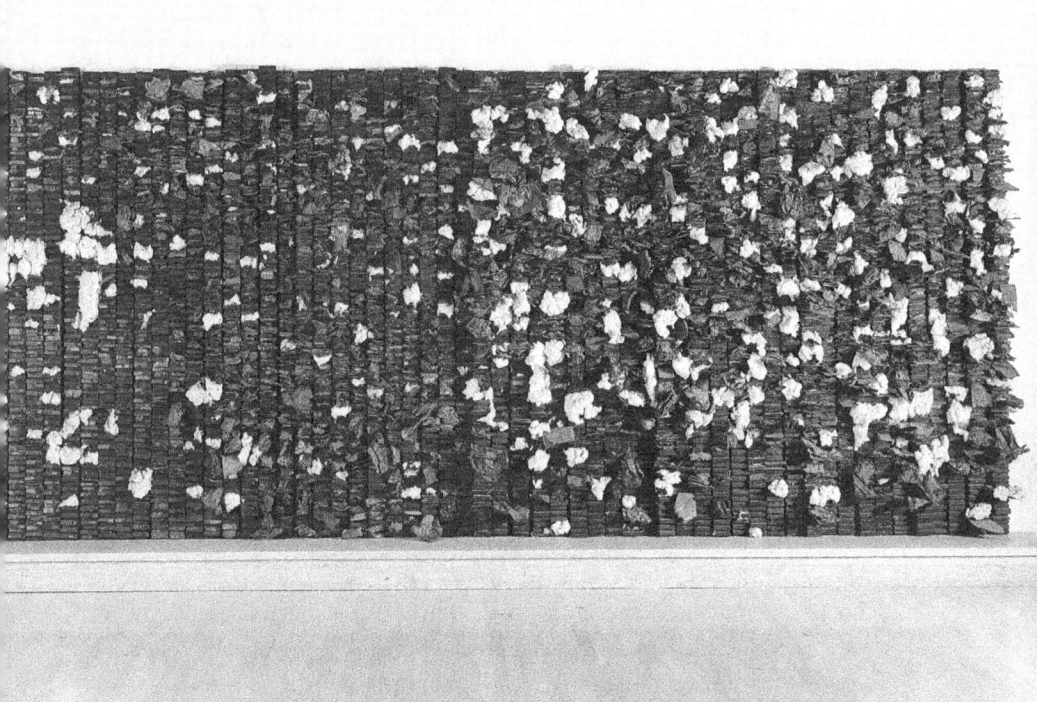

FIGURE 4.3. Leonardo Drew, *Number 24*, 1992; cotton, oxidized metal, paper, and wood; 96 × 240 × 13.5 in. (243.8 × 609.6 × 34.3 cm). The Metropolitan Museum of Art, gift of Barbara Schwartz, in memory of Eugene Schwartz, 2000; photography by John Berens.

pathology that originarily belongs to category. Here I think of the burning of trash by the housing projects Drew grew up in, fire as instrumentalized by capitalism toward destruction and removal.

To imagine fire's compositional work, its inherently transformational promise and possibility, means, then, following Ferreira da Silva once more, reimagining the elemental apart from its capitalist instrumentalization:

> Thinking with heat, I find, displaces Universal time (the time of the Human) toward a non-anthropocentric account of what exists or what happens. With heat, it is possible to figure change not as progression but as material transformation. . . . How then to interrupt the pervasiveness of Universal (Human) time? Lately I have been experimenting with the correspondence of the classic elements to the four typical phase transitions: solid/earth, liquid/water, gas/air, plasma/fire. Elemental thinking—in particular Empedocles's notion that all that exists is but a composition, re-composition or decomposition of the four classic elements (air, fire, water, earth)—I find, inspires a description of *what happens* which does not recall Universal time's presentation of change as a temporal progression. Instead, it figures change as *material* transformation, that is, as phase transition. (Ferreira da Silva 2018)

With respect to Drew, the simulation of fire doesn't eliminate; it transforms. Maybe what Drew does with his work is something akin to what Best (2018, 34) describes as "thinking like a work of art." That is, Drew thinks with fire. Early on, as a kid, he sat and thought with the fire, what it illuminated and how it transformed. This recalls Samiya Bashir's poetic engagement with thermodynamics whereby energy is generated at the interface of heat and entropy's increase. In other words, even as heat became something racist capitalism thought it could harness, extract, own, heat's cosmic reach in and as the universe's condition along with the fact that work is accompanied by disorder itself, that is, entropy, undoes that conceit. In some ways, heat has always been there, at the heart of the universe's deregulated togetherness. I wonder if this is why Drew uses the language of burning when describing the "attitude" of another one of his works, *Number 77* (figure 4.4). He muses, "That piece encompasses my energy level better than anything else I have created. When I look at it, I see myself. The work actually looks like me. And when I say it looks like me, more it feels like me, you know . . . I think that it burns. I think it's just the intensity of it. It's unharnessed, you know. It's out there. It's alive. It has an attitude you cannot avoid" (quoted in Schmuckli 2009, 14).

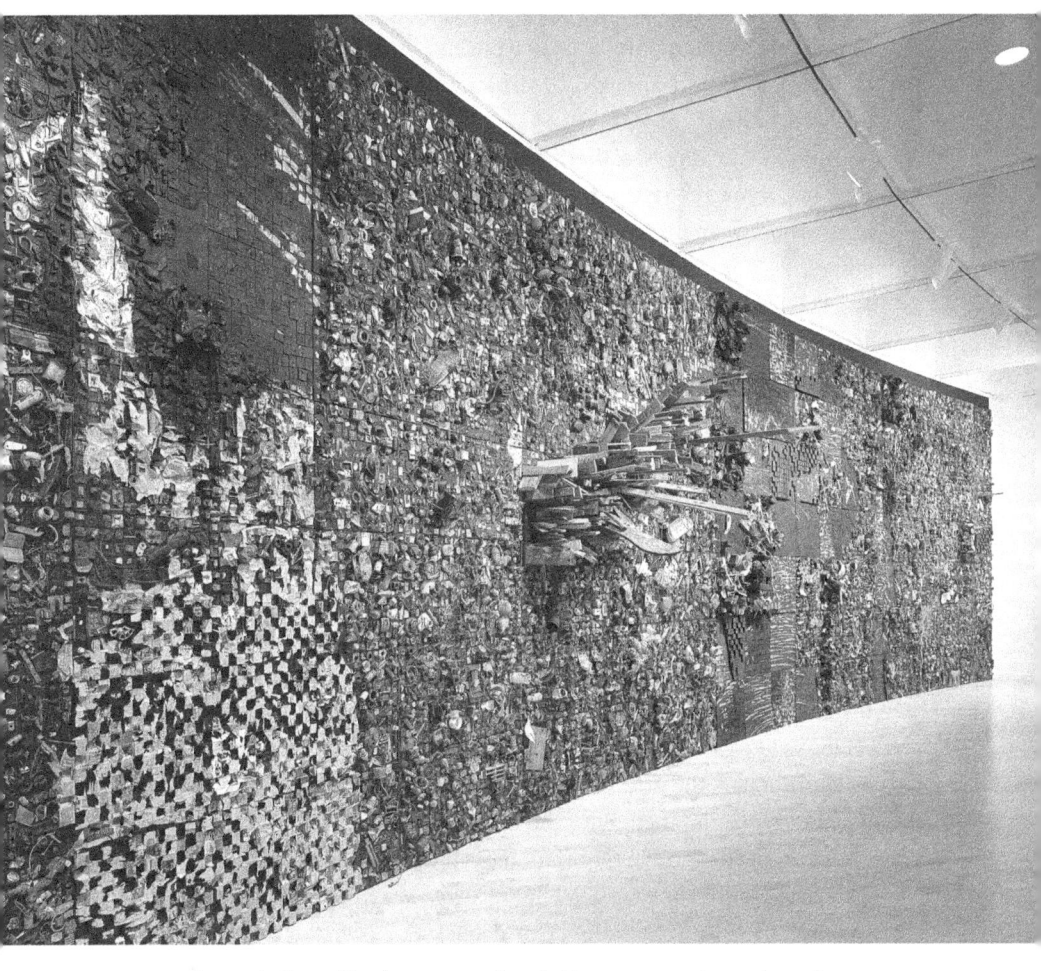

FIGURE 4.4. Leonardo Drew, *Number 77*, 2000; found objects, paper, paint, and wood; 168 × 672 × 53 in. (426.7 × 1706.9 × 147.3 cm). Courtesy of the artist; photography by Ansen Seale.

Measuring fourteen feet high by fifty-six feet long, *Number 77* is a stunning collection of found objects—spools of thread, appliance parts, electrical wire, broken combs, mousetraps, and the like—interspersed with shredded newspaper and spokes of wood. In places, the gatherings are painted over with black paint, creating the illusion that the piece came through a fire. *Washington Post* writer Michael O'Sullivan (2000) describes the work as "resemble[ing] topographic maps of a burned-out metropolis—sci-fi cityscapes of a nameless, post-apocalyptic urban wasteland," calling *Number 77* "positively orchestral."

Perhaps burning, weathering in Drew isn't just about the end's elucidation, but about the return to the beginning again. Even still, there's a tension in Drew between projects that destroy and those that are stolen back, rebuilt differently. For example, in *Number 77*, just as colorful arrangements of found objects nestle alongside spokes of wood, whole pages of newspapers stretch across while breaking under the canvas's momentary insistence on a grid. Indeed, as with a majority of Drew's other pieces, the Modernist grid forms the base of *77*. But on the other hand, *77*'s gatherings, as with Drew's other pieces, aren't entirely regulated by the grid; as with Mondrian's *Victory Boogie Woogie*, the creative use of paint and paper creates the illusion of an endlessly dispersing crowd that spills over the lines and edges of the grid itself. Moreover, the use of black paint simulates a burning that slowly and quietly moves across the piece, erasing any earthly trace of the grid's grip.

Rosalind Krauss (1979, 50) once famously argued that in the context of modernist art, grids connote order and aesthetic autonomy: "Flattened, geometricized, ordered, [they are] antinatural, antimimetic, antireal. It is what art looks like when it turns its back on nature. In the flatness that results from its coordinates, the grid is the means of crowding out the dimensions of the real and replacing them with the lateral spread of a single surface." As some critics argue, the grid in Drew attempts but fails to manage violent chaos and disorder (Krajewski 1999). While in *Number 23* the grid dissolves from the spillover of cotton, in *Number 77* it buckles under the relentless spread of wildfire. What repeats in pattern or order crumbles under the unpredictability of objects, their weightedness and undecidable rate of burning. One might say too that gathering itself subverts the grid and in so doing returns to greet nature and the universe itself in a kind of smoldering, ambient embrace.

If, for example, *Number 23* and *Number 24* evoke racial slavery's compulsively repetitive ordering and management of chattel, then what is at stake when such systems break down under the weight of objects? What is it about the gatherings themselves that perform that labor? To address this question

I return to the multiple meanings of gathering. As a verb, gathering signifies the act of collecting or a bringing together. As a noun, gathering refers to a collective of people, a crowd. Beginning with gathering as verb, part of what this act does—in bringing together discrete objects—is create a sense of wholeness that threatens "an impulse to name and represent" (Moten 2003, 139). For Moten, part of what the ensemble, or gathering, does is generate a music that dispenses with the "illusion of singularity and the illusion of its plurals' intersections and divergences" (139). In that way, *Number 23* and *Number 24* are more than their historically loaded elements, more than the cotton and tightly spaced compartments together. Like *Number 77*, their wholeness-in-gathering performs like an ensemble, "an entity whose apprehension demands the improvisation through any prior notions of ontology, epistemology, and ethics" (127). That is, this is a modality of organization that thrives because of its resistance to a notion of Western ontology that requires, as with value, the engulfment of the other, in the assertion of being (Ferreira da Silva 2007). Rather, the weightedness of being comes through precisely through a kind of deregulated togetherness.

Such gatherings powerfully pressure the very ordering structures that might be their very conditions, in the case of Drew's works, the grids. This is crucial given the violent captures and aggregations that inspired such pieces as *Number 23*, *Number 24*, and *Number 77*. Particularly, even if we assume a correlation among *Number 23*, *Number 24*, and Gorée Island, the aesthetic in the former undoes the taxonomizing, anatomizing, separating, and spatializing of the latter. That is, if slave castles, ships, and housing projects are brutally exemplary grids, then Drew's gatherings in *Number 23* and *Number 24* depart from their re-presentation.

This is to say, *Number 23* and *Number 24* are gatherings that demand another level of engagement along with the recognition that the works' ecological expanse exceeds the notion of engagement itself. Beginning with the former, to regard these pieces as complex wholes requires an attention to ruination, the decline of objects together: a communion of falling apartness, textures, sounds, and smells. As critic Lorraine Edwards (1997, 20) describes *Number 8*, "it reeks of decay." This odor derives not from one component, but from all of it singing and entering into the cosmic atmosphere together, just like the smells of summer that lingered from the garbage heaps of Drew's childhood. In this way, *Number 8* is more than charred pieces of rope and dead animals: perhaps, instead, a staggering, thick rainfall. *Number 23* is more than rows of boxes haphazardly fattened by cotton: maybe, too, a bumpy, dingy wall, falling apart (opening up) at the seams. And *Number 77* might amble somewhere between a disposed-of city and energies of another architectural impulse: glimmers of the future.

Moreover, with respect to the second assertion that Drew's pieces have in some ways already moved on, molecularly, spatiotemporally from the space of their beholding, how do we think about or not think about that? Is the not thinking, the impossible symbolization between *Number 77* and Bridgeport, Connecticut, and between *Number 8* and a homeless man's cart, also imbricated somehow in that otherwise ecology, the partial project to which Drew contributes? Put simply, what's at stake in building a city that looks like "the future" where all can live?

I conclude by asking: What if Drew's art experimentalized and experimentalizes another occasion for group living, providing the scene of collective engagement and a kind of momentary release from governance? In 1997, under the auspices of the art education initiative Projeto Axé, Drew went to Salvador, Brazil, to perhaps ask that question most directly. Projeto Axé was founded in 1990 by "the educator and attorney Cesare de Florio La Rocca in Salvador ... to address the devastating situation of the city's street children ... children "ranging in age from five to eighteen, mostly Black and poor, who live with the burden of centuries of racism, economic injustice, and physical, psychological, and social violence" (Quiet in the Land n.d.). During his residency, Drew chose to live in a poor, predominantly Black neighborhood called Candeal de Brotas. He recalls, "I grew up in a similar situation, which I had the chance to see by living in Candeal. I needed access to that, to those energies coming at you, which you digest and then give back" (Quiet in the Land n.d.). By merging a northern American housing project with a poor Brazilian neighborhood, Drew instructively links locales putatively regarded as dumping grounds, forgotten terrains of disposable, Black life.

How can we think about those energies? Do they emerge out of an experience of racialized, classed subjection and captivity? Or are they linked more closely to what Harris calls the "new energies" that potentiate in ruination, the door that opens on value's underside? Combining the two questions, perhaps it's the intimacies engendered by coercive deprivations of autonomy, whether in the hold of a slave ship or in the cramped quarters of the favela, that made for some ungovernable relation, momentary escape hatches for besieged gatherings. Moreover, the intimacies and energies engendered by these spaces, in the context of Candeal, should be considered in relation to maroonage, as Candeal was once a *quilombo*, a village formed by runaway slaves. In this way it was and continues to be the place where gatherings are reimagined, the flight from economic and ontological extractions/engulfments a collective enterprise.

This oscillation between gathering as subjection and isolation and gathering as liberation moves throughout Drew's works undertaken in Brazil. As part of their collaboration, for example, Drew asked the children of Projecto Axé to collect items from the street. Instead of placing them on a flat surface, Drew sewed the found objects onto a fishing net and suspended it above the ground. If you look closely, you might find an empty pan, a pair of gray jeans, soft drink cans, a yellow shirt, and a sun decoration. (See figure 4.5.) Moreover, regarding the work as an assemblage of discrete objects might open another order of discernment wherein spectacularized disposal, nonvalue, and captivity radiate just around the enclosure. But looking at the art as discrete singularities misses the wholeness of the piece. The wholeness as an ensemble, as a gathering that exceeds its netted constraints, again requires another kind of looking and listening, one that might reveal beautiful bunches of color augmenting a tired white wall.

I assert that this secondary vision—the reimagining of beauty beyond category, of color and life beyond the mourning of use—is the ethical promise of Drew's work. As I indicated earlier, part of what this artwork presumed is a different relation with disposability, the discarded energy found there. The children of Projecto Axé are from the street, what Lindon Barrett (2009, 99) refers to as the enabling absence of white, bourgeois civic order. More specifically, in his engagement with Ann Petry's novel *The Street*, Barrett argues that the street at once constitutes that "restricted economy in which 'refuse' is caught" and, as such, is future-less (98). Figured as without a future, imbricated with refuse itself, the children of Projecto Axé, following Barrett's argument, are not only from the street; they are the street.

On the one hand, being-the-street constitutes the radical outside, the excess or limit of normative life and value: open terrain for the search and seizure of the discarded "readymade." But if we think about the implications of Copeland's (2013, 19) claim that "the slave emerges as a thing-that-is-not one, a form of readymade that . . . challenges the status of the artwork," might we consider the not-oneness not just to suggest violent histories of fungibility but as multiplicities that precede and exceed exchange? Drew and the children's artful embrace of the latter bespeaks the other orders of beauty and life for objects no longer tethered to value. The other possibilities of group living, of living with, and of being a project (Projecto Axé translates into English as Project Spirit) that tries to release, ungive back what was stolen.

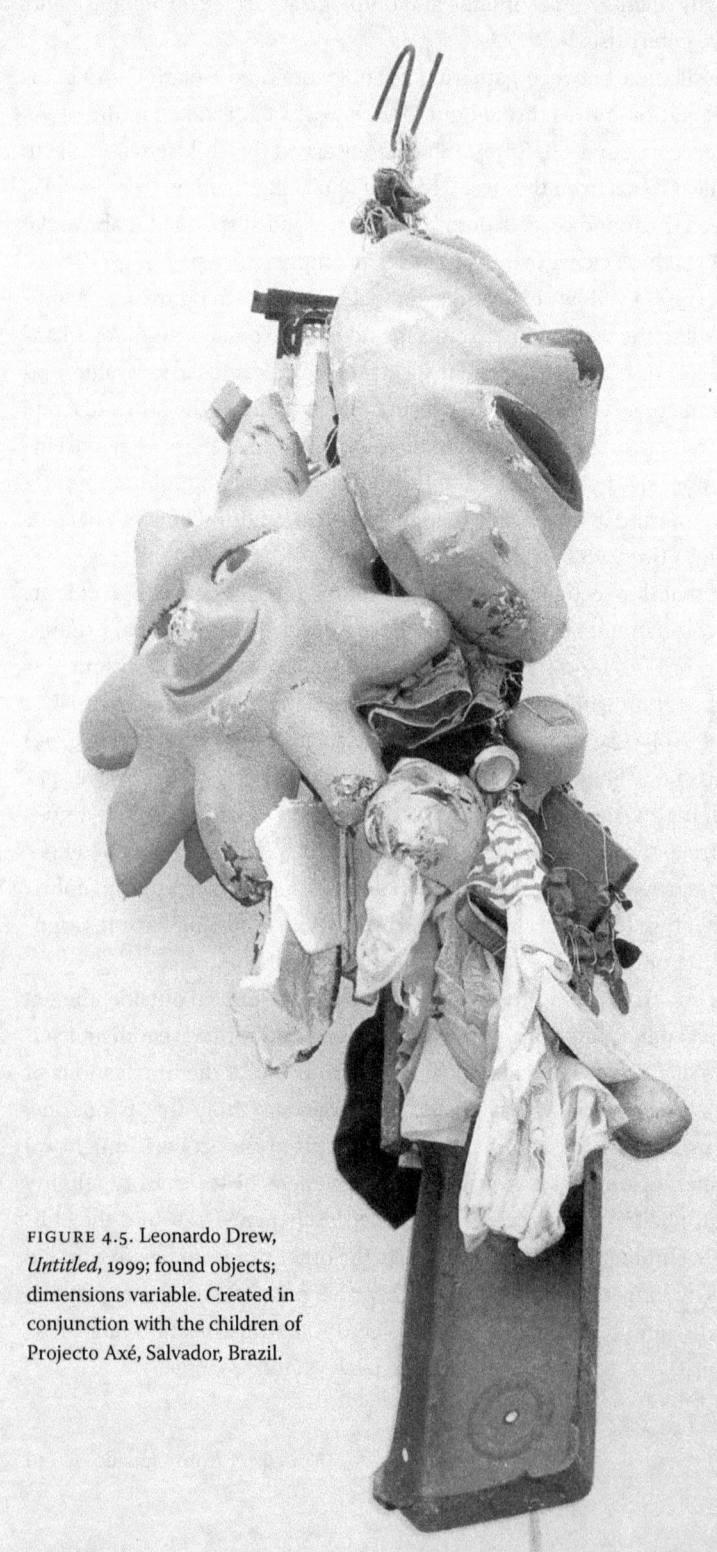

FIGURE 4.5. Leonardo Drew, *Untitled*, 1999; found objects; dimensions variable. Created in conjunction with the children of Projecto Axé, Salvador, Brazil.

Indeed, within Drew's gatherings the rejectable revel in their (overlooked and devalued) weightedness. Just as *Number 8*'s charred rope and dead animals move like a shimmering rainfall and *Number 23* and *Number 24* might burst into music, the Projecto Axé installation and *Number 77* burn as some place to dissemble, to come together once again between ruined city and cosmos. These are gatherings of life and love, irreducible artfulness. Life forces and forms that coalesce as arrangements of ungiven texture, color, smell and sound. Forms and relations that, for the artist, look like "the future" resembling nothing but themselves.

Clementine Hunter's Unscalable Field

To see the beauty to which th[e] work of art directs your gaze, in short,
would actually need a world without art.
—STEPHEN BEST, *None Like Us*

Writing a conclusion is hard. There's an expectation of resolution and reflection, a pointing toward the end of a project. But what if the end, and the fic-
tive beginning it presumes, is undone by the creativities blooming from the
book's elusive center, its wayward middle, creativities that themselves call for
forms of antiteleological and anticategorical engagement? Across this book,
gathering uneasily frames creativities that assert ways of being together without the regulative constraints that disrupt such gathering. Modes of creativity
that advance an idea, a feeling, a vision and dream of togetherness as open
and ongoing, irresolvable by the ends that ostensibly separate people from
trees, flesh from sky, earth from cosmos, art from life, the presumptive beginning of a scholarly meditation and its end.

The above quote from Stephen Best's (2018, 50) stunning meditation on the elusive shapes of "impossible black sociality" and Black nonbelonging in the abstract arrangements of artists El Anatsui and Mark Bradford resonates, for me, not just with the previous chapter on Leonardo Drew but also with the practice of offering conclusions on art that does so better itself. Put differently, I, too, wonder about the kinds of categorical and anticategorical engagement that Drew's art both invites and refuses, realizing, after reading Best and learning from the artists discussed herein, that any time you see a sociality in art you also don't or shouldn't, that sociality's possibility is also its impossibility, or, put differently, that sociality's contours are always more than the frame of the book, the poem, the painting, the gesture from which they are said to emerge. In that way, reflecting on the forms surveyed throughout this book, I think that, despite their differences, these forms share an experimentalism that makes it so that their presumptive flatness and/or availability to meaning is belied by an inaccessible buoyancy, cavernousness. Just as visual arts bear possibilities for an elusive communion, the literary arts harbor architectural and astral possibilities for unexhumable togetherness. Moreover, as I've argued, all of the artists surveyed in *Black Gathering* offer art that connects to what Ferreira da Silva (2014) describes as a black feminist poethical praxis of undivided, infinite canvasing.

Indeed, there are gender and ideological differences too among the artists, and I don't know whether or how each framed/frames their art as Black feminist. Even still, there's an offering of relation on pages and canvasses that seemingly moves against and outside an anti-Black, antifeminine extractive logic, which in turn, as Ferreira da Silva (2014, 85) argues, generates moments of Black feminist "radical praxis [that] acknowledges the creative capacity Blackness indexes." Beyond that, I'm hesitant to resolve the gathering engendered by this book with a potentially enclosing frame. I wonder then, along with refusing the possibility that the earth is given, that life is given, whether perhaps we might conclude by joining Best (2018, 46) in refusing "the givenness of the frame as an act that transfigures matter into form, an 'act of containment' necessary for matter or the world to be engendered with a significance, a meaning. A founding gesture of the artist. An act of sovereign assertion." Or, following Moten (2017b, 256), might we ask: What if gathering is an occasion of "art's insovereign social work" or if art is an occasion for gathering's "insovereign social work"? In refusing that frame, perhaps we can say that this conclusion isn't really one; perhaps it's another chapter, and if you're feeling experimental, go ahead and throw this book into a bucket of paint after the last word hits your eye.

I like ending with visual art because it seems to smuggle in some other beginning and because painting, especially runny paints in their blurring of forms that creep into and over the edge of a canvas, asserts a vitality in excess of the page. If, as Layli Long Soldier (2017, 61) muses, "pages are cavernous, white at entrance, black at absorption," perhaps the depths of the page arrive in what Moten (2008, 202) calls a "chromatic saturation," an inexhaustible, flowy weightedness that is nothing if not a many-roomed cascade of elemental return.

My head's been scattering as I write this. Thinking about the weight of a canvas, what's unavailable to extraction and use, makes me think about the weight of the earth. Why, despite being mined, fracked, cultivated, and extracted, all while Black and Brown kids everywhere die of thirst, its weight is of water. Like a mural by Louisiana artist Clementine Hunter, whose work is the focus of this conclusion, wherein paints run together, blurring the forms often centered on them, the earth insists on appearing aquatically saturated from space. Bright blue. I wonder whether the earth's insurgent blue, its ungiven vitality, is an aquatic reminder of relationality that cannot be exhausted, controlled, or extracted, suggesting something about what painting offers but doesn't give over. Responding to the question "Why is the sky blue?" NASA Science writes:

> Sunlight reaches Earth's atmosphere and is scattered in all directions by all the gases and particles in the air. Blue light is scattered in all directions by the tiny molecules of air in Earth's atmosphere. Blue is scattered more than other colors because it travels as shorter, smaller waves. This is why we see a blue sky most of the time. . . . Closer to the horizon, the sky fades to a lighter blue or white. The sunlight reaching us from low in the sky has passed through even more air than the sunlight reaching us from overhead. As the sunlight has passed through all this air, the air molecules have *scattered* and *rescattered* the blue light many times in many directions. (NASA Science [Space Place] n.d.)

This ongoing "scattering" and "rescattering" of light, along with the fact that oceanic depths ensure an enduring deep blue, is instructive. Further, according to volcanologist Jim Webster: "Earth contains huge quantities of water in its oceans, lakes, rivers, the atmosphere, and believe it or not, in the rocks of the inner Earth. Over millions of years, much of this water is recycled between the inner Earth, the oceans and rivers, and the atmosphere. This cy-

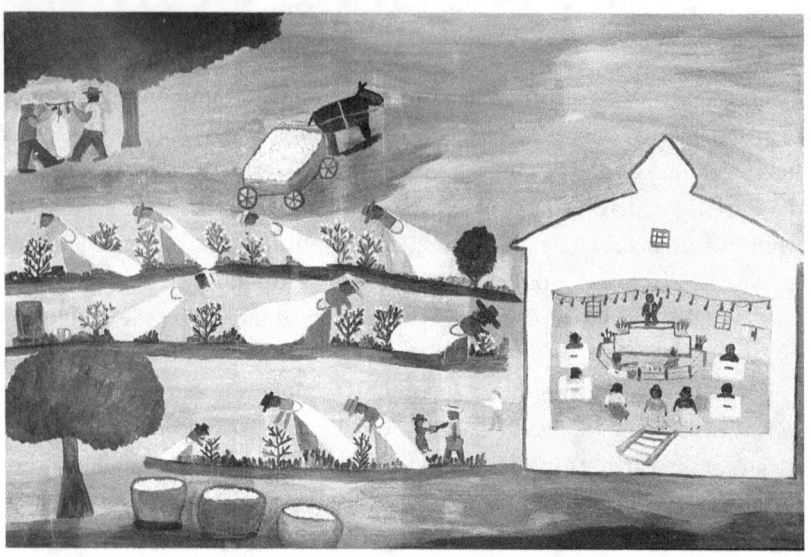

FIGURE C.1. Clementine Hunter, *Harvest Time Mural*, 1955. African House at Melrose Plantation, Natchitoches Parish, Louisiana. Rights held by Cane River Art Corporation. Special Thanks to Thomas N. Whitehead.

cling process means that freshwater is constantly made available to Earth's surface where we all live" (Webster n.d.).

The rescattering of light in conjunction with the recirculation of water points to the gatherings that linger long after the emissaries of extraction have their say: water and light, enduring blue, earth inside itself. By ending with an artist who worked in diluted paints to express Black gathering, I consider painting as the occasion of a similar kind of elemental circulation, the craft enacting another chromatic beginning in the depths of the canvas, an "insovereign social work" for earthly, fleshly, interspecies sociality's depiction and aquatic-like chemical derangement (Moten 2017b, 256). In Hunter's paintings, in their unscaling and blurring of form (see figure C.1), gatherings arrive in unruly circulation, a coming together that coalesces as release and as an elusive impression around the shape of sociality that might accrue to ungivable freedom.

Hunter largely composed figurative paintings of Black gatherings on and around Melrose Estate in Natchitoches Parish, Louisiana, the enclosed earth on which she and her family toiled and lived. In her murals, Black women are not painted to scale but famously are painted larger than the men with whom they share a canvas. Although she didn't work in watercolor, Hunter diluted her oils so much that they moved like watercolor, blurring the edges of forms, wavering the lines between people and the skies they gathered under.

Something about what Hunter does in her blurring of form, her figural subversions and innovations in scale, suggests something about the Black gatherings her paintings are said to bear. That is, following Moten, in the diffusion and expansion of pigment—with kerosene and turpentine in Hunter's case—Black gathering is a figural in-betweenness, moving between rescaled relations among people, animals, and plants as well as nonrepresentational blur: Black gathering as an experiment of material, elemental, and unframeable communion, a togetherness ungiven to art's own formal rendering, moving as possible and impossible sociality.[1] Returning to Best, the painting might be said to harbor Black gathering only insofar as the forms of such gatherings blur against their frames. And, finally—which is to say not finally—I like ending with Hunter's art because it elucidates how the plantation's perverse terroristic endurance, even if figured as touristic banality, is matched by an infinite canvas, or "Canvas Infinita," togethernesses ungiven to enclosure's presumptive finality (Ferreira da Silva 2014, 92).

The African House Murals

In 1955, Hunter completed a series of murals commissioned for the second-floor walls of African House, a structure on the working twentieth-century Melrose Plantation located in northwest Louisiana. On the walls of what was alternately remembered as a storehouse and a prison for enslaved people, Hunter painted scenes of fettered and unfettered gathering: Black women sharecroppers picking cotton and pecans, church services and baptisms, nighttime dancing (see figure C.2).[2] In these murals, Black gatherings appear as painterly vision, de- and repainted by someone whose own ancestors were violently gathered so that those walls could hold life apart: mother from child, lover from lover, unheld earth from ungiven hand. As with Morrison's *Beloved*, we might say that Hunter's murals moved in the interest of a cross-temporal rejoining.

Part of what's at stake for that rejoining, I argue, is the suspension of extraction. Indeed, an encounter with Hunter's African House murals involves participating in a postbellum plantation economy wherein her paintings are viewable after the purchase of a tour ticket and where prints of her paintings are sold in the plantation's gift shop. Given this, I'm interested in the unscalability of that rejoining, how the gatherings depicted in the paintings exceed the extractive logics presuming any kind of scalable separation.

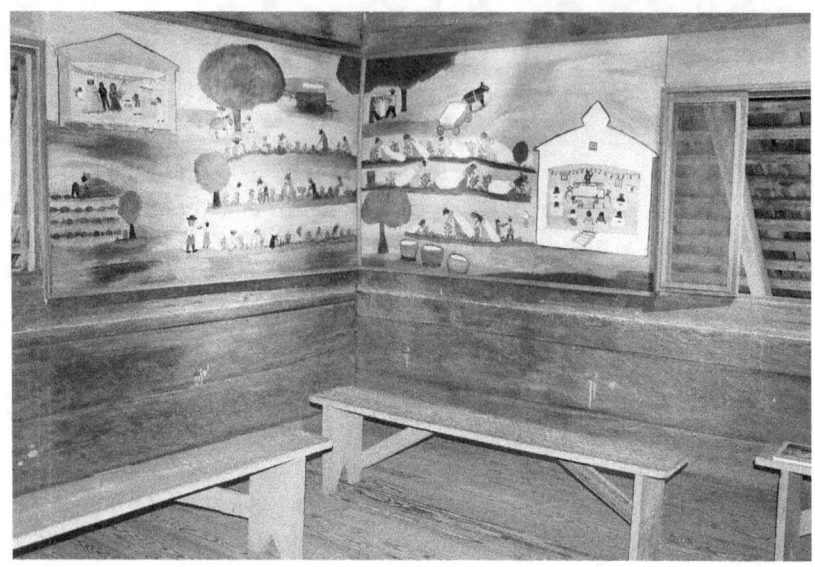

FIGURE C.2. Clementine Hunter, *African House Murals*, 1955. African House at Melrose Plantation, Natchitoches Parish, Louisiana. Photograph by Tom Whitehead, Cane River Art Corporation.

This is important because, with respect to Hunter, her encounter with art is indissociable from the extractive labors occurring on Melrose Estate. That is, for the first fifty years of her life, Hunter picked cotton and pecans, the former providing some enjoyment, according to the artist, and eventually moved inside as a housekeeper. Although she spent the second half of her life painting, using old cardboard, lampshades, and, most famously, the interior walls of African House, we might say Hunter never truly left the field. On the one hand, following the definition of *field* as verb, Hunter was born about twenty years after slavery's formal abolition into a family of sharecroppers/tenant farmers, a deeply racialized and gendered set of economic conditions that sustained Black poverty and indebtedness, a being regulated by somebody else's field, presumptively given-over and plotted ground. This is all compounded by the continuation of labor extraction that profited from her simultaneous labors as domestic worker/housekeeper and as working artist. Concerning the latter, as art historian Mary Lyons observes,

> the artist had little to say about the Association for the Preservation of Historic Natchitoches. In 1977 the association became the new owner of Melrose. It raised $7000 by selling her posters at a party held for her

hundredth birthday. The money was used to modernize her old cabin, paint it white, and move it closer to Melrose's big house. Hunter's former studio now sits prettily behind the big house. But one local person noted that the building "never looked that nice when Clementine lived there." It puzzles me that Hunter had to worry about payments on her new mobile home while her art financed an empty exhibit cabin. (Lyons 1998, 7)

This "empty exhibit cabin," where Hunter ostensibly did not live postrenovation, bespeaks the trace of her celebrated presence in the plantation's afterlife. As noted before, anyone wanting to see Hunter's original works must pay for the plantation tour.

What is more, the plantation's gift shop is filled with merchandise covered with reproductions of her mostly privately owned paintings. The one upside, I noted, is that her grandson James Hunter painted the reproductions; the idea that her family might receive income from the gift shop's proceeds somehow unsettles the reductions achieved by this museumification of her life and art. In that way, the shape of Hunter's innovation, which concerns an unsettling of the plantation as given-over ground with the nonscaled scenes of Black ecological enjoyment, bespeaks and, conceivably, does something to the field. On the one hand, *field* as verb indexes a state of being caught or held, as when the errancy of a ball or question is removed from the air and held. On the other hand, *field* as noun is defined alternately as enclosure and possibility: the unplanned-for life (and its attendant flourishes) that might take root there, the otherwise energy and intramural created between a Black woman laborer and the cotton she loved to be with (Shiver and Whitehead 2012, 17). This duality of the field, as enclosure and opening, undoubtedly animates the above meditations on the touristic afterlife of Hunter's art along with the belief that the life of her art exceeds the telos of any possible tour. Similarly, even the paints used by Hunter, the leftovers and castoffs of painters residing on the plantation during its mid-twentieth-century career as an artist colony, fugitively exceed their own formal constraints. That is, because there wasn't much paint left to work with in a thrown-away tube, Hunter had to dilute the paints so that they could move (Shiver and Whitehead 2012, 60). As with Leonardo Drew, what was thrown away engendered innovation against the kinds of arbitrary extractivist divisions animating a distinction between what can and can't be used and between who is or is not useful.

Still, I ask: What happens to anti-plantation innovation when one's art is subjected to the entrapments that animate the kinds of scalar logics integral to the plantation itself and, in this case, when the nonscalarity of Hunter's visions are printed on fans used by those on a plantation tour? Kept in a bucket by a small refrigerator carrying cold beverages, these fans sell for $2 and feature scenes from Hunter's artworks. The fan featured in figure C.3 depicts a scene from the *Harvest Time* mural.

Complicatedly, the fan traces an impossible gesture of scaling. The original scene was painted on one of African House's walls. Hunter received little compensation for its creation and completion (Shiver and Whitehead 2012, xiv). Her poverty while alive contrasts with the posthumous hyper-reproducibility of her work. Arguably the fan, as with the scene it is said to show, elucidates the promiscuities of scale integral to the plantation's ongoing economic operation. Anna Tsing (2012, 148–50) writes:

> Scalability . . . came into being with the European colonial plantation, as it emerged between the fifteenth and seventeenth centuries. Sugarcane plantations can show us how. Early plantations were not designed with modern blueprints, and there were many dead ends. When the Spanish first tried planting cane in the Caribbean, for example, they employed Native Americans and used their mound-planting methods. The cane grew, but the results were ordinary; in other words, nonscalable. When the Spanish saw what the Portuguese were doing in Brazil, they gave up mounds and copied the Portuguese. So it is to Portuguese experiments we might look to see how stable landscape elements were formed by contingency and friction. . . . In the New World . . . the cane had no history of either companion species or disease relations; it was isolated. Genetic isolates without interspecies ties: New World cane clones were the original nonsoels [or nonsocial] landscape elements without transformative relationships. They made fields ready for expansion. . . . Through doing away with native peoples and seizing their land, a vast terrain for experimentation with nonsoels spread out before the European planters. . . . Workers had to cut cane as fast as they could, and with full attention, just to avoid injury. Under these conditions, workers became autonomous units. Already considered commodities, there were given jobs made interchangeable by the monotonous regularity and coordinated timing engineered into the cane. Slaves were the next nonsoel, design elements engineered for expansion without change.

As a phrase, scalability originated in capitalism, but instructively Tsing frames it in the context of art, as in the capacity of a "picture" to retain its original shape when rescaled without pixilation. For Tsing, the digitally reproduced

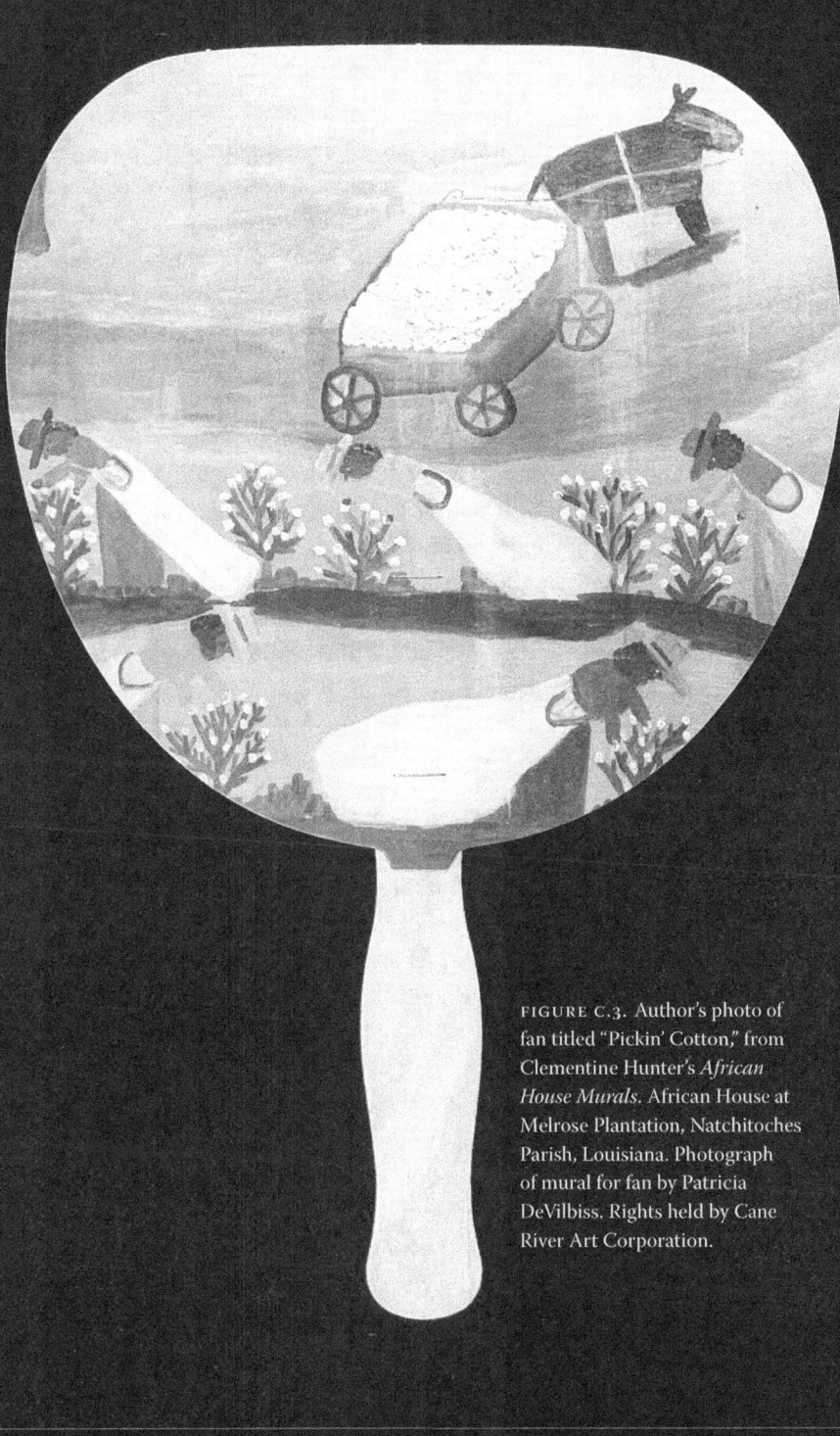

FIGURE C.3. Author's photo of fan titled "Pickin' Cotton," from Clementine Hunter's *African House Murals*. African House at Melrose Plantation, Natchitoches Parish, Louisiana. Photograph of mural for fan by Patricia DeVilbiss. Rights held by Cane River Art Corporation.

picture is threatened by the errancy of the pixel. Pixels must "remain uniform, separate and autonomous; they cannot bleed into each other" (146). Pixelation occurs when pixels become visible; in other words, their invisibility ensures the clarity of the picture. When you see the pixel, the picture as a series of pieces, shards of light, the art quality is said to be degraded. What is more, anxiety around the degradation of the view, given in concerns over pixelation, misses an even bigger picture, as it were. This is the life movement uncapturable in image, the purported "nonsocial landscape elements" removed from the picture so as to sustain its coherence and its ongoing cooperation in scalability (146). In other words, what is removed from this picture is the social life essential to its making. The gift shop fan, while not pixelated, nonetheless removes some of the art's social life—excerpting an image of five women from a gathering of ten—in order to become a reproducible and exchangeable commodity. To make the fan is to collapse the painting; put differently, the fan is the gathering's impossibility.

Powerfully, then, even after her death, Hunter's art continues to refuse scale in ways akin to the artist's own aesthetic strategies. For example, plantation curator Francois Mignon's evaluations of Hunter's paintings, as revealed in his diaries, include a lamentation about the problem of realism in Hunter's painting; the absence of architectural, ecological, pictorial realism and accurate scale figures, for Mignon, as Hunter's aesthetic deficit.

> "I did get a quick glimpse at the first panel. . . ." Mignon wrote. . . . "Architecturally it is not too hot, the buildings vaguely resembling the Big House and the African House but there is charm in the little trees" . . . and later "simplicity of concept and a delightful childishness of execution inject a certain charm that is characteristic of the artist," he wrote in his journal. (quoted in Shiver and Whitehead 2005, 30–31)

Mignon continues:

> I sat with her as she gave the Big House a fresh coat of paint, lightning it up wonderfully. And when that had been achieved, I casually jockeyed her into the cotton chopping section and asked her how she thought a white-ish line around the interior of the cabin, enclosing the wedding scene, would look? She liked the idea and proved her point that it would enhance the value of the wedding. [Then] I edged her over to the cotton picking section and after admiring it much, I asked her if she thought the horse, attached to the cotton wagon and originally painted the same reddish color would look better if said horse were darker to contrast with

the red wagon and white cotton heaped therein. It was as though the ideas were her own and lo! The horse metamorphosed from red to black in a jiffy. After a little further chat about the church in the same section, she somehow got the idea that there ought to be some black lines to indicate some steps and others to indicate a window, as the extent of whiteness seemed excessive. (quoted in Shiver and Whitehead 2005, 36)

The above passage from Mignon's journal bespeaks a managerial comportment both toward artist and artwork. Moreover, Mignon's investment in Melrose's lifelike realization (as if anything like life ever flourished in keeping the plantation to scale) arguably manifests in a certain kind of overseeing; even though Mignon and Hunter weren't literally entrapped in the field's bloody, racial, and sexual logics and violences, his edging her "over to the cotton chopping section" is difficult to separate from an extractivist relation.

Even still, the "excessive" whiteness of the canvas is ruptured by Hunter's innovation. "Black lines" build passage while they make possible the indication of a window, an architectural and ecological "opening up." That is, unenclosing what visionless curators figure as "childish" seemingly opens up windowless buildings along with larger innovations of relationalities, the chromatic nonpartitioning of people, atmosphere, animals, plants, and water. Keeping writers like Toni Morrison and Nikki Wallschlaeger in mind, for example, I see Hunter's innovations as a Black feminine ecological undoing wherein all earthly life returns to a prior intimacy somehow dreamed in excess of extraction's grip. Moreover, returning to an earlier argument I made in relation to Alexis De Veaux and June Jordan's conversation on poetry as housework, I aver that Hunter's murals further align with this ecoaesthetic tradition. In other words, on and against plantational, institutional, barricaded, and surveilled walls, Hunter's art joins this long tradition of Black women's artistic and literary innovation against home as racist, patriarchal enclosure and toward release.

In that way, returning to the fan, the murals already move against the racial, sexual, gender, and economic logics of her art's giftstorification, its complicity with the flattening out of Black women's art and creativity as well as with a plantational presumption of scalability. That is, once more, Hunter's surrealist art shows up as both scalar difference—Black women tend to be painted larger than men—and ecological reordering, a nondominative relation between people and the earth they're with (Shiver and Whitehead 2012, 28).

What observers of the art presume as error or expropriable belies that fact that Hunter herself claimed to paint what was "in her mind" (quoted in Shiver and Whitehead 2012, xiii). In that way, it's already unscalable—how is it possible to scale what the mind holds?—and reflects realism in only the ways memory can. That's why I wonder if we might think of Hunter's surrealism as wishes, ecological dreams, or, rather, as occasions for a kind of ecological dreaming. For example, in the case of the *Harvest Time* mural, Hunter's aerial view of the field ostensibly opens it, making it look less as a division than as the multiplication of ground. (See figure C.1.)

On the canvas's left side, beginning from the top, a pinkish blue sky descends into the green of grass. Underneath that sky Black women stand in three horizontal rows picking cotton. What's powerful is that, in Hunter's view, crop rows don't separate; they bring together. Thus the three rows of women form a galaxy of their own that outsizes, reducing comparatively in scale, the church occupying the same canvased space. While there is much to be said about the significance of an outside communion exceeding the size of an enclosed one, I think what's most significant is how Hunter's innovations in scale quite literally change the relation between flesh and earth. In *Harvest Time*, the rearrangement of the field intermixes it with atmosphere so that you see sky appear between, not above, each row. Powerfully, then, it seems as if the rearrangement and descaling of Black gathering here changes the gravitational field set in motion by the painting. Field ethereally and materially moves vis-à-vis oil paint from enclosure to atmospheric possibility, another relation with proximate flesh, air, and sky. Moreover, following Macarena Gómez-Barris (2017, 6), Hunter's horizontalization of the field "countervisuali[zes]" against extraction, as "vertical seeing" buttressed an understanding of space and time, and of earth as given over: "If settler colonialism and extractive capitalism reorganized space and time, then vertical seeing normalized violent removal."

In that way, we might say that the murals generate another kind of atmosphere, one where people and the earth share an intimacy that enables each to flourish, where the wavering lines of the unscaled forms of people, trees, horses, crops, and air generate an impossible communion somehow harbored in the unknowable, unvisualizable meeting ground of memory and canvas. What is more, returning to Hunter's interaction with Mignon, maybe when Hunter made those black lines, she was asserting that the whiteness of the canvas was never originary, that is, that its realism was predicated on the erasure of Black and interspecies assertions of passage and togetherness. The presumption that gathering's entrenchment in agricultural labor and extraction precludes other forms of communion, other forms of gathering: unscalable, horizontal modalities of ungiven relation that only the people in the painting can ever feel.

1   Throughout the book, I characterize aspects of gathering in art (i.e., unfinishedness) as "insistent." In some ways, my use of the word *insistent* is informed by Nathaniel Mackey's usage in *Bedouin Hornbook* (2010). For Mackey, *insistent* characterizes the sound of a "previousness," heard in the "clucking beat" of reggae (35). While *Black Gathering* does not engage substantively with Mackey's art and thought, I continued to pause at my use of *insistent* and in my thinking around its familiarity, I arrived at Mackey. What the usages—mine and Mackey's—share are a belief that art insists and such insistence is of a certain un/knowable relationality. See Mackey 2010.

2   See Stefano Harney and Fred Moten's *The Undercommons* (2013, 17) for their critique of settler colonialism manifest in the dual violent affectivities of feeling at home and surrounded.

3   Along with Cheryl Harris, Joanne Barker's (2006, 6-7) writing on the use of John Locke's settler colonialist theories among eighteenth-century US jurists was enormously helpful here.

4   I want to acknowledge books that were enormously helpful in my thinking about the enduring whiteness of mainstream environmentalism along with a recent expression of black ecology as that which is engendered by literature's disciplinary troubling of "the limits imposed by a disciplinary or otherwise aversion to thinking with nonhuman forms of life" (Bennett 2020, 8). These books are Carolyn Finney's *Black Faces, White Spaces* (2014) and Joshua Bennett's *Being Property Once Myself* (2020). Bennett conceives of black ecology as a place where "black literary study might take place . . . [in] largely unthought forms of interspecies collaboration, convergence and convivalit[y]" (Bennett 2020, 13). *Black Gathering* attends to interspecies sociality as it manifests in Morrison's literary engagement with flora and fauna. Although Bennett's focus is on human and nonhuman animal socialities, his advancement of the term

black ecology to describe environments experimentalized by literature is enormously important.

5 My use of "the extractive view" is informed by Macarena Gómez-Barris's brilliant elaboration of extraction's force as the violent reduction of earthly life into takeable resource. In *The Extractive Zone* (2017), Gómez-Barris elaborates on the extractive view accordingly: "Before the colonial project could prosper, it had to render territories and peoples extractible, and it did so through a matrix of symbolic, physical, and representational violence. Therefore, the extractive view sees territories as commodities, rendering land as for the taking, while also devalorizing the hidden worlds that form the nexus of human and nonhuman multiplicity. This viewpoint, similar to the colonial gaze, facilitates the reorganization of territories, populations, and plant and animal life into extractible data and natural resources for material and immaterial accumulation" (5).

6 My first encounter with Glissant's phrase "right to obscurity" was in reading Saidiya Hartman's *Scenes of Subjection*. Hartman's conceptual and methodological deployment of the phrase moves as part of her critique of the "coerced theatricality" of enslaved people (Hartman 1997, 37). This "coerced theatricality" not only manifested in the compulsion of dancing on the auction block but also presumed that performances by enslaved people were always already for the captor. For Hartman, the complexity of Black performance in subjection lies in refusing to "consider black song as an index or mirror of the slave condition" but rather as a place where "something in excess of the orchestrated amusements" moved (36).

And this something else, the white supremacist fear of it, suffered endless policing. As Hartman argues, an enduring feature of anti-Blackness was the "dominative imposition of transparency" exemplified in such postbellum violences as the Black Codes, which, among other things, policed any Black movement seen as without purpose or otherwise not sutured to capitalist accumulation (36).

As Hartman argues elsewhere (2018), the presumption of Black assembly as seditious, because unreadable and uncategorizable, further manifests in such anti-Black gathering ordinances as the 1901 Tenement House Law and the "five-second rule," imposed during the Ferguson protests of 2014.

With respect to the former ordinance, Hartman observes that in the early twentieth century, "Harlem was swarming with vice-investigators and undercover detectives and do-gooders who were all intent on keeping young black women off the streets, even if it meant arresting every last one of them. Street strollers, exhausted domestics, nocturnal creatures, wannabe chorus girls, and too loud colored women were arrested on a whim or suspicion or likelihood. In custody, the reasons for arrest were offered: Loitering. Riotous and Disorderly. Solicitation. Violation of the Tenement House Law. Who knew that being too loud, or loitering in the hallway of your building or on the front stoop was a violation of the law; or making a date with someone you met at the club, or arranging a casual hookup, or running the streets was prostitution? Or sharing a flat with ten friends was criminal anarchy? Or the place where you stayed was a disorderly house, and could be raided at any moment? The real offense was blackness" (Hartman 2018, 473). Given this history, an engagement with Black gatherings must not reproduce whiteness through an anti-Black "imposition of transparency" historically integral to whiteness as property's codification and violent endurance. My commitment to modes of relation on and with earth that are not governed by whiteness and property, as such moves, as both political and aesthetic forms of ethical comportment, that aver to think of reading not as a "dominative" critical imposition but as a thinking with.

7   Concerning Audre Lorde, the reference to language's geological capacities, its potential earth-building power, appears in her book *The Cancer Journals* (1980). In a dream, Audre Lorde finds herself in a small gathering, a class that includes herself, a teacher, and another woman. It is here where she ponders the relationship between words and rocks. There's something really beautiful about these geological ruminations in Lorde's dream, written in the context of her meditations on illness, environmental racism, and state-sanctioned suffering. Lorde gathers with her selves in the dream, and what flourishes is a planet with her survival in mind: "I dreamt I had begun to change my life, with a teacher who is very shadowy. I was not attending classes, but I was going to learn how to change my whole life, live differently, do everything in a new and different way. I didn't really understand, but I trusted this shadowy teacher. Another young woman who was there told me she was taking a course in 'language crazure' the opposite of discrazure (the cracking and wearing away of rock). I thought it would be very exciting to study the formation and crack and composure of words, so I told my teacher I wanted to take that course" (1980, 8).

8   My use of the word *otherwise*, as in "gathering otherwise" or "otherwise ecologies," is indebted to scholars Ashon Crawley and Denise Ferreira da Silva. In "Otherwise Ferguson," Crawley (2016) writes: "To begin with the otherwise as word, as concept, is to presume that whatever we have is not all that is possible. Otherwise. It is a concept of internal difference, internal multiplicity. The otherwise is the disbelief in what is current and a movement towards, and an affirmation of, imagining other modes of social organization, other ways for us to be with each other. Otherwise as plentitude. Otherwise is the enunciation and concept of irreducible possibility, irreducible capacity, to create change, to be something else, to explore, to imagine, to live fully, freely, vibrantly. Otherwise Ferguson. Otherwise Gaza. Otherwise Detroit. Otherwise Worlds. Otherwise expresses an unrest and discontent, a seeking to conceive dreams that allow us to wake laughing, tears of joy in our eyes, dreams that have us saying, *I hope this comes true.*"

9   Denver is the name of a character in Toni Morrison's *Beloved*, who finds and gathers with other earthly life outdoors. What if this photograph named Den-

ver is at once and perhaps never a character, at once and never a geographic, ecological relation? Denver as person, as place, as categorically evasive? Denver as partially disclosed togetherness? Maybe Denver is an arrangement of letters, a bringing together whose "epoch-making" sociality remains earthly, fleshly, geologically un-notionable and yet to come.

10   In addition to recalling "Black Topographic Existence" (Moten 2017c), I'm reminded of a line from a conversation among Moten, Robin D. G. Kelley, Afua Cooper, and Rinaldo Walcott. Moten shares, "I think that Black studies has on a fundamental level a specific, though not necessarily exclusive, mission to try to save the Earth, and on a secondary level, to try to save the possibility of human existence on Earth. That's a big statement, but I think maybe it is important to just leave that big statement out there for a minute and just make sure you know that I knew that I said it when I said it" (quoted in Cooper, Walcott, and Hughes 2018, 156).

11   My use of "more than" here indicates both nonhuman vitalities and what Erin Manning refers to as the "more-than" of experience. In *The Minor Gesture* (2016, 30), Manning writes: "To reorient toward the radically empirical is to profoundly challenge the knower-known relation as it is customarily defined. Neither the knower nor the known can be situated in advance of the occasion's coming to be. . . . Like Deleuze's insistence that the virtual, while not actual, is real, radical empiricism emphasizes that experience is made up of more than what actually takes form. Experience is alive with the more-than, the more-than as real as anything else directly experienced."

12   My thinking here on Black art's capacity to transform an environment, to "aerate" a space as suffocating as a plantation prison, as in Hunter's murals, is inspired by Moten's (2013, 778–79) beautiful writing: "There is an ethics of the cut, of contestation, that I have tried to honor and illuminate because it instantiates and articulates another way of living in the world, a black way of living together in the other world we are constantly making in and out of this world, in the alternative planetarity that the intramural, internally differentiated presence—the (sur)real presence—of blackness serially brings online as persistent aeration, the incessant turning over of the ground beneath our feet that is the indispensable preparation for the radical overturning of the ground that we are under."

ONE. "FOR A WHILE AT LEAST"

1   In the preface to *Beloved*, Morrison (2004, xvi–xvii) shares: "I think now it was the shock of liberation that drew my thoughts to what 'free' could possibly mean to women. In the eighties, the debate was still roiling: equal pay, equal treatment, access to professions, schools and choice without stigma. To marry or not. To have children or not. Inevitably these thoughts led me to the different history of Black women in this country—a history in which marriage was discouraged, impossible, or illegal; in which birthing children was required,

but 'having' them, being responsible for them—being, in other words, their parent was as out of the question as freedom. Assertions of parenthood under conditions peculiar to the logic of institutional enslavement were criminal."

2 My argumentation here is informed by Fred Moten's phrase "trace of human inhabitation" spoken in response to Saidiya Hartman's arguments about petit maroonage and the modes of living and survival predicated on leaving no "trace of human inhabitation." See Duke Franklin Humanities Institute 2016.

3 In Jones's *Eva's Man* (1976), much of the oikic energies of the novel centers around a hotel room, and in Toni Cade Bambara's *The Salt Eaters* (1980), the story largely takes place, radiates, and constellates around the shared space of a community center.

4 When I consider the "relational aesthetics" of *Beloved*, I think about Barbara Smith's (1978) foundational text, "Toward a Black Feminist Criticism." In this essential text, Smith argues for the centrality of Black women's literature toward Black feminist consciousness. Her engagement with Morrison's novel *Sula* (1973) powerfully anticipates what Miles calls "relational aesthetics" buttressing ecoaesthetic philosophies long advanced by Black women's writing. Smith (1978, 24) writes: "Morrison depicts in literature the necessary bonding that has always taken place between Black women for the sake of barest survival. Together the two girls can find the courage to create themselves." In relation, through their gathering, Sula and Nel create. They create themselves in relation to the world and each other. Among other powerful interventions, Smith significantly asserts that relational creativity moves at the heart of Black feminist literary praxis.

For another beautiful meditation of the relational aesthetics of Sula, see Kevin Quashie's *Black Women, Identity, and Cultural Theory* (2004).

I also recently read a beautiful essay by Gervais Marsh on Black feminist relationality in a Sola Olulode painting. See Marsh 2020. Marsh engages the "Black womxn" (Marsh's term to include non-cisgender women) as they appear on Olulode's canvases in painterly and erotic relation while respecting the quiet of that intimacy.

5 With respect to the question of madness in relation to Margaret Garner's murder of her child, I want to acknowledge the important scholarship on madness and Black creativity, particularly that of La Marr Jurelle Bruce and his *How to Go Mad without Losing Your Mind* (2021). In an earlier work, Bruce offers a complicated engagement with the term *madness*. In "'The People Inside My Head, Too,'" Bruce (2012, 372) argues that madness might be understood in four ways: "First is phenomenal madness: a severe unwieldiness or chaos of mind. . . . Second is clinical madness: an informal shorthand for any range of psychotic, psychopathic, or severely neurotic disorders . . . (as diagnosed or misdiagnosed by clinicians) that may or may not coincide with phenomenal madness. Third is madness as anger. . . . Fourth and most capacious of these categories is psychosocial alterity: radical divergence from the 'normal' within a given psychosocial context. This iteration of madness functions as variable

foil to normative notions of reason and order. Indeed, any person, idea, or be-havior that perplexes and vexes dominant psychosocial logics is vulnerable to the ascription of 'crazy.' In this fourth category, madness is less a measure of a 'mad' mind than it is an index of the limits of a 'reasonable' majority in pro-cessing radical difference." The fourth definition that seeks less to diagnose mental illness than it is to think normativity's own violence might be said to correlate to Garner's infamous act. Put differently, how much does a figuration of her purported madness depend on stabilizing chattel slavery's flesh- and earth-killing violences as rational? Instead, I learn from Bruce here in thinking about how the figuration of "madness" elucidates and moves against what oth-erwise violently traffics as the normative.

Too often I have facilitated and witnessed conversations on the novel where readers feel entitled to morally arbitrate infanticide. Indeed, I think Morrison's instruction "not to pass on" might also be a word of caution against such an evaluative move.

6   Much has been written about *Beloved*, but I want to highlight some import-ant writing on the question of ecology, nature, and home in the novel: Victo-ria Kennedy's "Native Americans, African Americans, and the Space That Is America" (2006); Lorie Watkins Fulton's "Hiding Fire and Brimstone in Lacy Groves" (2005); Barbara Christian's "Community and Nature" (1980); Toni Morrison's "Rootedness" (1999); Valerie Sweeney Prince's *Burnin' Down the House* (2004); Samira Kawash's "Haunted Houses, Sinking Ships" (2001).

7   This aesthetic notion of healing that smells "like earth" and feels "like hands" resonates for me with a scene of healing from Toni Cade Bambara's powerful novel *The Salt Eaters* (1992). In an exchange between Minnie, a healer, and her patient Velma, Minnie feels Velma's readiness to finally be well. Equally power-ful for the healer is how she experiences another's healing of a body-mind as a new feel of earth and of cosmos. Minnie relates: "I'm getting a message. . . . Minnie moving quickly, pressing her tongue down hard away from her back molars. It was coming to her like a siren, not at all like instructions. A fre-quency not used before more shrill than the signal from Saturn's rings, less timbre that the telling from the Ring of Wisdom, more static than the CBS or traffic waves. A wiry, shrill siren that spun in her head like a gyroscope. She was holding her jaws and heading toward the path, moving swiftly through the woods not cloistered now at the crest by the sheltering branches but thrown open, clear. Gliding over the lemon grass damp against her legs, her shoes squishy like never before. . . . Velma would remember it as the moment she started back toward life, the moment when the healer's hand had touched some vital spot" (276–78).

8   Lorie Watkins Fulton offers a powerful meditation on the complex, symbolic role of trees in *Beloved*. Fulton (2005, 198) concludes, "Just as she [Morrison] describes Sweet Home as a place where 'fire and brimstone' hid in 'lacy groves,' she intimates that things in this world that hurt also contain the potential to heal."

9   My use of *ecoethical* is informed by Chelsea Frazier's usage of *ecoethic* as it
    pertains to Black feminist critiques of colonialist forms of relationality. See
    Frazier's "Repurposing Queens" (2019).
10 I learned of Alexis De Veaux's interview with June Jordan from Black feminist
    poet-scholar Alexis Pauline Gumbs. Gumbs kindly emailed me a PDF of the
    interview from *Essence* magazine. I thank her here for it.
11 See Freeman's beautiful essay "How My Grandfather's Garden Taught Me to
    Survive while Black and Queer" (2018). Freeman's writing here, along with es-
    says in the Black Ecology series published on the African American Intellectual
    History Studies website on long-overlooked Black ecologies and Black ecolog-
    ical epistemologies forged in the Black South, is enormously important. Edited
    by J. T. Roane, Justin Hosbey, and Leah Kaplan, the Black Ecology series docu-
    ments and centers on long-overlooked practices of southern Black/earthly re-
    lation and survival. Particularly noteworthy is a recent essay by Roshad Meeks,
    "The Bond of Live Things Everywhere" (2020).
12 *Houses* powerfully meditates on the little details of a home and how they hold
    the power to change an environment for better or worse for those living inside.
    In Wallschlaeger's poem "Black House," the poet centers an image of children
    gathering amid flowers in an "invisible" house. That image of gathering, the
    beauty it bears, contrasts starkly with the disregard paid to the home by "pa-
    trolling" neighbors. Even still, the kids gather with the flowers whether they
    are seen or not. This attention to detail, to beauty's ecological, alchemical ca-
    pacity to somehow protect and celebrate that togetherness is powerfully hon-
    ored and celebrated by Black women writers, most notably Christina Sharpe
    and Elizabeth Alexander. I post two passages, respectively, from the authors'
    writings, where their attention to detail, to the little things, bears elusive in-
    struction on how to survive in an anti-Black world.
        I begin with an excerpt from Sharpe's "Beauty Is a Method" (2019): "What
    is beauty made of? Attentiveness whenever possible to a kind of aesthetic that
    escaped violence whenever possible—even if it is only the perfect arrangement
    of pins. I continue to think about beauty and its knowledges. . . . If the ceiling
    was falling down and you couldn't do anything about it, what you could do was
    grow and arrange peonies and tulips and zinnias; cut forsythia and mock or-
    ange to bring inside."
        And now, from Elizabeth Alexander's *The Black Interior* (2004, 3–4): "In
    my mother's living room, there are shelves upon which she has arranged many
    beautiful and extraordinary objects. . . . My mother calls them 'the shelves,' the
    objects perhaps 'treasures.' I call the six shelves together an altar where her in-
    tuitive and artful arrangement divines power; the power of beauty itself; the
    power of precious objects put together to add up more than their mere sum;
    the power of the stories behind each object; the power of a family and those
    who have blessed them and their home. Those shelves may be the presentation
    piece of the living room and our family's home but my mother alone arranged
    them; they speak of her aesthetic and her eye—an aesthetic made collective as

it speaks for my family to announce that this is our home, sacred and beautiful. The living room is where she reveals who we are."

13 Email correspondence with the author, November 10, 2019.

14 There is a powerful literary account of anti-Blackness as affective, ecological positioning and weight in Morrison's *The Bluest Eye* (1970). And it revolves around the racialized, gendered, sexualized onto-ecological estrangement presented in the phrase "being put outdoors." It's this concept, I think, that resonates with the "invisibility" that atmospherically surrounds and condemns "Black House." Morrison (2007 [1970], 17) writes: "Outdoors was the end of something, an irrevocable and physical fact, defining and complementing our metaphysical condition. Being a minority in both caste and class, we moved about anyway on the hem of life, struggling to consolidate our weaknesses and hang on, or to creep singly up into the major folds of the garment. . . . But the concreteness of being outdoors was another matter—like the difference between the concept of death and being, in fact, dead. Dead doesn't change and outdoors was here to stay."

TWO. THE ART OF THE MATTER

1 I am, without a doubt, deeply indebted to Dionne Brand's book of poems *The Blue Clerk* (2018). Through her devotion to earthly color, texture, and smell—to what falls out of prose's enclosing pretense—Brand comports toward the poem as another modality of earthly perception and as a place for unfettered dwelling. In some ways, following Brand, the poem's quantum and earthly rearrangements generate another space of togetherness without arbitrary interruption.

2 The phrase "minor science" is coined by Britt Rusert. Drawing on the idea of an "eccentric science" theorized by Gilles Deleuze and Félix Guattari, Rusert historicizes such "minor science" as a Black radical project of empiricism intervening against the world-historical violences of state measure. She argues, "This eccentric science is a 'minor science' that rejects the theorems, metrics, and categorizations of state science. Minor sciences refuse to count or to be held accountable. They 'pose more problems than they solve': problematics are their only mode. Minor science proceeds by a radical empiricism that, instead of selecting and reducing experience into static epistemological categories, works to amplify experiences and build ever-proliferating connections and relations. State science captures and appropriates minor science, but minor science, which also goes under the name of 'nomad' and 'itinerant' science for Deleuze and Guattari, continually escapes the sovereignty imposed on its inventions. While state science establishes itself as a rigid and autonomous domain, minor science is constantly on the move, linking up nonscientific collectivities, marking and extending a territory, and tracing a line of flight. In other words, minor science is animated by the praxis of fugitivity. Oriented toward ongoing experiments in mapping, movement, and escape, minor science might also go under the name of fugitive science" (Rusert 2017, 17).

Bashir's first poem in *Field Theories* (2017, 3), "Consequences of the laws of thermodynamics," begins as follows:

> When Albert Murray said
> the second law adds up to
> the blues that in other words
> ain't nothing nothing he meant it.

Moreover, also in this sentence, I want to acknowledge that my use of the word *anoriginal* is indebted to Fred Moten (2013, 789): "blackness's anoriginal displacement of ontology." I quote the longer passage later in the chapter.

3 Karen Barad's *Meeting the Universe Halfway* (2007) was helpful for my thinking about measurement here.

4 I want to thank Samiya Bashir for directing me to physicist Richard Feynman's famous lectures on theoretical concepts of physics. Inasmuch as I am not adept at science, these lectures aided my understanding of entropy, thermodynamics, Planck's constant, and the Carnot cycle.

5 This promotion video for *Field Theories* is titled "This Is the World Spinning in the Vast Dark" (Bashir 2016).

6 In addition to Keyon Gaskin (choreographer of the dance featured in the promotion of *Field Theories*), Samiya Bashir, and Toni Cade Bambara, I want to acknowledge Mikael Owunna's beautiful artwork wherein Black people are photographed as celestial beings. In a 2019 article for NPR titled "Every Black Person Deserves to See Themselves This Way," Owunna tells writer Becky Harlan, "'If the majority of images that you see of yourself are negative, if people who look like you are dead or dying or captured in a negative light, how do those images enter your body?'" Karlan continues, "Owunna wanted to counteract the pain of those photos [of the death of Michael Brown in Ferguson, Missouri], to create imagery that showed the black body not as a site of death, but as a site of magic." Karlan reports that Owunna's project "was inspired by Chinua Achebe's writing on traditional Igbo spirituality, its supreme deity, Chukwu, and the concept of *chi*, the spirit guide found in every person." As Owunna tells her, "'Each of our spirits is just one ray of the infinite essence of the sun. And in my photography, [I'm] shooting that UV light, trying to capture that spiritual dimension that we're all on.'" The artist continues: "'How can I capture a piece or fragment or a shadow in that land of magic? That's what I'm grounding the project in and that's what I'm capturing, the spiritual guide for the individual models.'"

7 As stated previously, Bambara writes about the healing process of a Black woman community activist. In the slowed down elaboration of that healing, Bambara (1980, 19) highlights Velma Henry's (the main character) intrinsic starriness: "So she would be light. Would go back to her beginnings in the stars and be star light, over and done with, but the flame traveling where it pleased. . . . Sound broke glass. Light could cut through even steel. There was no escaping the calling, the caves, the mud mothers, the others. No escape."

A section of this chapter appeared as "Gayl Jones, Barricaded Feeling and Un-stately Black Life," *Capacious: Journal of Emerging Affect Theory* 1, no. 1 (2017): 77–81.

1   I want to thank Renee Gladman for recommending Susan Bernstein's book, *Housing Problems* (2008).

2   Therí Pickens's definition of madness is particularly useful with respect to Jones's deployment of the term in the title of the essay, "Take Refuge in Madness." In *Black Madness :: Mad Blackness*, Pickens (2019, 51) argues, "I deploy the term madness because of the critical possibilities it offers in its vagueness. It operates as a way to describe impairments such as cognitive disability or mental illness as well as a catchall phrase de-signed to reference those not be-having according to culturally prescribed norms."

I wonder here, following Pickens, if Jones's use of the "vague" term *madness* further helps move attention away from her besieged main character, redi-recting the reader to consider how medical attempts at understanding are in-terruptive of gathering. What vagueness allows for, too, is more space for the main character's linguistic-architectural arrangements outside the enclosures of diagnosis.

3   The title of the story appears as "The Seige"; it is unclear if this is a publication error or not, but I wanted to indicate that that's how the story's title is origi-nally spelled.

4   I am grateful to LaMonda Horton Stallings for helping me think through the episodic nature of Jones's storytelling.

5   Here I want to thank Raj Chetty. When we discussed "The Siege," he men-tioned that the beginning of the short story sounded like a police report. I agree, and it has since resonated with me.

6   Against a "hierarchy of forms" implied by the word *species*, Erin Manning (2013, 88) offers "speciation, [which] is not a question of scale but of mode: it binds the organic and the inorganic in an infinity of micropercetible yet tangible ways, creating new forms of life-living barely categorizable as form or matter." Speciation in the context of "The Siege" might refer to the elusive gatherings of imperceptible vitality that infuse the barricaded room, the un-shareable pleasures of an onion.

7   I'm thankful for Lisa Stevenson's brilliant meditations on wellness as state compulsion and violence in her book *Life beside Itself* (2014).

This chapter is derived, in part, from my article "Black Gathering: 'The Weight of Being' in Leonardo Drew's Sculpture," *Women and Performance: A Journal of Feminist Theory* 26, no. 1 (2016): 1–16, https://www.tandfonline.com/doi/abs /10.1080/0740770X.2016.1185242.

1 The title of this chapter is culled from Fred Moten's poem "The Gramsci Monument" (2014a, 117). Note the following passage:

> If the projects become a project from outside,
> then the projects been a project forever. held in
> the projects we the project they stole. we steal
> the project back and try to give it back to them.

Held in the projects we the project they stole. The poetic and artful rendering of "stolen life" is a project to which Fred Moten and sculptor Leonardo Drew make offerings. *Try to give it back to them. A project forever* stealing back, stealing away from anti-Blackness and its architectural, sculptural, propertied expression as a "project" that kills. *Held in the projects we the project they stole* (Moten 2014a, 117). As artwork, as experimental housing, "The Gramsci Monument" indicates that, even as it has/they have been sustained through repeated exercises in holding and stealing, housing projects are more than their world-historical interpretations, more than the repeating, racializing, and architecturalizing violences that uphold the modern text and its terrible avatars—slave ship, public housing. The monument for which the poem is named "is the fourth and last in Thomas Hirschhorn's series of 'monuments' dedicated to major writers and thinkers . . . . This fourth monument pays tribute to the Italian political theorist and Marxist Antonio Gramsci (1891–1937), famous for his *Letters from Prison and Prison Notebooks.* The Gramsci Monument is based on Hirschhorn's will 'to establish a definition of monument,' to provoke encounters, to create an event, and to think Gramsci today. [As Hirschhorn himself claims:] My love for Antonio Gramsci is the love of philosophy, the love of the infinitude of thought. It is a question of sharing this, affirming it, defending it, and giving it form" (*Mousse Magazine* n.d.).

The location of the monument is at Forest Houses, a housing project in the Morrisania section of the Bronx. Returning to Moten's poetic insights, Hirschhorn's architectural-philosophical desire identified with the spirit of that other project, already undergone and ongoing in public housing. More precisely, the Gramsci Monument's featuring of "children's art classes, a local newspaper, a radio station, a library, a computer lab, and a grill," extended public housing itself in its experimentalization of deregulated togethernesses (Kimball 2014). Togethernesses where individual ownership is not an option and collectivities stay "protect[ed] . . . with our open hands" (Moten 2014a, 117).

2 I thank my friend and co-conspirator J. Kameron Carter for his writing and engagement with the phrase "god-term" in Hortense Spillers's thought. See Carter 2020.

3 In addition to the authors named here, information about Drew's artwork is derived from commentary by curator Claudia Schmuckli on the exhibit "Existed: Leonardo Drew," February 6–May 9, 2010, Weatherspoon Art Museum, UNC-Greensboro, Greensboro, NC. See Schmuckli 2009.

4 In addition to Ferreira da Silva's important writing on anti-blacknesss's expropriative force, I want to acknowledge Katherine McKittrick's (2014, 20) engagement with mathematics' brutal archival expression in "the violence of transatlantic slavery," "a numerical moment through which anti-blackness was engendered and came to underwrite post-slave emancipation promises."

5 In thinking about the question of the autonomous in art as it relates to Black gathering, I return again to scholars Saidiya Hartman and Denise Ferreira da Silva. As I argue earlier via Hartman, after emancipation, Black autonomy figured as impossible due to enduring forms of racist, civic, and economic subjection. For example, Black indebtedness, as Hartman writes, was an enduring feature of postbellum Black life. Moreover, as Ferreira da Silva argues via the concept of affectability in *Toward a Global Idea of Race* (2007), because Black people have historically and philosophically been regarded as incapable of self-governance, autonomy remains definitionally buttressed by whiteness (as does rational endowment/capacity to self-govern). Even still, Greenberg's use of the term evokes autonomy to mean self-referentiality. Thinking about both uses of the term—the historical-philosophical and the art-historical—I wonder, then, is autonomy's aesthetic opposite not representation, but interdependence? What if art was both abstract and dependent? How might that art-philosophical intervention lend itself to an aesthetic critique of whiteness' relation-killing violences? I don't know the answers to these questions but am trying to think it through.

6 Even though Harris is considering Aubrey Williams's abstract painting strategies here, the futurity or other landscapes for fantastic production seems to exist as a potential of all abstract art. In particular, if the ruination of form enacts an openness, perhaps, too, there exists a domain of fantasy—bright lights, warm textures, sweet smells, and music—just on the other side of his broken-down works (Mackey 2006).

CONCLUSION

1 Here I'm thinking of a line from Moten's *Black and Blur* (2017, 246): "Over the past few years, I've been thinking and writing about contemporary art and the phenomenon of blur that sometimes happens both in and between artworks. You could think about it as a kind partition in refusal of partition; a general assertion of inseparability."

2 Information about the African House was derived from a photograph by M. P. Wolcott published on the Library of Congress website, accessed July 2016, https://www.loc.gov/item/2017804399/.

Alexander, Elizabeth. 2004. *The Black Interior: Essays by Elizabeth Alexander.* Minneapolis, MN: Graywolf Press.

Allewaert, Monique. 2013. *Ariel's Ecology: Plantations, Personhood, and Colonialism in the American Tropics.* Minneapolis: University of Minnesota Press.

Bambara, Toni Cade. [1980] 1992. *The Salt Eaters.* New York: Vintage.

Barad, Karen. 2007. *Meeting the Universe Halfway: Quantum Physics and the Entanglement of Matter and Meaning.* Durham, NC: Duke University Press.

Barker, Joanne. 2006. *Sovereignty Matters: Locations of Contestation and Possibility in Indigenous Struggles for Self-Determination.* Lincoln: University of Nebraska Press.

Barrett, Lindon. 2009. *Blackness and Value: Seeing Double.* Cambridge: Cambridge University Press.

Bashir, Samiya. 2016. "This Is the World Spinning in the Vast Dark." *Field Theories-Six* promotion video. Vimeo.com. https://vimeo.com/203384009.

Bashir, Samiya. 2017. *Field Theories.* Brooklyn: Nightboat Books.

Bassett, P. S. 1856. "A Visit to the Slave Mother Who Killed Her Child by Rev. P. S. Bassett." *National Anti-slavery Standard*, March 15.

Baudelaire, Charles. [1851] 2010. *On Wine and Hashish.* London: Hesperus.

Benjamin, Andrew. 1996. *What Is Abstraction?* London: Wiley.

Benjamin, Walter. 2006. *The Writer of Modern Life: Essays on Charles Baudelaire.* Edited by Michael W. Jennings. Cambridge, MA: Harvard University Press.

Bennett, Joshua. 2020. *Being Property Once Myself: Blackness and the End of Man.* Cambridge, MA: Harvard University Press.

Bernstein, Susan. 2008. *Housing Problems: Writing and Architecture in Goethe, Walpole, Freud, and Heidegger.* Stanford, CA: Stanford University Press.

Best, Stephen. 2018. *None Like Us: Blackness, Belonging, Aesthetic Life.* Durham, NC: Duke University Press.

Blomley, Nicholas. 2005. "The Borrowed View: Privacy, Propriety and the Entanglements of Property." *Law and Social Inquiry* 30, no. 4: 617–61.

Brand, Dionne. 2018. *The Blue Clerk.* Durham, NC: Duke University Press.

Brown, Simone. 2015. *Dark Matters: On the Surveillance of Blackness.* Durham, NC: Duke University Press.

Bruce, La Marr Jurelle. 2012. "'The People Inside My Head, Too': Madness, Black Womanhood, and the Radical Performance of Lauryn Hill." *African American Review* 45, no. 3: 371–89.

Bruce, La Marr Jurelle. 2021. *How to Go Mad without Losing Your Mind: Madness and Black Radical Creativity.* Durham, NC: Duke University Press.

Carlson, Licia, and Eva Feder Kittay. 2010. "Introduction: Rethinking Philosophical Presumptions in Light of Cognitive Disability." In *Cognitive Disability and Its Challenge to Moral Philosophy*, edited by Licia Carlson and Eva Feder Kittay, 1–25. Malden, MA: Wiley-Blackwell.

Carter, J. Kameron. 2020. "Other Worlds, Nowhere (or, The Sacred Otherwise)." In *Otherwise Worlds: Against Anti-Blackness and Settler Colonialism*, edited by Tiffany Lethabo King, Andrea Smith, and Jenell Navarro, 158–209. Durham, NC: Duke University Press.

Carter, J. Kameron. n.d. "Black Rapture: A Poetics of the Sacred."

Catanzano, Amy. 2011. "Excerpt from Quantum Poetics: Writing the Speed of Light," pt. 3. *Poems and Poetics* blog, December 23. http://poemsandpoetics.blogspot.com/2011/12/amy-catanzano-from-quantum-poetics.html.

Cervenak, Sarah Jane. 2014. *Wandering: Philosophical Performances of Racial and Sexual Freedom.* Durham, NC: Duke University Press.

Ceyan, Tasha. 2017. "Leonardo Drew in Conversation with Tasha Ceyan." NYAQ, no. 6, March 13. https://www.sfaq.us/2017/03/leonardo-drew-in-conversation-with-tasha-ceyan.

Christian, Barbara. 1980. "Community and Nature: The Novels of Toni Morrison." *Journal of Ethnic Studies* 7, no. 4: 65–78.

Clabough, Casey. 2006. "'Toward an All-Inclusive Structure': The Early Fiction of Gayl Jones." *Callaloo* 29, no. 2: 634–57.

Cohen, Jeffrey Jerome. 2013. Introduction to *Prismatic Ecology: Ecotheory beyond Green*, edited by Jeffrey Jerome Cohen, xv–xxxv. Minneapolis: University of Minnesota Press.

Conrad, Joseph. [1899] 2018. *The Heart of Darkness.* Project Gutenberg e-book. https://www.gutenberg.org/files/219/219-h/219-h.htm#link2H_4_0001.

Cooper, Afua, Rinaldo Walcott, and Lekeisha Hughes. 2018. "Robin D. G. Kelley and Fred Moten in Conversation." *Journal of the Critical Ethnic Studies Association* 4, no. 1: 154–72.

Copeland, Huey. 2013. *Bound to Appear: Art, Slavery, and the Site of Blackness in Multicultural America.* Chicago: University of Chicago Press.

Crawley, Ashon. 2016. "Otherwise, Ferguson." *Interfictions Online: A Journal of Interstitial Arts*, no. 7 (October). http://interfictions.com/otherwise-fergusonashon-crawley/.

Crawley, Ashon. 2017. "Resonance: Neutrinos and Black Life." *Critical Ethnic Studies* 3, no. 1: 48–58.

Cuevas, Ofelia O. 2012. "Welcome to My Cell: Housing and Race in the Mirror of American Democracy." *American Quarterly* 64, no. 3: 605–24.

Despain, Cara. 2012. "Surveyor. An Interview with Xaviera Simmons." *Art Pulse*, April 20. http://artpulsemagazine.com/surveyor-an-interview-with-xaviera -simmons.

De Veaux, Alexis. 1981. "Creating Soul Food: June Jordan." *Essence*, April, 82, 138–50.

Dobrzynski, Judith. 2000. "Artist at Work: Extracting Metaphors from Life's Detritus: A Sculptor Entwines Found Objects with His Experiences and Human History." *New York Times*, February 2.

Drew, Leonardo. 2015. "Finding Piet Mondrian." Video short. *Art 21*, May 15. https://art21.org/watch/extended-play/leonardo-drew-finding-piet-mondrian -short.

Duffy, Andrew. 1999. "Heat Transfer." Lecture notes published online. Boston University Physics Department, December 6. http://physics.bu.edu/~duffy/py105 /Heattransfer.html.

Duke Franklin Humanities Institute. 2016. "Black Outdoors: Fred Moten and Saidiya Hartman at Duke University." October 5. https://www.youtube.com /watch?v=t_tUZ6dybrc.

Dungy, Camille T., ed. 2009. *Black Nature: Four Centuries of African American Nature Poetry*. Athens: University of Georgia Press.

Edwards, Brent Hayes. 2006. "Astral Caption (after an etching by Howardena Pindell, Cassiopeia, Andromeda [2003])." *Callaloo* 29, no. 1: 32–33.

Edwards, Lorraine. 1997. "Navigating a Sea of Chaos." *Sculpture* 16, no. 2: 18–21.

Erevelles, Nirmala. 2002. "(Im)Material Citizens: Cognitive Disability, Race, and the Politics of Citizenship." *Disability, Culture, and Education* 1, no. 1: 5–25.

Farmer, John Alan, and France Morin. 2000. *The Quiet in the Land*. Museo de Arte Moderna de Bahia, Salvador, Brazil.

Ferreira da Silva, Denise. 2007. *Toward a Global Idea of Race*. Minneapolis: University of Minnesota Press.

Ferreira da Silva, Denise. 2009. "No-Bodies: Law, Raciality and Violence." *Griffith Law Review* 18, no. 2: 212–36.

Ferreira da Silva, Denise. 2014. "Toward a Black Feminist Poethics: The Quest(ion) of Blackness toward the End of the World." *Black Scholar* 44, no. 2: 81–97.

Ferreira da Silva, Denise. 2016. "On Difference without Separability." In *Incerteza Viva* (Living uncertainty), catalog of the 32nd Biennial of São Paulo, ISSUU.com, 57–66. https://issuu.com/bienal/docs/32bsp-catalogo-web-en.

Ferreira da Silva, Denise. 2017. "1 (life) ÷ 0 (blackness) = ∞ − ∞ or ∞ / ∞: On Matter beyond the Equation of Value." *e-flux*, no. 79 (February). https://www.e-flux .com/journal/79/94686/1-life-0-blackness-or-on-matter-beyond-the-equation -of-value.

Ferreira da Silva, Denise. 2018. "On Heat." *Canadian Art*, October 29. https:// canadianart.ca/features/on-heat.

Ferris, Timothy. 2003. *Coming of Age in the Milky Way*. New York: HarperCollins.

Feynman, Richard. 1963. "The Laws of Thermodynamics." *The Feynman Lectures on Physics*, vol. 1, chap. 44. California Institute of Technology website. http://www.feynmanlectures.caltech.edu/I_44.html.

Finney, Carolyn. 2014. *Black Faces, White Spaces: Reimagining the Relationship of African Americans to the Great Outdoors*. Chapel Hill: University of North Carolina Press.

Frampton, Noelle. 2009. "P. T. Barnum Residents: We Don't Feel Safe." CT *Post*, November 16. https://www.ctpost.com/news/article/P-T-Barnum-residents-We-don-t-feel-safe-254444.php.

Frazier, Chelsea Mikael. 2019. "Repurposing Queens: Excavating a Black Feminist Eco-Ethic in a Time of Ecological Peril." PhD diss., Northwestern University.

Freeman, Amirio. 2018. "How My Grandfather's Garden Taught Me How to Survive While Black and Queer." *Drome* 3, April. https://www.wearedrome.com/features-2/grandfathers-garden-amirio-freeman.

Fröschels, Emil. 1932. *Psychological Elements in Speech*. Boston: Expression Co.

Fulton, Lorie Watkins. 2005. "Hiding Fire and Brimstone in Lacy Groves: The Twinned Trees of *Beloved*." *African American Review* 39, nos. 1–2: 189–99.

Gladman, Renee. 2017. *Prose Architectures*. Seattle: Wave Books.

Gladman, Renee. 2018. "Slowly We Have the Feeling #9 and #10." *Gulf Coast* 30, no. 2. http://gulfcoastmag.org/journal/30.2-summer/fall-2018/slowly-we-have-the-feeling-number-9-and-10/.

Glave, Dianne. 2010. *Rooted in the Earth: Reclaiming the African American Environmental Heritage*. Chicago: Chicago Review Press.

Goddard, Henry H. 1914. *Feeblemindedness: Its Causes and Consequences*. New York: Macmillan.

Gómez-Barris, Macarena. 2017. *The Extractive Zone: Social Ecologies and Decolonial Perspectives*. Durham, NC: Duke University Press.

Greenberg, Clement. 1960. "Modernist Painting." In *Forum Lectures*. Washington, DC: Voice of America. Accessed May 1, 2015. https://www2.southeastern.edu/Academics/Faculty/jbell/greenbergmodernist.pdf.

Hare, Nathan. 1970. "Black Ecology." *Black Scholar* 1, no. 6: 2–8.

Harlan, Becky. 2019. "Every Black Person Deserves to See Themselves This Way." NPR, March 3. https://www.npr.org/sections/pictureshow/2019/03/03/696969592/transforming-the-pain-of-black-lives-lost-into-portraits-of-magic-embodied.

Harney, Stefano, and Fred Moten. 2013. *The Undercommons: Fugitive Planning and Black Study*. Brooklyn: Minor Compositions.

Harney, Stefano, and Fred Moten. 2017. "Base Faith." *e-flux*, no. 86 (November). https://www.e-flux.com/journal/86/162888/base-faith.

Harper, Michael. 1977. "Gayl Jones: An Interview." *Massachusetts Review* 18, no. 4: 692–715.

Harper, Philip Brian. 2015. *Abstractionist Aesthetics: Artistic Form and Social Critique in African American Culture*. New York: New York University Press.

Harris, Cheryl. 1993. "Whiteness as Property." *Harvard Law Review* 106, no. 8: 276–91.

Hartman, Saidiya V. 1997. *Scenes of Subjection: Terror, Slavery, and Self-Making in Nineteenth-Century America*. New York: Oxford University Press.

Hartman, Saidiya. 2016. "The Belly of the World: A Note on Black Women's Labors." *Souls* 18, no. 1: 166–73.

Hartman, Saidiya. 2018. "The Anarchy of Colored Girls Assembled in a Riotous Manner." *South Atlantic Quarterly* 117, no. 3: 465–90.

Herzogenrath, Bernd. 2013. "White." In *Prismatic Ecology: Ecotheory beyond Green*, edited by Jeffrey Jerome Cohen, 1–21. Minneapolis: University of Minnesota Press.

Hinshelwood, Brad. 2013. "The Carolinian Context of John Locke's Theory of Slavery." *Political Theory* 41, no. 4: 562–90.

Jackson, Zakiyyah Iman. 2018. "'Theorizing in a Void': Sublimity, Matter, and Physics in Black Feminist Poetics." *South Atlantic Quarterly* 117, no. 3: 617–48.

Jarman, Michelle. 2012. "Dismembering the Lynch Mob: Intersecting Narratives of Disability, Race, and Sexual Menace." In *Sex and Disability*, edited by Robert McRuer and Anne Mollow, 89–107. Durham, NC: Duke University Press.

Jones, Gayl. 1973. "Toward an All-Inclusive Structure." PhD diss., Brown University.

Jones, Gayl. 1975. *Corregidora*. Boston: Beacon.

Jones, Gayl. 1976. *Eva's Man*. Boston: Beacon.

Jones, Gayl. 1977. *White Rat*. New York: Harlem Moon Classics.

Jones, Gayl. 1982. "The Siege." *Callaloo*, no. 16: 89–94.

Jones, Gayl. 1994. "From The Quest for Wholeness: Re-Imagining the African-American Novel: An Essay on Third World Aesthetics." *Callaloo* 17, no. 2: 507–18.

Jordan, June. 2005. "1977: Poem for Miss Fannie Lou Hamer." In *Directed by Desire: The Collective Poems of June Jordan*, 276–78. Port Townsend, WA: Copper Canyon Press.

Kafer, Allison. 2013. *Feminist, Queer, Crip*. Bloomington: Indiana University Press.

Kawash, Samira. 2001. "Haunted Houses, Sinking Ships: Race, Architecture and Identity in Beloved and Middle Passage." CR: *The New Centennial Review* 1, no. 3: 67–86.

Kant, Immanuel. [1785] 2005. *Foundational Principles of the Metaphysics of Morals*. Mineola, NY: Dover Publications.

Kelley, Robin D. G. 2003. *Freedom Dreams: The Black Radical Imagination*. Boston: Beacon.

Kennedy, Victoria. 2006. "Native Americans, African Americans, and the Space That Is America: Indian Presence in the Fiction of Toni Morrison." In *Crossing Waters, Crossing Worlds: The African Diaspora in Indian Country*, edited by Tiya Miles and Sharon Holland, 196–217. Durham, NC: Duke University Press.

Kimball, Whitney. 2014. "How Do People Feel about the Gramsci Monument One Year Later?" *Art F City*, August 20. http://artfcity.com/2014/08/20/how-do-people-feel-about-the-gramsci-monument-one-year-later.

King, Tiffany Lethabo. 2016. "The Labor of (Re)Reading Plantation Landscapes Fungible(ly)." *Antipode* 00, no. 0: 1–18.

Kluchin, Rebecca. 2009. *Fit to Be Tied: Sterilization and Reproductive Rights in America, 1950–1980*. New Brunswick, NJ: Rutgers University Press.

Koppes, Steve. 2004. "Astrophysicists Attempt to Answer Mystery of Entropy." *University of Chicago Chronicle* 24, no. 5 http://chronicle.uchicago.edu/041118/entropy.shtml.

Krajewski, Sara. 1999. "Matter and Memory: The Evocative Sculpture of Leonardo Drew." In *Leonardo Drew*, edited by Sara Krajewski, 9–31. Madison, WI: Madison Art Center.

Krauss, Rosalind. 1979. "Grids." *October*, no. 9: 50–64.

Locke, John. [1689] 2015. *Two Treatises of Government and a Lesson Concerning Toleration (with an introduction by Henry Morley)*. Overland Park, KS: Digireads.

Lorde, Audre. 1980. *The Cancer Journals*. San Francisco: Aunt Lute Books.

Lubrin, Canisia. 2018. "Q&A: Canisia Lubrin Speaks to Dionne Brand about Her Two New Books, *The Blue Clerk* and *Theory*." *Quill and Quire*, September 13. https://quillandquire.com/omni/qa-canisia-lubrin-speaks-to-dionne-brand-about-her-two-new-books-the-blue-clerk-and-theory.

Lyons, Mary. 1998. *Talking with Tebe: Clementine Hunter, Memory Artist*. New York: Houghton Mifflin Harcourt.

Mackey, Nathaniel. 2006. "Quantum Ghosts: An Interview with Wilson Harris." In *Discrepant Abstraction*, edited by Kobena Mercer, 206–21. Cambridge, MA: MIT Press.

Mackey, Nathaniel. 2009. "A Night in Jaipur." *Conjunctions*, no. 53: 288–90.

Mackey, Nathaniel. 2010. *From a Broken Bottle Traces of Perfume Still Emanate: Bedouin Hornbook, Djbot Baghostus's Run, Atet A.D.* Vols. 1-3. New York: New Directions.

Manning, Erin. 2013. *Always More Than One: Individuation's Dance*. Durham, NC: Duke University Press.

Manning, Erin. 2016. *The Minor Gesture*. Durham, NC: Duke University Press.

Marsh, Gervais. 2020. "Being Otherwise: Notes on Black Feminist Relationality in Sola Olulode's *Where the Ocean Meets the Beach*." *Arts.Black*, July 6. https://arts.black/essays/2020/07/sola-olulodes-where-the-ocean-meets-the-beach.

Mathers, Kathryn. 2010. *Travel, Humanitarianism and Becoming American in Africa*. New York: Palgrave.

McCray, Rebecca. 2014. "A Disturbing Trend in Agriculture: Prisoner-Picked Vegetables." *Take Part*, April 14. http://www.takepart.com/article/2014/04/14/prison-ag-labor.

McKittrick, Katherine. 2006. *Demonic Grounds: Black Women and the Cartographies of Struggle*. Minneapolis: University of Minnesota Press.

McKittrick, Katherine. 2014. "Mathematics Black Life." *Black Scholar* 44, no. 2: 16-28.

McRuer, Robert. 2004. "Composing Bodies; or, De-Composition: Queer Theory, Disability Studies, and Alternative Corporealities." *JAC* 24, no. 1: 47–78.

Meeks, Roshad Demetrie. 2020. "The Bond of Live Things Everywhere: What Black Nature Might Look Like." *Black Perspectives*, July 21. http:www.aaihs.org /the-bond-of-live-things-everywhere-what-black-nature-might-look-like.

Metzl, Jonathan. 2011. *The Protest Psychosis: How Schizophrenia Became a Black Disease*. New York: Beacon.

Miles, Malcolm. 2014. *Eco-Aesthetics: Art, Literature and Architecture in a Period of Climate Change*. London: Bloomsbury.

Mills, Charles. 1999. *The Racial Contract*. Ithaca, NY: Cornell University Press.

Morrison, Toni. 1997. "Home." In *The House That Race Built: Original Essays by Toni Morrison, Angela Y. Davis, Cornel West, and Others on Black Americans and Politics in America Today* edited by Wahneema Lubiano, 3–12. New York: Pantheon.

Morrison, Toni. 1999. "Rootedness: The Ancestor as Foundation." In *African American Literary Criticism: 1773 to 2000*, edited by Hazel Arnett Ervin, 198–202. New York: Twayne.

Morrison, Toni. [1987] 2004. *Beloved*. New York: Vintage.

Morrison, Toni. [1970] 2007. *The Bluest Eye*. New York: Vintage.

Morrison, Toni. 2019. "On *Beloved*." In *The Source of Self-Regard: Selected Essays, Speeches, and Meditations*, 280–86. New York: Knopf.

Moten, Fred. 2003. *In the Break: The Aesthetics of the Black Radical Tradition*. Minneapolis: University of Minnesota Press.

Moten, Fred. 2008. "The Case of Blackness." *Criticism* 50, no. 2: 177–218.

Moten, Fred. 2013. "Blackness and Nothingness: Mysticism in the Flesh." *South Atlantic Quarterly* 112, no. 4: 732–80.

Moten, Fred. 2014a. "The Gramsci Monument." *Social Text* 32, no. 1 (118): 117–18.

Moten, Fred. 2014b. "Notes on Passage: The New International of Sovereign Feelings." *Palimpsest: A Journal on Women, Gender, and the Black International* 3, no. 1: 51–74.

Moten, Fred. 2015. "Blackness and Poetry: Evening Will Come." *Arcade: Literature, The Humanities, and the World*, no. 55. July 1. https://arcade.stanford.edu /content/blackness-and-poetry-0.

Moten, Fred. 2017a. Afterword to *Prose Architectures* by Renee Gladman, 109–14. Seattle: Wave Books.

Moten, Fred. 2017b. *Black and Blur*. Durham, NC: Duke University Press.

Moten, Fred. 2017c. "Black Topographical Existence." In press packet for Arthur Jafa's installation "A Series of Utterly Improbable, Yet Extraordinary Renditions," June 8 through September 10, 2017, Serpentine Sackler Gallery, London.

Moten, Fred. 2018. *Stolen Life*. Durham, NC: Duke University Press.

Mousse Magazine. n.d. "Thomas Hirschhorn 'Gramsci Monument' in New York." http://moussemagazine.it/thomas-hirschhorn-gramsci-monument/.

MSNBC.com. 2005. "Hurricane Katrina: Wrath of God?" *Morning Joe* (transcript), MSNBC.com, October 5. https://www.nbcnews.com/id/wbna9600878.

Musser, Amber. 2020. "The Limits of Desire: Jacolby Satterwhite and the Maternal Elsewhere." *Black Scholar* 50, no. 2: 37–42.

Mutlaq, Jasem. n.d. "Blackbody Radiation." AstroInfo Project. Accessed August 2019. https://docs.kde.org/trunk5/en/extragear-edu/kstars/ai-blackbody .html.

NASA Science (Space Place). n.d. "Why Is the Sky Blue?" Accessed August 2019. https://spaceplace.nasa.gov/blue-sky/en.

National Park Service. 2019. "Grand Canyon: Geologic Formations." Last updated March 4. https://www.nps.gov/grca/learn/nature/geologicformations.htm.

Nguyen, Mimi. 2012. *The Gift of Freedom: War, Debt, and Other Refugee Passages.* Durham, NC: Duke University Press.

Ostriker, Jeremiah P., and Simon Mitton. 2013. *Heart of Darkness: Unraveling the Mysteries of the Hidden Universe.* Princeton, NJ: Princeton University Press.

O'Sullivan, Michael. 2000. "A Trash Course in Sculpture: Leonardo Drew Elevates the Value of Junk." *Washington Post*, March 26. https://www.washingtonpost .com/wp-srv/WPcap/2000-03/26/004r-032600-idx.html.

Patterson, Tom. 2010. "Transience: Influence of Artist's Early Life Evident in Work." *Winston-Salem Journal*, April 26.

Pickens, Therí Alyce. 2019. *Black Madness :: Mad Blackness.* Durham, NC: Duke University Press.

Posmentier, Sonya. 2017. *Cultivation and Catastrophe: The Lyric Ecology of Modern Black Literature.* Baltimore, MD: John Hopkins University Press.

Prince, Valerie Sweeney. 2004. *Burnin' Down the House: Home in African American Literature.* New York: Columbia University Press.

Purdy, Jedediah. 2015. "Environmentalism's Racist History." *New Yorker*, August 13. https://www.newyorker.com/news/news-desk/environmentalisms-racist -history.

Quashie, Kevin Everod. 2004. *Black Women, Identity, and Cultural Theory: (Un) Becoming the Subject.* New Brunswick, NJ: Rutgers University Press.

Quashie, Kevin. 2012. *The Sovereignty of Quiet: Beyond Resistance in Black Culture.* New Brunswick, NJ: Rutgers University Press.

The Quiet in the Land. n.d. "The Story." Representation of a story originally published in *Art Journal*, fall 2000. Last accessed November 18, 2020. http://www .thequietintheland.org/brazil/category.php?id=the-story.

Ralambo-Rajerison, Gabrielle. 2017. "To What Do I Owe This Pleasure." Prose poem originally accessed on Pitt University's Department of Physics and Astronomy website. Last accessed November 12, 2020. https://www.physicsand astronomy.pitt.edu/gabrielle-ralambo-rajerison.

Rancière, Jacques. 1999. *Disagreement: Politics and Philosophy.* Translated by Julie Rose. Minneapolis: University of Minnesota Press.

Rankine, Claudia. 2013. "After David Hammons." Poets.org. https://poets.org/poem /after-david-hammons.

Reed, Anthony. 2014. *Freedom Time: The Poetics and Politics of Black Experimental Writing.* Baltimore, MD: Johns Hopkins University Press.

Roberts, Dorothy. 1997. *Killing the Black Body: Race, Reproduction and the Meaning of Liberty.* New York: Vintage.

Rood, Daniel. 2017. *The Reinvention of Atlantic Slavery: Technology, Labor, Race, and Capitalism in the Greater Caribbean*. New York: Oxford University Press.

Ruffin, Kimberly N. 2010. *Black on Earth: African American Ecoliterary Traditions*. Athens: University of Georgia Press.

Rusert, Britt. 2017. *Fugitive Science: Empiricism and Freedom in Early African American Culture*. New York: New York University Press.

Schmuckli, Claudia. 2009. "Being and Somethingness." In *Existed: Leonardo Drew*, edited by Claudia Schmuckli, 9–17. London: D. Giles.

Schrijver, Karel, and Iris Schrijver. 2015. *Living with the Stars: How the Human Body Is Connected to the Life Cycles of the Earth, the Planets, and the Stars*. New York: Oxford University Press.

Scott, David. 2004. *Conscripts of Modernity: The Tragedy of Colonial Enlightenment*. Durham, NC: Duke University Press.

Sexton, Jared. 2014. "The *Vel* of Slavery: Tracking the Figure of the Unsovereign." *Critical Sociology* 42, nos. 4–5: 583–97.

Sexton, Jared. 2017. "All Black Everything." *e-flux*, no. 79 (February). https://www.e-flux.com/journal/79/94158/all-black-everything.

Sharpe, Christina. 2016. *In the Wake: On Blackness and Being*. Durham, NC: Duke University Press.

Sharpe, Christina. 2019. "Beauty Is a Method." *e-flux*, no. 105 (December). https://www.e-flux.com/journal/105/303916/beauty-is-a-method.

Sharpe, Christina. 2020. "Provisions #8: 'If I Could Just Leave the Old Things to Their Trembling.'" *Jewish Currents*, July 20. https://jewishcurrents.org/provisions-8-if-i-could-just-leave-the-old-things-to-their-trembling.

Shiver, Art, and Tom Whitehead. 2005. *Clementine Hunter: The African House Murals*. Natchitoches, LA: Association for the Preservation of Historic Natchitoches.

Shiver, Art, and Tom Whitehead. 2012. *Clementine Hunter: Her Life and Art*. Baton Rouge: Louisiana State University Press.

Simplican, Stacy Clifford. 2015. *The Capacity Contract: Intellectual Disability and the Question of Citizenship*. Minneapolis: University of Minnesota Press.

Smith, Barbara. 1978. "Toward a Black Feminist Criticism." *Radical Teacher*, no. 7: 20–27.

Sneathen, Eric. 2015. "Review: *Houses* by Nikki Wallschlaeger." *The Volta Blog*, December 1. https://thevoltablog.wordpress.com/tag/eric-sneathen.

Soldier, Layli Long. 2017. *Whereas*. Minneapolis, MN: Graywolf Press.

Spillers, Hortense J. 1987. "Mama's Baby, Papa's Maybe: An American Grammar Book." *Diacritics* 17, no. 2: 64–81.

Spillers, Hortense J. 2003. "'All the Things You Could Be by Now, If Sigmund Freud's Wife Was Your Mother': Psychoanalysis and Race." In *Black, White and in Color: Essays on American Literature and Culture*, edited by Hortense J. Spillers, 376–427. Chicago: University of Chicago Press.

Stevenson, Lisa. 2014. *Life beside Itself: Imagining Care in the Canadian Artic*. Berkeley: University of California Press.

Sutton, Christine. n.d. "Z Particle." *Encyclopedia Britannica* online. Accessed July 2017. https://www.britannica.com/science/Z-particle.

Takle, Eugene, and Don Hofstrand. 2015. "Global Warming: Agriculture's Impact on Greenhouse Gas Emissions." *Ag Decision Maker Newsletter* 12, no. 6, art. 1. https://lib.dr.iastate.edu/agdm/vol12/iss6/1/?utm_source=lib.dr.iastate .edu%2Fagdm%2Fvol12%2Fiss6%2F1&utm_medium=PDF&utm_campaign =PDFCoverPages.

Tate, Claudia. 1979. "An Interview with Gayl Jones." *Black American Literature Forum* 13, no. 4: 142–48.

Taussig, Michael. 1999. *Defacement: Public Secrecy and the Labor of the Negative*. Stanford, CA: Stanford University Press.

Taylor, Dorceta E. 2002. *Race, Class, Gender and American Environmentalism*. General Technical Report PNW-GTR-534. April. Portland, OR: US Department of Agriculture, Forest Service, Pacific Northwest Research Station.

Tinsley, Omise'eke. 2008. "Black Atlantic, Queer Atlantic: Queer Imaginings of the Middle Passage." *GLQ: A Journal of Lesbian and Gay Studies* 14, nos. 2–3: 191–215.

Tsing, Anna. 2012. "On Nonscalability: The Living World Is Not Amenable to Precision-Nested Scales." *Common Knowledge* 18, no. 3: 505–24.

Tsing, Anna. 2013. "More-Than-Human Sociality: A Call for Critical Description." In *Anthropology and Nature*, edited by Kristen Hastrup, 27–42. London: Routledge.

Tsing, Anna. 2015. *The Mushroom at the End of the World: On the Possibility of Life in Capitalist Ruins*. Princeton, NJ: Princeton University Press.

University of Southern Denmark. 2017. "How Does It Look When Earth Is Bombarded with Dark Matter?" *Science Daily*, December 6. https://www.science daily.com/releases/2017/12/171206122507.htm.

University of the Arts. 2018. "Artist Profile: Toyin Ojih Odutola." MFA Studio Art Department Visiting Artists Lecture Series, University of the Arts, Philadelphia, July 26. http://studioartmfa.uarts.edu/visiting-artist/toyin-ojih-odutola.

Varnedoe, Kirk. 2006. *Pictures of Nothing: Abstract Art since Pollock*. Princeton, NJ: Princeton University Press.

Wallschlaeger, Nikki. 2015. *Houses*. Galesburg, IL: Horse Less Press.

Webster, Jim. n.d. "Will the Earth Ever Run Out of Water?" American Museum of Natural History online. Accessed August 2019. https://www.amnh.org/explore /ology/earth/ask-a-scientist-about-our-environment/will-earth-run-out-of -water.

Weheliye, Alexander G. 2014. *Habeas Viscus: Racializing Assemblages, Biopolitics, and Black Feminist Theories of the Human*. Durham, NC: Duke University Press.

Weiss, Allen S. 2009. "Dust to Dust." In *Existed: Leonardo Drew*, edited by Claudia Schmuckli, 19–25. London: D. Giles.

Weiss, Haley. 2016. "Leonardo Drew and the Mother." *Interview Magazine*, September 29. https://www.interviewmagazine.com/art/leonardo-drew.

Williams, Lindsey, and Melanie Nind. 1999. "Insiders and Outsiders: Normalization and Women with Learning Difficulties." *Disability and Society* 14, no. 5: 659–72.

Williamson, Terrion. 2015. "In the Life: Black Women and Serial Murder." *Social Text* 33, no. 1 (122): 95–114.

Wynter, Sylvia. 2003. "Unsettling the Coloniality of Being/Power/Truth/Freedom: Towards the Human, after Man, Its Overrepresentation—An Argument." *CR: The New Centennial Review* 3, no. 3: 257–337.

Yusoff, Kathryn. 2019. *A Billion Black Anthropocenes or None.* Minneapolis: University of Minnesota Press.

www.ingramcontent.com/pod-product-compliance
Lightning Source LLC
Chambersburg PA
CBHW072153290526
45794CB00004B/1500